ORDER YOUR YELLOW & ORANGE TAX ANNUALS 2001-02

It's easy to lose your way in the wake of a new Budget a[nd] changes to tax legislation. **Tolley** can assist by providin[g] an unbeatable price. All the titles are leading tax annuals **Yellow & Orange Tax Annuals 2001-02** have an unriva[lled] and other professionals for providing clear, concise and [authoritative] practice in each individual area of tax. No practitioner sh[ould]

Yellow & Orange Tax Annuals Set 2001-02

TA01MW

ISBN 0 406 94116 5 £180.00

Yellow Tax Handbook 2001-02

"The tax practitioner's bible. Bigger than ever"   Taxation Practitioner

Publication date: June 2001   BYTH1
ISBN 0 406 93998 5   £53.95

Orange Tax Handbook 2001-02

"Is an invaluable and welcome sight every year"   Taxation

Publication date: June 2001   BOTH1
ISBN 0 406 94006 1   £49.95

BDO Stoy Hayward's Yellow Tax Guide 2001-02

BDO Stoy Hayward, Chartered Accountants

"are invaluable companions to that other pair of fiscal indispensables, Butterworths Yellow and Orange Tax Handbooks"   Solicitor's Journal

Publication date: October 2001   BDYT1
ISBN 0 406 93910 1   £65.00

BDO Stoy Hayward's Orange Tax Guide 2001-02

BDO Stoy Hayward, Chartered Accountants

Publication date: October 2001   BDOT1
ISBN 0 406 93911 X   £45.00

Whillans's Tax Tables 62nd Edition

Edited by Sheila Parrington, LLB and Gina Antczak, FCA ATII

"The publication of these tables twice each year is always a welcome event"
New Law Journal

Publication date: October 2001   WTT201
ISBN 0 406 94457 1   £13.95

Order your copies of the 2001-02 editions TODAY

TO ORDER SIMPLY COMPLETE THE ORDER FORM OVERLEAF

ORDER FORM

Please supply me with the following:

Title	Code	Qty	Price	Total
Yellow and Orange Tax Annuals Set 2001-02 ISBN 0 406 94116 5	TA01MW		£180.00	
Yellow Tax Handbook 2001-02 ISBN 0 406 93998 5	BYTH1		£53.95	
Orange Tax Handbook 2001-02 ISBN 0 406 94006 1	BOTH1		£49.95	
BDO Stoy Hayward's Yellow Tax Guide 2001-02 ISBN 0 406 93910 1	BDYT1		£65.00	
BDO Stoy Hayward's Orange Tax Guide 2001-02 ISBN 0 406 93911 X	BDOT1		£45.00	
Whillans's Tax Tables 62nd Edition ISBN 0 406 94457 1	WTT201		£13.95	

Orders are subject to a charge of £2.50 in the UK and £3.50 p&p for overseas customers.
Prices may be subject to change on publication

Total Amount due £
(inc p&p)

SIMPLY COMPLETE AND RETURN THIS CARD – NO STAMP NEEDED

Matthew Rowe, Butterworths Tolley,
Marketing Department, FREEPOST 6983, London WC2A 1BR
Telephone 020 8662 2000 Fax: 020 7400 2570

I WOULD LIKE TO PAY (Please tick as appropriate)
☐ using my Butterworths Tolley account no.

_____

☐ By credit card as follows
　☐ Mastercard　　☐ American Express
　☐ Barclaycard or other Visa card
My credit card no. is

and its expiry date is _____

☐ with attached cheque for　£ _____
　(made payable to Butterworths Tolley)

☐ Please supply the above on 21 days money back guarantee (EU countries only)

Signed _____

Date _____

MY FIRM / ORGANISATION IS
_____
Address _____
_____
_____ Country _____
Postcode _____ DX _____
VAT Reg No _____
and it has _____ partners/employees

MY DETAILS ARE
Name _____
Job Title _____
Telephone number _____

We like to keep our customers informed of other relevant books, journals and information services produced by Butterworths Tolley or by companies approved by Butterworths Tolley.
If you do not wish to receive such information, please tick the box. ☐

Tolley
LexisNexis

Butterworths Tolley, 35 Chancery Lane, London WC2A 1EL
A division of Reed Elsevier (UK) Ltd
Registered office　25 Victoria Street　London SW1H 0EX
Registered in England number 2746621
VAT Registered No. GB 730 8595 20

Whillans's Tax Tables

Sixty-second edition

Edited by Sheila Parrington LLB
and
Gina Antczak FCA ATII

Members of the LexisNexis Group worldwide

United Kingdom	Butterworths Tolley, a Division of Reed Elsevier (UK) Ltd, Halsbury House, 35 Chancery Lane, LONDON, WC2A 1EL, and 4 Hill Street, EDINBURGH EH2 3JZ
Argentina	Abeledo Perrot, Jurisprudencia Argentina and Depalma, BUENOS AIRES
Australia	Butterworths, a Division of Reed International Books Australia Pty Ltd, CHATSWOOD, New South Wales
Austria	ARD Betriebsdienst and Verlag Orac, VIENNA
Canada	Butterworths Canada Ltd, MARKHAM, Ontario
Chile	Publitecsa and Conosur Ltda, SANTIAGO DE CHILE
Czech Republic	Orac sro, PRAGUE
France	Editions du Juris-Classeur SA, PARIS
Hong Kong	Butterworths Asia (Hong Kong), HONG KONG
Hungary	Hvg Orac, BUDAPEST
India	Butterworths India, NEW DELHI
Ireland	Butterworths (Ireland) Ltd, DUBLIN
Italy	Giuffrè, MILAN
Malaysia	Malayan Law Journal Sdn Bhd, KUALA LUMPUR
New Zealand	Butterworths of New Zealand, WELLINGTON
Poland	Wydawnictwa Prawnicze PWN, WARSAW
Singapore	Butterworths Asia, SINGAPORE
South Africa	Butterworths Publishers (Pty) Ltd, DURBAN
Switzerland	Stämpfli Verlag AG, BERNE
USA	LexisNexis, DAYTON, Ohio

© Reed Elsevier (UK) Ltd 2001

All rights reserved. No part of this publication may be reproduced in any material form (including photocopying or storing it in any medium by electronic means and whether or not transiently or incidentally to some other use of this publication) without the written permission of the copyright owner except in accordance with the provisions of the Copyright, Designs and Patents Act 1988 or under the terms of a licence issued by the Copyright Licensing Agency Ltd, 90 Tottenham Court Road, London, England W1P 0LP. Applications for the copyright owner's written permission to reproduce any part of this publication should be addressed to the publisher.

Warning: The doing of an unauthorised act in relation to a copyright work may result in both a civil claim for damages and criminal prosecution.

Any Crown copyright material is reproduced with the permission of the Controller of Her Majesty's Stationery Office. Any European material in this work which has been reproduced from EUR-lex, the official European Communities legislation website, is European Communities copyright.

A CIP Catalogue record for this book is available from the British Library.

ISBN 0 406 94457-1

Typeset by Wyvern 21 Ltd, Bristol
Printed by Antony Rowe Ltd, Chippenham, Wiltshire

Visit Butterworths LexisNexis direct at www.butterworths.com

Overseas
Average rates of exchange

Average for year ending	31.12.98	31.3.99	31.12.99	31.3.00	29.12.00	30.3.01
Algeria (Dinar)	97·8645	99·2018	107·1554	109·3333	112·7047	111·9071
Argentina (Peso)	1·658	1·6539	1·6171	1·6102	1·5153	1·4787
Australia ($A)	2·638	2·6643	2·5075	2·5	2·6092	2·661
Austria (Schilling)	20·5069	20·2487	20·8987	21·4907	22·5939	22·4336
Bahrain (Dinar)	0·6254	0·6239	0·6099	0·6073	0·5716	0·5578
Bangladesh (Taka)	77·9876	78·6191	79·3028	80·0803	79·0938	78·2862
Barbados (BD$)	3·3458	3·334	3·2303	3·2114	3·0195	2·9467
Belgium (Franc)	60·1307	59·3682	61·2658	63·0014	66·2402	65·7704
Bolivia (Boliviano)	9·1699	9·2559	9·344	9·4378	9·3162	9·2479
Botswana (Pula)	7·0147	7·2987	7·4751	7·5101	7·7717	7·8691
Brazil (Real)	1·9252	2·1975	2·9494	2·9227	2·7724	2·8004
Brunei ($)	2·7657	2·7821	2·7381	2·7277	2·6169	2·5729
Burma (Myanmar) (Kyat)	10·3702	10·3445	9·9981	9·9297	9·7314	9·647
Burundi (Franc)	733·8387	775·3835	918·7623	965·6341	1,087·1708	1,106·252
Canada (Can$)	2·4588	2·4873	2·4041	2·3706	2·2505	2·2238
Cayman Islands (CI$)	1·3762	1·3714	1·3332	1·3163	1·2442	1·2207
Chile (Peso)	764·0855	777·2736	824·1754	830·0176	816·8918	821·4341
China (Renminbi Yuan)	13·7424	13·6737	13·3652	13·3267	12·5381	12·2233
Colombia (Peso)	2,367·175	2,451·284	2,843·8825	2,987·0423	3,174·5532	3,216·9658
Congo Dem Rep (Zaire) (Congolese Franc)	224,147·7	223,581·9	67,151·89	11,061·44	6·8223	6·6577
Costa Rica (Colon)	427·8467	436·6955	461·3303	470·6506	466·4669	462·2145
Cuba (Peso)	38·1782	37·9873	35·5282	34·6202	30·9054	30·107
Cyprus (£)	0·8596	0·8521	0·8843	0·9083	0·9448	0·9372
Czech Republic (Koruna)	53·3515	53·0363	54·606	55·4834	58·5144	57·5581
Denmark (Krone)	11·1015	10·9556	11·2926	11·616	12·2386	12·1593
Ecuador (Sucre)	9,258·9275	11,008·15	19,895·9167	26,233·83	37,859·2583	27,843·72
Egypt (£)	5·6636	5·6512	5·5326	5·5143	5·358	5·393
El Salvador (Colon)	14·5292	14·4518	14·1085	14·0693	13·2329	12·8998
EMS (ECU)	1·4783					
Ethiopia (Birr)	11·472	11·5096	11·99	12·38	12·2714	12·0439
European Union (Euro)		1·4647	1·5207	1·563	1·6237	1·6114
Fiji (F$)	3·3017	3·3113	3·1856	3·1921	3·2249	3·2331
Finland (Markka)	8·8624	8·7562	9·0356	9·2933	9·788	9·7153
France (Franc)	9·7681	9·6473	9·9624	10·2445	10·7706	10·6942
French Cty/Africa (CFA franc)	979·1458	967·5958	1,002·7792	1,031·958	1,079·9175	1,069·841
French Pacific Is (CFP franc)	177·7411	175·5382	181·8722	187·2139	197·1027	195·4233
Gambia (Dalasi)	17·0422	17·3619	18·6287	18·961	19·848	20·6167
Germany (Deutsche mark)	2·9147	2·878	2·9702	3·0548	3·2114	3·1886
Ghana (Cedi)	3,846·755	3,869·185	4,013·507	4,826·704	8,362·358	9,498·54
Greece (Drachma)	489·8869	486·6462	495·3136	513·2787	553·1315	552·1486
Grenada/Wind. Isles (EC$)	4·4788	4·4677	4·3689	4·3503	4·0935	3·9947
Guyana (G$)	244·0337	249·2911	271·0854	278·7615	280·418	274·0524
Honduras (Lempira)	22·3154	22·518	23·0901	23·3034	22·456	22·0814
Hong Kong (HK$)	12·8378	12·8158	12·5548	12·5157	11·8145	11·5332
Hungary (Forint)	357·4845	363·4616	386·3691	399·6829	428·9736	428·6946
Iceland (Krona)	117·9762	117·0532	117·2219	117·5749	119·2531	121·3855
India (Rupee)	68·432	69·5958	69·6492	69·7983	68·0779	67·5606
Indonesia (Rupiah)	16,894	16,511·01	12,734·4	12,111·46	12,687·52	13,292
Iran (Rial)	4,976·34	4,964	4,602·872	4,058·152	2,629·251	2,587·011
Iraq (Dinar)	0·5157	0·5144	0·7034	0·7221	0·4931	0·4615
Ireland (Rep. of) (Punt)	1·1635	1·1529	1·2004	1·2324	1·2932	1·284
Israel (Shekel)	6·3147	6·4948	6·7024	6·6725	6·1811	6·0609

Average rates of exchange — continued

Average for year ending	31.12.98	31.3.99	31.12.99	31.3.00	29.12.00	30.3.01
Italy (Lira)	2,876·52	2,843·76	2,929	3,012·31	3,179·27	3,156·72
Jamaica (J$)	59·378	60·0323	62·1793	63·397	64·0371	64·0382
Japan (Yen)	216·6834	211·499	183·969	179·386	163·378	163·482
Jordan (Dinar)	1·1796	1·1771	1·1508	1·1452	1·0771	1·0512
Kenya (Shilling)	100·1734	100·8518	114·1545	117·7128	115·3867	114·6715
Korea South (Won)	2,269·7583	2,133·946	1,915·9317	1,875·842	1,723·1075	1,742·825
Kuwait (Dinar)	0·5057	0·5036	0·4927	0·4915	0·4825	0·4716
Laos (New Kip)	4,477·095	5,453·88	9,561·205	10,934·47	11,545·9667	11,216·97
Lebanon (£)	2,515·233	2,501·539	2,436·964	2,424·005	2,289·722	2,237·333
Libya (Dinar)	0·6447	0·6703	0·7323	0·7374	0·7533	0·7621
Luxembourg (Franc)	60·1307	59·3713	61·2658	63·0014	66·2364	65·7666
Malawi (Kwacha)	52·1602	60·5949	70·0759	70·8686	89·3763	99·8568
Malaysia (Ringgit)	6·477	6·4056	6·1488	6·1226	5·7611	5·6221
Malta (Lira)	0·6449	0·64	0·6473	0·6511	0·6542	0·6529
Mauritius (Rupee)	39·7329	40·4902	45·9016	45·9791	39·6999	39·6706
Mexico (Peso)	15·2139	15·8026	15·478	15·1846	14·349	14·1202
Morocco (Dirham)	15·9401	15·7773	15·8869	16·109	16·1161	15·8934
Nepal (Rupee)	99·6421	101·4974	109·7453	110·2098	107·5093	106·9198
Netherlands (Guilder)	3·2854	3·2438	3·3469	3·4416	3·6184	3·589
N'nd Antilles (Guilder)	2·9713	2·9546	2·8569	2·8465	2·69	2·6223
New Zealand (NZ$)	3·0946	3·1402	3·0555	3·1036	3·3285	3·3641
Nicaragua (Gold Cordoba)	17·05	17·4486	19·105	19·4643	18·7369	18·4729
Nigeria (Naira)	36·3062	40·8369	131·9738	158·8655	158·8476	160·0406
Norway (Krone)	12·5117	12·5348	12·6194	12·7918	13·323	13·2635
Oman (Rial Omani)	0·6387	0·6371	0·6228	0·6202	0·5837	0·5697
Pakistan (Rupee)	77·9532	80·1179	82·7123	83·2222	81·5945	82·5336
Papua New Guinea (Kina)	3·4923	3·6339	4·1831	4·4518	4·2012	4·19
Paraguay (Guarani)	4,488·0871	4,650·0563	5,044·431	5,243·9173	5,289·0655	5,250·9205
Peru (New Sol)	4·8575	5·0689	5·4651	5·4964	5·2868	5·1815
Philippines (Peso)	67·8068	65·6731	62·0974	63·843	66·9936	68·5464
Poland (Zloty)	5·8184	5·9455	6·4571	6·5556	6·6123	6·4235
Portugal (Escudo)	298·5344	294·9011	304·48	313·0858	329·1632	326·8482
Qatar (Riyal)	6·0411	6·0242	5·89	5·8646	5·5195	5·3865
Romania (Leu)	14,935·4667	16,801·7	25,176·975	27,460·78	33,138·1833	35,363·23
Russia (Rouble) (Market)						
1.4.97–31.12.97	17·6101	24·9644	40·5494	42·1773	42·7404	41·6317
1.1.98–31.3.98						
Rwanda (R Franc)	538·8919	525·5502	538·7893	547·4084	539·3179	538·3299
Saudi Arabia (Riyal)	6·2222	6·2069	6·0673	6·0412	5·6864	5·5492
Seychelles (Rupee)	8·7357	8·7682	8·6127	8·6233	8·6478	8·8073
Sierra Leone (Leone)	2,083·987	2,358·464	2,806·673	2,950·364	3,024·77	2,938·786
Singapore (S$)	2·7692	2·7791	2·742	2·7278	2·6127	2·57
Solomon Islands (SI$)	7·9247	7·9434	7·9444	8·0168	7·7079	7·5651
Somalia (Shilling)	4,348·9917	4,327·245	4,208·7617	4,194·893	3,966·2592	3,868·396
South Africa (Rand)	9·1681	9·6233	9·8932	9·9319	10·4972	10·8197
Spain/Balearic Islands (Peseta)	247·4537	244·5556	252·6969	259·8556	273·1989	271·2611
Sri Lanka (Rupee)	107·5062	110·1795	114·381	115·5974	116·3355	118·2743
Sudan (Dinar)	289·0171	301·7498	378·191	401·4363	390·8893	382·0302
Surinam (Guilder)	665·6281	662·2998	947·3155	1,109·188	1,288·1075	1,319·532
Swaziland (Lilangeni)	9·2103	9·6606	9·905	9·9719	10·5756	10·868
Sweden (Krona)	13·1769	13·1419	13·3732	13·5666	13·869	13·9687
Switzerland (Franc)	2·4011	2·376	2·4307	2·5026	2·5572	2·5092

Average rates of exchange — continued

Average for year ending	31.12.98	31.3.99	31.12.99	31.3.00	29.12.00	30.3.01
Syria (Pound)	68·6522	70·0802	72·1322	72·1909	78·9066	80·1564
Taiwan (New T$)	55·4635	55·1962	52·1951	60·403	56·5057	46·844
Tanzania (Shilling)	1,081·67	1,099·416	1,200·421	1,240·899	1,211·789	1,190·039
Thailand (Baht)	68·2186	64·3246	61·2617	61·222	60·8115	61·4603
Tonga Islands (Pa Anga)	2·6455	2·6829	2·5087	2·5073	2·6282	2·6823
Trinidad and Tobago (TT$)	10·3313	10·322	10·0452	9·9933	9·4465	9·2274
Tunisia (Dinar)	1·8879	1·8719	1·9211	1·9689	2·0742	2·067
Turkey (Lira)	436,113·253	483,958·502	682,515·902	767,547·854	945,505·394	1,014,631·97
Uganda (New Shilling)	2,041·597	2,131	2,353·274	2,401·505	2,490·5547	2,525·946
United Arab Emirates (Dirham)	6·0927	6·0776	5·9416	5·9154	5·5062	5·3736
Uruguay (Peso Uruguayo)	17·3546	17·6704	18·3411	18·5613	18·3314	18·2361
USA (US$)	1·6573	1·6542	1·6181	1·6114	1·5163	1·4793
Venezuela (Bolivar)	908·8414	931·5492	980·4513	1,009·818	1,030·271	1,022·147
Vietnam (Dong)	22,094·9167	22,451·46	22,519·5417	22,521·63	21,471·7083	21,115·76
Yemen (Rial)	218·2828	222·6623	241·5695	249·2783	244·0709	237·9881
Zambia (Kwacha)	3,177·2307	3,508·3228	4,024·737	4,183·863	4,935·725	5,178·623
Zimbabwe (Dollar)	39·4382	48·2683	62·1361	61·5445	67·1213	71·8766

Rates of exchange on year-end dates

	31.12.98	31.3.99	31.12.99	31.3.00	29.12.00	30.3.01
Australia ($A)	2·7126	2·5563	2·4631	2·6282	2·6884	2·9117
Austria (Schilling)	19·4965	20·5755	22·1255	22·9406	21·894	22·1294
Belgium (Franc)	57·1561	60·3193	64·8634	67·2528	64·1847	64·8747
Canada (Can$)	2·5555	2·4421	2·3391	2·3161	2·2437	2·2386
Denmark (Krone)	10·589	11·1137	11·9658	12·4123	11·8756	12·0122
European Union (Euro)		1·4953	1·608	1·6672	1·5911	1·6082
France (Franc)	9·294	9·8084	10·5473	10·9359	10·4369	10·5491
Germany (Deutsche mark)	2·7711	2·9245	3·1448	3·2607	3·112	3·1454
Hong Kong (HK$)	12·8895	12·5101	12·5286	12·4218	11·6515	11·0878
Ireland (Rep. of) (Punt)	1·1159	1·1776	1·2664	1·313	1·2531	1·2666
Italy (Lira)	2,743·43	2,895·26	3,113·37	3,228·06	3,080·79	3,113·91
Japan (Yen)	187·671	191·182	164·966	163·622	170·592	178·161
Luxembourg (Franc)	57·1561	60·3193	64·8634	67·2528	64·1847	64·8747
Netherlands (Guilder)	3·1224	3·2952	3·5434	3·674	3·5064	3·544
Norway (Krone)	12·6761	12·4765	12·9535	13·4631	13·1731	12·95
Portugal (Escudo)	284·055	299·776	322·359	334·235	318·986	322·416
South Africa (Rand)	9·7875	9·9845	9·9241	10·4413	11·3081	11·3875
Spain/Balearic Islands (Peseta)	235·746	248·793	267·536	277·391	264·736	267·582
Sweden (Krona)	13·486	13·2744	13·7688	13·7834	14·0948	14·6707
Switzerland (Franc)	2·2852	2·3894	2·5799	2·6525	2·4207	2·4538
USA (US$)	1·6638	1·6143	1·6117	1·5953	1·4938	1·4217

Note: The material on pages 3 to 5 is Crown Copyright.

Double taxation agreements (including protocols and regulations)
Taxes on income and capital gains

Agreements terminated or superseded within the last six years are printed in italic. Amending protocols and exchanges of notes are printed in square brackets. Entry into force after 5.4.70 is indicated in the third column.

Country	SI/SR & O	Entry into force	Country	SI/SR & O	Entry into force
Antigua & Barbuda	1947/2865		Finland	1970/153	
	[1968/1096]			[1980/710]	25.4.81
Argentina	1997/1777	1.8.97		[1985/1997]	20.2.87
Armenia†	1986/224	30.1.86		[1991/2878]	23.12.91
Australia§§	1968/305	3.10.95		[1996/3166]	8.8.97
	[1980/707]	21.5.80	France*§§	1968/1869	
	(talks 2001)			[1973/1328]	6.8.73
Austria*	1970/1947	17.12.70		[1987/466]	7.4.87
	[1979/117]	6.2.79		[1987/2055]	23.12.87
	[1994/768]	1.12.94		(text agreed)	
Azerbaijan	*1986/224*	*30.1.86*			
	1995/762	3.10.95	Gambia	1980/1963	5.7.82
			Georgia†§§	1986/224	30.1.86
Bangladesh	1980/708	8.7.80		(talks 2001)	
Barbados	1970/952	26.6.70	German Federal	1967/25	
	[1973/2096]	12.12.73	Republic*	[1971/874]	1.6.71
Belarus†	1986/224	30.1.86	Ghana	1993/1800	10.8.94
	1995/2706		Greece*	1954/142	
Belgium*	1987/2053	21.10.89	Grenada	1949/361	
Belize	1947/2866			[1968/1867]	
	[1968/573]		Guernsey	1952/1215	
	[1973/2097]	12.12.73		[1994/3209]	3.1.95
Bolivia	1995/2707	23.10.95	Guyana	1992/3207	18.12.92
Bosnia Herzegovina‡	1981/1815	16.9.82			
Botswana	1978/183	9.2.78	Hungary	1978/1056	27.8.78
	(talks 1998)				
Brazil	(talks 1997)		Iceland	1991/2879	19.12.91
Brunei	1950/1977		India	1993/1801	25.10.93
	[1968/306]		Indonesia	1994/769	14.4.94
	[1973/2098]	12.12.73		(talks 2000)	
Bulgaria	1987/2054	28.12.87	Irish Republic*	1976/2151	23.12.76
				[1976/2152]	23.12.76
Canada§§	1980/709	17.12.80		[1995/764]	21.9.95
	[1980/1528]	18.12.80		[1998/3151]	23.12.98
	[1985/1996]	23.12.85	Isle of Man	1955/1205	
	1980/780 (dividend)	*1.7.80*		[1991/2880]	19.12.91
	[1987/2071]	*1.1.88*		[1994/3208]	3.1.95
	1996/1782	30.7.96	Israel	1963/616	
	(talks 2000)			[1971/391]	25.3.71
Chile§§	(talks 2001)		Italy	1990/2590	31.12.90
China◊	1984/1826	23.12.84	Ivory Coast	1987/169	10.2.87
	[1996/3164]	4.3.97			
Croatia‡§§	1981/1815	16.9.82	Jamaica	1973/1329	31.12.73
	(talks 2001)		Japan	1970/1948	25.12.70
Cyprus	1975/425	18.3.75		[1980/1530]	31.10.80
	[1980/1529]	15.12.80	Jersey	1952/1216	
Czech Republic§	1991/2876	20.12.91		[1994/3210]	3.1.95
			Jordan§§	(agreement signed)	
Denmark	1980/1960	17.12.80			
	[1991/2877]	19.12.91	Kazakhstan	1994/3211	15.7.96
	[1996/3165]	20.6.97		[1998/2567]	2.11.98
			Kenya*	1977/1299	18.10.77
Ecuador	(text agreed)		Kiribati	1950/750	
Egypt	1980/1091	23.8.80		[1968/309]	
Estonia	1994/3207	19.12.94		[1974/1271]	25.7.74
European	(Convention and		Korea	*1978/786*	*31.5.78*
Economic	Directives 90/434/			1996/3168	30.12.96
Community	EEC, 90/435/EEC,		Kuwait	1999/2036	1.7.2000
	90/436/EEC: see		Kyrgyzstan†	1986/224	30.1.86
	TA 1988 s 815B)	23.7.90			
Falkland Islands	*1984/363*	*27.6.84*	Latvia	1996/3167	30.12.96
	[1992/3206]	*30.12.92*	Lesotho	*1949/2197*	
	1997/2985	18.12.97		*[1968/1868]*	
Faroe Islands**	*1950/1195*			1997/2986	23.12.97
	[1961/579]		Lithuania§§	(agreement signed)	
	1969/1068	31.5.71	Luxembourg*	1968/1100	
	[1971/717]	*31.5.71*		[1980/567]	21.5.80
	1973/1326	*19.12.75*		[1984/364]	19.3.84
	[1975/2190]	*19.12.75*			
Fiji*	1976/1342	17.8.76			

Double taxation agreements — continued

Country	SI/SR & O	Entry into force
Macedonia‡	1981/1815	16.9.82
Malawi	1956/619	
	[1964/1401]	
	[1968/1101]	
	[1979/302]	14.3.79
Malaysia	1973/1330	13.9.73
	[1987/2056]	26.1.88
	1997/2987	8.7.98
Malta	1995/763	27.3.95
Mauritius*	1981/1121	19.10.81
	[1987/467]	26.10.87
Mexico	1994/3212	15.12.94
Moldova†	1986/224	30.1.86
Mongolia	1996/2598	4.12.96
Montserrat	1947/2869	
	[1968/576]	
Morocco	1991/2881	29.11.90
Myanmar*	1952/751	
Namibia*§§	1962/2352	
	[1962/2788]	
	[1967/1489]	
	[1967/1490]	
	(agreement initialled)	
Netherlands*§§	1967/1063 (dividend)	
	1980/1961	6.4.81
	[1990/2152]	20.12.90
	(talks 2001)	
New Zealand	1984/365	16.3.84
Nigeria	1987/2057	27.12.87
Norway*	1985/1998	20.12.85
	2000/3247	21.12.2000
Oman◇◇	1998/2568	9.11.98
Pakistan	1987/2058	8.12.87
Papua New Guinea	1991/2882	20.12.91
Philippines	1978/184	9.2.78
Poland	1978/282	25.2.78
Portugal*	1969/599	
Qatar§§	(talks 2001)	
Romania	1977/57	17.1.77
Russian Federation†	1994/3213	18.4.97
St Christopher and Nevis	1947/2872	
Serbia and Montenegro‡	1981/1815	16.9.82
Sierra Leone	1947/2873	
	[1968/1104]	
Singapore	1967/483	
	[1978/787]	4.8.78
	1997/2988	19.12.97
Slovakia§	1991/2876	20.12.91
Slovenia‡§§	1981/1815	16.9.82
Solomon Islands	1950/748	
	[1968/574]	
	[1974/1270]	25.7.74
South Africa*§§	1969/864	
	(talks 2000)	
Spain	1976/1919	25.11.76
	[1995/765]	26.5.95
Sri Lanka	1980/713	21.5.80
Sudan	1977/1719	25.10.77
Swaziland*	1969/380	
Sweden	1984/366	26.3.84
	(talks 1998)	
Switzerland*	1978/1408	7.10.78
	[1982/714]	18.5.82
	[1994/3215]	19.12.94
Tajikistan†	1986/224	30.1.86
Thailand	1981/1546	20.11.81
Trinidad and Tobago	1983/1903	22.12.83
Tunisia	1984/133	8.2.84
Turkey	1988/932	26.10.88
Turkmenistan†	1986/224	30.1.86
Uganda	1993/1802	21.12.93
Ukraine	1993/1803	11.8.93
United Arab Emirates§§	(text agreed)	
USA	1946/1331 (dividend)	
	[1955/499]	
	[1961/985]	
	[1980/779]	22.5.80
	1980/568	25.4.80
	[1994/1418] (dividend)	16.6.94
	[1996/1781] (dividend)	30.7.96
	(new agreement signed)	
Uzbekistan	1994/770	10.6.94
Venezuela	1996/2599	31.12.96
Vietnam	1994/3216	15.12.94
Zambia*	1972/1721	29.3.73
	[1981/1816]	14.1.83
Zimbabwe	1982/1842	11.2.83

* Individuals resident in these countries are entitled to personal reliefs, similar to the relief under TA 1988 s 278, under the provisions of double taxation treaties between these countries and the UK. Non-resident nationals of all EEA countries are entitled to personal allowances as from 6 April 1996: see FA 1996 s 145.

** Following its termination by Denmark, the agreement ceased to have effect in the UK from 1 April 1997 for corporation tax and 6 April 1997 for income tax.

† SP 3/92: as an interim measure the Convention with the former USSR is to be regarded as applicable pending negotiation of new Conventions with the successor states. Such conventions have been concluded and are in force with Azerbaijan, Kazakhstan, Russia, Ukraine and Uzbekistan. A convention has been concluded with Belarus, but this has not yet been ratified.

‡ SP 6/93: the treaty with former Yugoslavia is treated as remaining in force between the UK and, respectively, Croatia and Slovenia, until bilateral agreements are signed. The UK also applies that treaty to Bosnia Herzegovina, Macedonia and 'rump' Yugoslavia (i.e. Serbia and Montenegro). Macedonia applies the treaty vis à vis the UK, but the Inland Revenue is not aware of the position taken by Bosnia Herzegovina or Serbia and Montenegro.

§ SP 5/93: the treaty with the former Czechoslovakia is treated as remaining in force between the UK and, respectively, the Czech Republic and Slovakia.

§§ Negotiations with these countries, and with Taiwan, Iran and Saudia Arabia, are seen as a priority (IR Press Release of 30 March 2001).

◇ The 1984 Agreement does not apply to the Hong Kong Special Administrative Region.

◇◇ Certain provisions relating to profits, income and gains from ships and aircraft operated in international traffic take effect from 1 January 1979 (Article 29(2)).

Double taxation agreements — continued
Shipping and air transport profits

Country	SI or SR & O	Country	SI or SR & O
Algeria (air)	1984/362	Iran (air)	1960/2419
Argentina	*1949/1435*	Jordan	1979/300
Armenia (USSR air)*	1974/1269	Kuwait (air)**	1984/1825
Bahrain (air)	(text agreed)	Kyrgyzstan (USSR air)*	1974/1269
Belarus (USSR air)*	1974/1269	Lebanon	1964/278
Brazil	1968/572	Moldova (USSR air)*	1974/1269
Cameroon (air)	1982/1841	Qatar (air)	(text agreed)
China (air)	1981/1119	*Russia (USSR air)**	*1974/1269*
Congo Democratic Republic	1977/1298	Saudi Arabia (air)	1994/767
Ethiopia (air)	1977/1297	Tajikistan (USSR air)*	1974/1269
Georgia (USSR air)*	1974/1269	Turkmenistan (USSR air)*	1974/1269
Hong Kong (air)	1998/2566	United Arab Emirates (air)	(text agreed)
(shipping)	2000/3248	*USSR (air)**	*1974/1269*

* The Revenue has confirmed that this Arrangement will be treated in the same way as the Convention covering income and capital gains SI 1986/224. See note † on p 7.

** Superseded by the comprehensive Agreement (SI 1999/2036, Art. 30) which entered into force on 1 July 2000, p 6 above.

Estates, inheritances and gifts

France*	1963/1319	South Africa	1979/576
India*	1956/998	Sweden	1981/840
Ireland	1978/1107		1989/986
Italy*	1968/304	Switzerland	*1957/426*
Netherlands	1980/706		1994/3214
	[1996/730]	USA	1979/1454
Pakistan*	1957/1522		(talks 2000)

* Agreements pre-date UK inheritance tax/capital transfer tax.

Income arising abroad — Schedule D assessment

	Case IV	Case V		
	Securities	Professions, trades, etc	Pensions	Possessions
NON-RESIDENTS	Exempt	Exempt	Exempt	Exempt
RESIDENTS				
1) **Foreign domicile**	Remittance	Remittance	Remittance	Remittance
2) **UK domicile**				
(a) Non Commonwealth citizen[1]	Arising	Arising	90%[3] arising	Arising
(b) Commonwealth citizen[2]				
(i) ordinarily resident	Arising	Arising	90%[3] arising	Arising
(ii) not ordinarily resident	Remittance	Remittance	Remittance	Remittance

[1] But not citizen of the Republic of Ireland.
[2] Or citizen of the Republic of Ireland.
[3] Pensions paid by the governments of the Federal Republic of Germany or of Austria to victims of Nazi persecution are exempt.

Schedule E liability of non-resident employees see p 72.

Tax-free (FOTRA) securities

Under FA 1996 s 154 interest on certain securities ('FOTRA securities') issued by the Treasury is exempt from tax where the beneficial owner is not ordinarily resident in the UK. Except in the case of 3½% War Loan 1952 or after, the exemption does not apply where the securities are held for the purposes of a trade or business carried on in the UK. From 6 April 1998, FOTRA status has been extended to all government stock on the terms of FA 1996 s 154 (FA 1998 s 161).

General

Certificates of tax deposit

The Series 7 Prospectus came into operation on 1 October 1993.

From 1 October 1993, certificates are not available for purchase for use against corporation tax liabilities, although certificates purchased before that date can be used before 1 October 1999 and set against all liabilities listed in the schedule to the Series 6 Prospectus.

Certificates are available to individuals, trustees, companies or other persons or bodies for the payment of any taxes or other liabilities listed in the schedule to the Prospectus. Minimum first deposit £2,000; subsequent deposits not less than £500.

Interest is paid without deduction of tax and is assessed under Schedule D Case III. It will only be paid for the first 6 years of a deposit. Under the Series 7 Prospectus a deposit bears interest for the first year at the rate in force at the time of the deposit and for each subsequent year at the rate in force on the anniversary of the deposit. No bonus or interest supplement is payable.

Series 7

Deposits of £100,000 or over: rate varies according to number of months held for in relevant year:

A = under £100,000
B = £100,000 or over

From	Amount	Held for (mths in yr)	Pay't of tax %	Cashed %	From	Amount	Held for (mths in yr)	Pay't of tax %	Cashed %
Series 7 (1.10.93)					6.11.98	A	no limit	3¼	1¾
14.12.95	A	no limit	2½	1¼		B	under 1	3¼	1¾
	B	under 1	2½	1¼			1-under 3	5¾	3
		1-under 3	5½	2¾			3-under 6	5¼	2¾
		3-under 9	5	2½			6-under 9	5	2½
		9-12	4¾	2½			9-12	4¾	2½
19. 1.96	A	no limit	2¾	1½	11.12.98	A	no limit	3¼	1¾
	B	under 1	2¾	1½		B	under 1	3	1½
		1-under 3	5¼	2¾			1-under 3	5¼	2¾
		3-under 9	4¾	2½			3-under 6	4¾	2½
		9-12	4½	2¼			6-under 9	4½	2¼
11. 3.96	A	no limit	2½	1¼			9-12	4¼	2¼
	B	under 1	2½	1¼	8. 1.99	A	no limit	2½	1¼
		1-under 3	5	2½		B	under 1	2½	1¼
		3-under 9	4¾	2½			1-under 3	5	2½
		9-12	4½	2¼			3-under 6	4½	2¼
7. 6.96	A	no limit	2¼	1¼			6-12	4	2
	B	under 1	2¼	1¼	5. 2.99	A	no limit	1¾	1
		1-12	4¾	2½		B	under 1	1¾	1
31.10.96	A	no limit	2½	1¼			1-under 3	4½	2¼
	B	under 1	2½	1¼			3-under 6	4	2
		1-under 3	5¼	2¾			6-12	3¾	2
		3-12	5	2½	9. 4.99	A	no limit	1¾	1
7. 5.97	A	no limit	2¾	1½		B	under 1	1¾	1
	B	under 1	2¾	1½			1-under 3	4¼	2¼
		1-under 3	5½	2¾			3-under 6	4	2
		3-under 6	5¼	2¾			6-12	3¾	2
		6-under 9	5½	2¾	11. 6.99	A	no limit	1½	¾
		9-12	5¼	2¾		B	under 1	1½	¾
9. 6.97	A	no limit	3	1½			1-12	4	2
	B	under 1	3	1½	9. 9.99	A	no limit	1¾	1
		1-12	5½	2¾		B	under 1	1¾	1
11. 7.97	A	no limit	3¼	1¾			1-12	4½	2¼
	B	under 1	3¼	1¾	4.11.99	A	no limit	2	1
		1-under 3	6	3		B	under 1	2	1
		3-under 9	5¾	3			1-under 3	5	2½
		9-12	6	3			3-under 12	4¾	2½
8. 8.97	A	no limit	4½	2¼	14. 1.00	A	no limit	2¼	1¼
	B	under 1	4½	2¼		B	under 1	2¼	1¼
		1-under 9	6	3			1-under 9	5	2½
		9-12	5¾	3			9-12	5¼	2¾
7.11.97	A	no limit	4	2	11. 2.00	A	no limit	2½	1¼
	B	under 1	4	2		B	under 1	2½	1¼
		1-under 6	6½	3¼			1-under 3	5¼	2¾
		6-12	6¼	3¼			3-under 6	5	2½
5. 6.98	A	no limit	4	2			6-12	5¼	2¾
	B	under 1	4	2	9. 2.01	A	no limit	2¼	1¼
		1-under 3	6½	3¼		B	under 1	2¼	1¼
		3-under 9	6¼	3¼			1-under 3	4¾	2½
		9-12	6	3			3-under 9	4¼	2¼
9.10.98	A	no limit	3¾	2			9-12	4	2
	B	under 1	3¾	2	6. 4.01	A	no limit	2	1
		1-under 3	6¼	3¼		B	under 1	2	1
		3-under 6	5¾	3			1-under 3	4¼	2¼
		6-under 9	5½	2¾			3-under 6	4	2
		9-12	5¼	2¾			6-under 9	3¾	2
							9-12	3½	1¾
					11. 5.01	A	no limit	2	1
						B	under 1	2	1
							1-under 6	4	2
							6-12	3¾	2

Due dates of tax

Capital gains tax

From 1996–97:
(TMA 1970 s 59B. There are no provisions for payment on account for capital gains tax.)
Normally 31 January following end of year of assessment.
(See also *Extended due dates* under **Income tax**, below)
Before 1996–97:
Later of *(a)* 1 December following end of year of assessment, and
(b) 30 days after issue of notice of assessment.

Corporation tax

Generally (accounting periods ending after 30 September 1993: pay and file and self assessment)
(TMA 1970 s 59D, substituted by FA 1998 Sch 19 para 29 for accounting periods ending after 30 June 1999.)
9 months and 1 day after end of accounting period.
Instalments for larger companies (TMA 1970 s 59E, SI 1998/3175)
(Large: profits exceeding upper relevant maximum amount in force at end of accounting period, subject to certain restrictions: reg 3.)
    1st instalment: 6 months and 13 days from start of accounting period (or date of final instalment if earlier);
    (2nd instalment: 3 months after 1st instalment, if length of accounting period allows);
    (3rd instalment: 3 months after 2nd instalment, if length of accounting period allows);
    Final instalment: 3 months and 14 days from end of accounting period.
Transitional provisions (reg 4) percentage of total liability payable by instalments for accounting periods ending:
    after 30 June 1999 but before 1 July 2000: 60%
    after 30 June 2000 but before 1 July 2001: 72%
    after 30 June 2001 but before 1 July 2002: 88%
(balance due and payable in accordance with *Generally* above).
Advance corporation tax (abolished from 6 April 1999) (FA 1998 ss 31, 32, Sch 3)
Tax in respect of franked payments to be included in a return is due 14 days after a return period ends.
Return periods end on 31 March, 30 June, 30 September, 31 December and at the end of each accounting period, when not one of the above.
Close companies: tax on loans to participators
Loans etc made in accounting periods ending after 30 March 1996: 9 months and 1 day after the end of the accounting period. Previously 14 days after the end of the accounting period in which the loan was made. To be included in instalment payments for large companies in respect of accounting periods ending after 30 June 1999 (TMA 1970 s 59E(11), see above).

Income tax

From 1997–98:
(1)   *Payment on account* (TMA 1970 s 59A)*
A payment on account is required where a taxpayer was assessed to income tax in respect of the immediately preceding year in an amount exceeding the amount of tax deducted at source in respect of that year (subject to a de minimis limit, see below). This excess is known as the "relevant amount".
The payment on account is made in 2 equal instalments due on –
    (a) 31 January during the year of assessment, and
    (b) 31 July in the following year of assessment.
No payments on account are required where–
    (a) the aggregate of the relevant amount (see above) and the Class 4 NIC liability for the preceding year is less than £500; or
    (b) more than 80% of the taxpayer's income tax and Class 4 NIC liability for the immediately preceding year was met by tax deducted at source.

From 1996–97:
(2)   *Payment of income tax* (TMA 1970 s 59B, Sch 3ZA)
Balance of income tax due for a year of assessment (after deducting payments on account, tax deducted at source and credits in respect of dividends, etc) is due on:
31 January following end of year of assessment (TMA 1970 s 59B(4)).
Extended due dates:
    (a) If a taxpayer has given notice of liability within 6 months of the end of the year of assessment (as required by TMA 1970 s 7), but a notice to make a return is not given until after 31 October following the end of the year of assessment, the final payment is not due until 3 months after the notice is given (TMA 1970 s 59B(3)).
    (b) If tax is payable as a result of a taxpayer's notice of amendment, a Revenue notice of correction or a Revenue notice of closure following enquiry, in each case given less than 30 days before the due date (or the extended due date at (*a*) above) the additional tax is due on or before the day following the end of a 30-day period beginning on the day on which the notice is given (TMA 1970 s 59B(5), Sch 3ZA as amended/inserted by FA 2001, Sch 29 paras 14–16).
    (c) If an assessment other than a self-assessment is made, tax payable under the assessment is due on the day following the end of a 30-day period beginning on the day on which notice of the assessment is given (TMA 1970 s 59B(6)).
The extensions under (b) and (c) do *not* alter the due date *for interest purposes* (see p 11).

*(For 1996–97 only:**
(1)   *Payment on account* (TMA 1970 s 59A as amended by FA 1995 Sch 21 para 2)
A payment on account was required where a taxpayer was assessed to income tax in respect of 1995–96 in an amount exceeding the aggregate of (a) the amount of higher-rate tax charged on any income not subject to PAYE or income from which tax had been deducted or was treated as deducted, and which was attributable to the difference between the higher rate and the basic rate (or lower rate in the case of dividend income); (b) tax deducted at source; and (c) the excess of any Schedule E liability over tax deducted under PAYE etc (subject to a de minimis limit, see below). This excess was known as the "relevant amount".
The payment on account was to be made in 2 instalments as follows–
    (*a*) due on 31 January 1997:
        (i)   100% of 1995–96 tax charged under Schedule A and Schedule D Cases III to VI and
        (ii) 50% of the remainder (including Class 4 NIC)
    excluding tax deducted at source, and
    (*b*) due on 31 July 1997: 50% of the remainder (including Class 4 NIC).
No payments on account were required where the aggregate of the relevant income (see above) and the Class 4 NIC liability for 1995–96 was less than £500.)
** These rules do not apply to partnership businesses commenced before 6 April 1994 where there has been no subsequent deemed cessation and recommencement. For 1996–97, such partnerships were required to pay tax in two instalments on 1 January and 1 July 1997, as under the old rules (see p 12).

Interest on overdue tax see p 11.   **Repayment supplement** see p 15.
Remission of tax see p 14.

Before 1996–97 (These rules applied also, in the case of Schedule D Cases I, II and V, for 1996–97 to partnerships commenced before 6 April 1994 and which had not undergone a deemed cessation and recommenced subsequently):

Schedule A   Later of   *(a)*   1 January in year of assessment, and
                                (b)   30 days after issue of notice of assessment.

Schedule C   Tax deducted by paying agent and due within 30 days of issue of notice of assessment.

Schedule D Cases I, II and V *(trades, professions, etc)*: 2 equal payments due –
                                (a)   1 January in year of assessment (or 30 days after issue of notice of assessment, if later) and
                                (b)   1 July following year of assessment (or 30 days after issue of notice of assessment, if later).

Schedule D Cases III, IV, V *(other than trades, professions)* and VI: Later of –
                                (a)   1 January in year of assessment, and
                                (b)   30 days after issue of notice of assessment.

Schedule E   Deductible from emoluments under PAYE
                    Assessments: 14 days after application by collector.

Higher rate   on income from which income tax has been deducted (other than under PAYE), or is treated as having been deducted or paid, or income chargeable under Schedule F
               Later of   *(a)*   1 December following end of year of assessment, and
                               (b)   30 days after issue of notice of assessment.

Inheritance tax (capital transfer tax)

Chargeable transfers other than on death, made between:
6 April and 30 September – 30 April in next year.
1 October and 5 April   – 6 months after end of month in which chargeable transfer is made.

Chargeable events following conditional exemption for heritage etc property and charge on disposal of trees or underwood before the second death
                            – 6 months after end of month in which chargeable event occurs.

Transfers on death
Earlier of   *(a)*   6 months after end of month in which death occurs, and
               (b)   delivery of account by personal representatives.

Tax or extra tax becoming payable on death: (1)   chargeable transfers and potentially exempt transfers within 7 years of death, or
                                                            (2)   gifts in excess of £100,000 made to political parties before 15 March 1988 and within 1 year of death:
                                                            due 6 months after end of month in which death takes place.

Interest on overdue tax

Interest on overdue income tax and capital gains tax

(NB: These rules apply with respect to liabilities for 1996–97 and subsequent years and to liabilities for 1995–96 and earlier years assessed after 5 April 1998. However, for partnerships with trades, etc set up and commenced before 6 April 1994, the previous rules continued to apply for the year 1996–97.)

For payments on account (under TMA 1970 s 59A(2)), tax not postponed pending an appeal (under TMA 1970 s 55) and balancing payments (under TMA 1970 s 59B), interest runs from the due date to the date of payment, on the amount outstanding. For the due date, see pp 10, 11. In respect of payments on account, interest is charged on the difference between the amount that ought to have been paid and the amount actually paid.

For tax resulting from amendments/corrections to returns and from discovery assessments (under TMA 1970 s 29), interest normally runs from the annual filing date for the relevant tax year.

Where a claim made under TMA 1970 s 59A(3) or (4) to reduce payments on account proves to be excessive, an underpayment may arise. In such a case, interest is charged on the difference between the amount actually paid and the amount that ought to have been paid if the claim had been made correctly.

Surcharge on unpaid income tax and capital gains tax (TMA 1970 s 59C, amended by FA 1995 s 109)

Applies from 1996-97, and for assessments for 1995–96 or an earlier year of assessment made after 5 April 1998 (FA 1995 s 109(2)). (Tax taken into account in determining certain other penalties (under TMA 1970 ss 7, 93(5), 95 and 95A) is ignored for the purposes of calculating the surcharge.)

28 days: Where income tax or capital gains tax becomes payable and all or part of it remains unpaid the day following 28 days after the due date, the taxpayer is liable to a surcharge of 5% of the unpaid tax.

6 months: The taxpayer is liable to a further surcharge of 5% on any of the tax remaining unpaid 6 months and 1 day from the due date.

Interest is payable on surcharge from the expiry of 30 days beginning on the day on which the surcharge is imposed until the date of payment. It is charged at the rate applying to overdue income tax and capital gains tax (see p 13).

Interest on overdue corporation tax (accounting periods ending after 30 September 1993)

Interest runs from the due date (see p 10) to the date of payment: TMA 1970 s 87A (wording amended by FA 1994 Sch 19 para 24 and SI 1998/3175 reg 7 for accounting periods ending after 30 June 1999) and ss 59D (substituted from the same date) and 59E (inserted from the same date).

For instalment payments by large companies for accounting periods ending after 30 June 1999, a special rate of interest runs from the due date to the earlier of the date of payment and nine months after the end of the accounting period (after which the normal rate applies): SI 1989/1297 regs 32A and 32B (inserted by SI 1998/3176 reg 6).

Interest on inheritance tax

Interest runs from the due date (see above) to the date of payment.

Interest on overdue tax — continued

Interest on PAYE and national insurance

Employer's tax and Class 1 national insurance payable under PAYE (1992–93 and future years)	19 April following deduction year to date of payment
(Settlement agreement: Income Tax (Employments) Regulations 1993 Part VI Ch V)	19 October following year to which agreement relates to date of payment
Class 1A national insurance	19 April following year in which contributions due to date of payment
Class 4 national insurance	See under income tax on p 10

'Old' rules:

Period for which interest runs: default interest charged under TMA 1970 s 88 (*repealed* with effect for assessments in respect of 1996–97 and subsequent years (1997–98 and subsequent years if the taxpayer is a partnership whose trade etc commenced before 6 April 1994), and for assessments in respect of 1995–96 and earlier years where such assessments are made after 5 April 1998.)

Advance corporation tax	Not applicable
Capital gains tax	1 December following end of tax year for which charged to date of payment
Income tax	
Schedule A	1 January in tax year for which charged to date of payment
Schedule C	*1 January in tax year for which charged to date of payment*
Schedule D Cases I, II and V (foreign trades and professions)	One-half from 1 January in tax year for which charged; one-half from following 1 July to date of payment
Schedule D Cases III, IV, V (other than trades etc), VI	1 January in tax year for which charged to date of payment
Schedule E	1 January in tax year for which charged to date of payment
Higher rate tax	1 December following end of tax year for which charged to date of payment

Period for which interest runs: non-default interest (for partnerships with trades, etc set up and commenced before 6 April 1994, in respect of years before 1997–98, and generally for liabilities in respect of 1995–96 and earlier years assessed before 6 April 1998, only)
(*For due date see pp 10 and 11, above)

Advance corporation tax	Due date* to date of payment
Capital gains tax	See p 12 (below)
Capital transfer tax	Due date* to date of payment
Corporation tax (accounting periods ending after 30 September 1993)	Due date to date of payment
Development land tax	3 months after event giving rise to liability to date of payment
Employer's tax and Class 1 national insurance payable under PAYE (1992–93 and subsequent years)	19 April following deduction year to date of payment
Class 1A national insurance	19 April following year in which contributions due to date of payment
Class 4 national insurance	See p 12 (below)
Income tax	
Schedule A	See p 12 (below)
Schedule C	See p 12 (below)
Schedule D	See p 12 (below)
Schedule E	Due date to date of payment
Higher rate tax	See p 12 (below)
Inheritance tax	Due date* (see above) to date of payment

Capital gains tax, income tax under Schedules A, C, D (for partnerships with trades, etc set up and commenced before 6 April 1994, or liabilities in respect of 1995–96 and earlier years assessed before 6 April 1998, only)

Interest runs from due date for payment (see pp 10, 11) until paid *unless* the assessment is under appeal *and* an application is made to postpone the tax (*or* if additional tax not charged by the assessment is found payable on appeal), when the interest runs from the *later* of—
(a) the original due date (see column (a) below), and
(b) the *earlier* of— (i) the date on which the tax actually becomes due (see column (b) (i) below), and
               (ii) the date given in TMA 1970 s 86(4) Table (see column (b) (ii) below).

Tax	(a)	(b)(i)		(b)(ii)
		(1)	(2)	
	Original due date	*Tax not postponed*	*Tax postponed but payable or additional tax determined payable*	*Date given in TMA 1970 s 86(4) Table*
Capital gains tax	1 December following y of a†	Due date (a), or 30 days after the determination of the postponement application, if later	Due date (a), or 30 days after issue of notice of total tax due, if later	1 June after end of *next* y of a
Higher rate tax				
Schedule A Schedule D Cases III (except public/foreign dividends) IV, V (other than trades, professions), VI	1 January in y of a†	As above	As above	1 July following y of a
Schedule C Schedule D Case III (public/foreign dividends etc)	30 days from issue of notice of assessment	30 days after determination of postponement application	30 days after issue of notice of total tax due	6 months after due date (a)
Schedule D Cases I,II (including Class 4 national insurance contributions), V (foreign trades, professions)	2 equal instalments: 1 Jan in y of a† and 1 July following y of a†	Each instalment: appropriate due date (a), or 30 days after determination of application, if later	Each instalment: appropriate due date (a), or 30 days after issue of notice of total tax due, if later	1 July following y of a

† Or 30 days after issue of notice of assessment, if later; not applicable for the purposes of column (b) (i) or (ii).

Prescribed rate

	Rate	Period
Income tax, capital gains tax and Class 1, 1A and 4 national insurance contributions and stamp duty and stamp duty reserve tax: from 1 October 1999 (SI 1999/2538; SI 1999/2536)	7.5% 8.5% 7.5% 8.5% 9.5% 8.5% 6.25% 7% 6.25% 5.5% 6.25%	from 6 May 2001 6 February 2000–5 May 2001 6 March 1999–5 February 2000 6 January 1999–5 March 1999 6 August 1997–5 January 1999 31 January 1997–5 August 1997 6 February 1996–30 January 1997 6 March 1995–5 February 1996 6 October 1994–5 March 1995 6 January 1994–5 October 1994 6 March 1993–5 January 1994
Corporation tax self assessment: (accounting periods ending after 30 June 1999) (a) Instalment payments (except where tax still unpaid nine months after end of accounting period)	6.25% 6.5% 6.75% 7% 8% 7.75% 7.5% 7.25% 7% 7.25% 7.5% 8% 8.25%	from 21 May 2001 16 April 2001–20 May 2001 19 February 2001–15 April 2001 20 April 2000–18 February 2001 21 February 2000–19 April 2000 24 January 2000–20 February 2000 15 November 1999–23 January 2000 20 September 1999–14 November 1999 21 June 1999–19 September 1999 19 April 1999–20 June 1999 15 February 1999–18 April 1999 18 January 1999–14 February 1999 7 January 1999–17 January 1999
(b) Payments other than instalment payments (or for instalment payments still unpaid nine months after end of accounting period)	7.5% 8.5% 7.5%	from 6 May 2001 6 February 2000–5 May 2001 6 March 1999–5 February 2000
Corporation tax pay and file: (accounting periods ending after 30 September 1993)	6% 6.75% 5.75% 6.5% 7.5% 6.25% 7% 6.25% 5.5% 6.25%	from 6 May 2001 6 February 2000–5 May 2001 6 March–5 February 2000 6 January 1999–5 March 1999 6 August 1997–5 January 1999 6 February 1996–5 August 1997 6 March 1995–5 February 1996 6 October 1994–5 March 1995 6 January 1994–5 October 1994 1 October 1993–5 January 1994
Corporation tax: (accounting periods ending before 1 October 1993)	5.75% 6.5% — 6.25% 7% 6.25% 5.5% 6.25%	from 6 May 2001 6 March 2001–5 May 2001 31 January 1997–5 March 2001 6 February 1996–30 January 1997 6 March 1995–5 February 1996 6 October 1994–5 March 1995 6 January 1994–5 October 1994 6 March 1993–5 January 1994
Income tax on company payments (due on or after 14 October 1999)	7.5% 8.5% 7.5%	from 6 May 2001 6 February 2000–5 May 2001 14 October 1999–5 February 2000
Income tax on company payments (due before 14 October 1999), **advance corporation tax, development land tax, petroleum revenue tax** (including **advance petroleum revenue tax**) and **stamp duty reserve tax** (before 1 October 1999)	5.75% 6.5% 5.75% 6.5% 7.25% 6.25% 7% 6.25% 5.5% 6.25%	from 6 May 2001 6 February 2000–5 May 2001 6 March 1999–5 February 2000 6 January 1999–5 March 1999 6 August 1997–5 January 1999 6 February 1996–5 August 1997 6 March 1995–5 February 1996 6 October 1994–5 March 1995 6 January 1994–5 October 1994 6 March 1993–5 January 1994

Prescribed rate – continued

	Rate	Period
Inheritance tax and **capital transfer tax:** The rates for periods before 16 December 1986 applied *unless* the transfer was one of those mentioned below	4%	from 6 May 2001
	5%	6 February 2000–5 May 2001
	4%	6 March 1999–5 February 2000
	5%	6 October 1994–5 March 1999
	4%	6 January 1994–5 October 1994
	5%	6 December 1992–5 January 1994
	6%	6 November 1992–5 December 1992
	8%	6 July 1991–5 November 1992
	9%	6 May 1991–5 July 1991
	10%	6 March 1991–5 May 1991
	11%	6 July 1989–5 March 1991
	9%	6 October 1988–5 July 1989
	8%	6 August 1988–5 October 1988
	6%	6 June 1987–5 August 1988
	8%	16 December 1986–5 June 1987
	11%	1 May 1985–15 December 1986
	8%	1 December 1982–30 April 1985
	12%	1 January 1980–30 November 1982
	9%	before 1 January 1980
Inheritance tax: chargeable transfers on death or potentially exempt transfers **Capital transfer tax:** chargeable transfers on death *only*	9%	1 May 1985–15 December 1986
	6%	1 December 1982–30 April 1985
	9%	1 January 1980–30 November 1982
	6%	before 1 January 1980

Remission of tax

By concession, arrears of tax may be waived if they result from the Revenue's failure to make proper and timely use of information supplied by the taxpayer or, where it affects the taxpayer's coding, by his or her employer. From 26 April 1994 the concession also applies to information supplied by the DSS affecting the taxpayer's entitlement to a retirement or widow's pension (see Concession A19). The concession only applies where the taxpayer could reasonably have believed that his or her affairs were in order and (unless the circumstances are exceptional) where the taxpayer is notified of the arrears more than 12 months after the end of the tax year in which the Revenue received the information indicating that more tax was due.

Repayment supplement

Calculated as simple interest on the amount of tax repaid. The supplement is tax free. (From 31 January 1997 the rate is determined under SI 1989/1297 as amended by SI 1996/3187, see below.)

These rates apply also to overpaid Class 1, 1A and 4 national insurance contributions but not to overpaid corporation tax for accounting periods ending after 30 September 1993 (see p 16). The rates also apply to overpaid stamp duty and stamp duty reserve tax from 1 October 1999.

Period to which supplement relates	*Rate*
from 6 May 2001	3·5%
6 February 2000–5 May 2001	4%
6 March 1999–5 February 2000	3%
6 January 1999–5 March 1999	4%
6 August 1997–5 January 1999	4·75%
6 February 1997–5 August 1997	4%
6 February 1996–5 February 1997	6·25%
6 March 1995–5 February 1996	7%
6 October 1994–5 March 1995	6·25%
6 January 1994–5 October 1994	5·5%
6 March 1993–5 January 1994	6·25%
6 December 1992–5 March 1993	7%
6 November 1992–5 December 1992	7·75%
6 October 1991–5 November 1992	9·25%
6 July 1991–5 October 1991	10%
6 May 1991–5 July 1991	10·75%
6 March 1991–5 May 1991	11·5%
6 November 1990–5 March 1991	12·25%
6 November 1989–5 November 1990	13%
6 July 1989–5 November 1989	12·25%
6 January 1989–5 July 1989	11·5%
6 October 1988–5 January 1989	10·75%
6 August 1988–5 October 1988	9·75%
6 May 1988–5 August 1988	7·75%
6 December 1987–5 May 1988	8·25%
6 September 1987–5 December 1987	9%
6 June 1987–5 September 1987	8·25%
6 April 1987–5 June 1987	9%
6 November 1986–5 April 1987	9·5%
6 August 1986–5 November 1986	8·5%
6 May 1985–5 August 1986	11%
6 December 1982–5 May 1985	8%
6 January 1980–5 December 1982	12%
6 April 1974–5 January 1980	9%
Before 6 April 1974	6%

'New' rules:
Income tax (TA 1988 s 824; FA 1997 s 92)
From 1996–97 (1997–98 for partnerships whose trade, profession or business commenced before 6 April 1994) repayment supplement applies to:
    (a) amounts paid on account of income tax
    (b) income tax paid by or on behalf of an individual
    (c) surcharges on late payments of tax
    (d) penalties incurred by an individual under any provision of TMA 1970
but excluding amounts paid in excess of the maximum the taxpayer is required to pay.

Except for tax deducted at source, the repayment supplement runs *from* the date on which the tax, penalty or surcharge was paid *to* the date on which the order for repayment is issued. For tax deducted at source, repayment supplement runs from 31 January after the end of the tax year for which the tax was deducted.

Capital gains tax (TCGA 1992 s 283; FA 1997 s 92)
From 1996–97 repayment supplement runs *from* the date on which the tax was paid *to* the date on which the order for repayment is issued.

'Old' rules:
Individuals, personal representatives and trusts. (Before 1996–97, or before 1997–98 for partnerships whose trade, profession or business commenced before 6 April 1994.)
Repayments of IT, surtax or CGT made over 12 months after year of assessment to which repayment relates. Calculated *from* later of
    (a) end of year of assessment following that for which repayment is made, and
    (b) end of year of assessment in which overpayment of tax was made,
to end of tax month in which repayment order issued (TA 1988 s 824 as originally enacted).

Companies: interest on tax overpaid (accounting periods ending after 30 September 1993 and before 1 July 1999) (TA 1988 s 826)

Repayments of corporation tax, repayments of ACT in respect of foreign income dividends, repayments of income tax in respect of payments received, and payments of tax credits in respect of franked investment income received, made after the material date. Advance corporation tax is abolished from 6 April 1999 (FA 1998 ss 31, 32, SI 1999/358).

Calculated *from* the material date *to* the date the repayment order is issued.

For corporation tax, the material date is the later of

(a) the date on which the tax was paid and

(b) the date on which the tax became, or would have become, due and payable – generally, nine months and one day after the end of the accounting period.

For ACT, the material date is the date on which corporation tax for the accounting period in which the distribution was made became, or would have become, due and payable – generally, nine months and one day after the end of the accounting period.

For repayments of income tax in respect of payments received and payments of tax credits in respect of franked investment income received, the material date is the date on which corporation tax for the accounting period in which the payments or the franked investment income were received became, or would have become, due and payable. Again, this is generally nine months and one day after the end of the accounting period.

This rule is qualified in instances where there is a carry-back of surplus ACT or a carry-back of trading losses for more than 12 months.

Surplus ACT (s 826(7) repealed for accounting periods beginning on or after 6 April 1999 by FA 1998 Sch 3)

Where there is in any accounting period ('the later period') an amount of surplus ACT and a claim is made under TA 1988 s 239(3) to carry this surplus ACT back to an earlier accounting period ('the earlier period'), then interest on any repayment of corporation tax for the earlier period (or of income tax on a payment received in the earlier period) resulting from the claim under s 239(3) begins to run only after the date on which the corporation tax for the *later* period (the period in which the surplus ACT arose) became due and payable.

This rule is in itself subject to modification where the surplus ACT arises because of a trading loss carried back (see below).

A similar rule (s 826(7C)) applies to the carry-back of a non-trading deficit on a company's loan relationships as applies to the carry-back of surplus ACT.

Trading losses carried back for more than 12 months (s 826(7A), (7B))

Where a claim is made under TA 1988 s 393A(1) to set off a loss incurred in a later period against the profits of an earlier period not falling within the 12 months immediately preceding the later period, and

(a) a repayment of corporation tax in respect of that earlier period or a repayment of income tax in respect of a payment received in the earlier period; or

(b) following a claim under TA 1988 s 242 to include surplus franked investment income in profits available for set-off, a payment of the whole or part of the tax credit comprised in franked investment income of the earlier period,

is made, interest in respect of that part of the repayment due to the claim under TA 1988 s 393A(1) or TA 1988 s 242 (so far as it relates to the claim under s 393A(1)) begins to run only after the date on which the corporation tax in respect of the later period (the lossmaking period) became, or would have become, due and payable.

Carry-back of trading loss giving rise to carry-back of surplus ACT (s 826(7AA) repealed for accounting periods beginning on or after 6 April 1999 by FA 1998 Sch 3)

Where

(a) a trading loss carried back under s 393A(1) from a later period ('the lossmaking period') gives rise to an amount of surplus ACT, and that surplus ACT is then carried back under s 239(3) to a still-earlier period and

(b) as a result a repayment of corporation tax for the still-earlier period (or of income tax on a payment received in the still-earlier period) falls to be made

then interest on those repayments begins to run only after the date on which the corporation tax for the *lossmaking period* became due and payable.

A similar rule (s 826(7CA)) applies to the carry-back of surplus ACT following the carry-back of a non-trading deficit on a company's loan relationships.

Rates	
from 6 May 2001	2.75%
6 February 2000–5 May 2001	3.5%
6 March 1999–5 February 2000	2.75%
6 January 1999–5 March 1999	3.25%
6 August 1997–5 January 1999	4%
6 February 1996–5 August 1997	3.25%

Corporation tax for accounting periods ending after 30 June 1999

SI 1989/1297 regs 3BA and 3BB (inserted by SI 1998/3176 reg 8)

For instalment payments by large companies and early payments by other companies, a special rate of interest runs from the date the excess arises (but not earlier than the due date of the first instalment) to the earlier of the date the repayment order is issued and nine months after the end of the accounting period after which the normal rate of interest applies.

Rates on overpaid instalment payments and on corporation tax paid early (but not due by instalments):	
from 21 May 2001	5%
16 April 2001–20 May 2001	5.25%
19 February 2000–15 April 2001	5.5%
21 February 2000–18 February 2001	5.75%
24 January 2000–20 February 2000	5.5%
15 November 1999–23 January 2000	5.25%
20 September 1999–14 November 1999	5%
21 June 1999–19 September 1999	4.75%
19 April 1999–20 June 1999	5%
15 February 1999–18 April 1999	5.25%
18 January 1999–14 February 1999	5.75%
7 January 1999–17 January 1999	6%

Rates on overpaid corporation tax in respect of periods after normal due date (SI 1989/1297 reg 3BB):

from 6 May 2001	4%
6 February 2000–5 May 2001	5%
6 March 1999–5 February 2000	4%

Penalties

A) Personal tax returns: offences by taxpayers

Offence	Penalty
Failure to give notice of chargeability to income or capital gains tax within 6 months from end of year of assessment (TMA 1970 s 7).	Amount not exceeding tax assessed (either self-assessed under TMA 1970 s 9 or under a TMA 1970 s 29 'discovery' assessment) for that year and not paid before 1 February following that year.
(From 1996–97) Failure to comply with notice requiring return for income tax or capital gains tax (TMA 1970 s 93).	(a) Initial penalty of £100; and (b) upon direction by Commissioners, further penalty not exceeding £60 for each day on which failure continues after notification of direction; (c) if failure continues after six months following filing date, and no application for a direction under (b) has been made, a further penalty of £100. (d) In addition, if failure continues after first anniversary of filing date, and there would have been a liability to tax shown in the return, a penalty not exceeding the liability that would have been shown in the return. (e) If the taxpayer can prove that the liability to tax shown in the return would not have exceeded a particular amount, the sum of penalties under (a) and (c) above are not to exceed that amount.
(From 1996–97) Failure to comply with notice requiring partnership return (TMA 1970 s 93A).	(a) Initial penalty on each 'relevant partner' of £100; and (b) upon direction by Commissioners, further penalty on each relevant partner not exceeding £60 for each day on which failure continues after notification to representative partner of direction; (c) if failure continues after six months following filing date, and no application for a direction under (b) has been made, a further penalty on each relevant partner of £100. NB: A 'relevant partner' is any person who was a partner at any time during the period for which the return is required.
Fraudulently or negligently delivering incorrect return or accounts or making an incorrect statement in connection with a claim for an allowance, deduction or relief (TMA 1970 s 95).	Penalty not exceeding the difference between the amount payable under the return etc and the amount which would have been payable if the return etc had been correct.
(From 1996–97) Fraudulently or negligently delivering incorrect partnership return or accounts or making an incorrect statement or declaration in connection with such a return (TMA 1970 s 95A).	Penalty on each relevant partner not exceeding the difference between the amount payable by him or her under the return, etc and the amount that would have been payable by him or her if the return, etc had been correct. For the meaning of 'relevant partner', see under TMA 1970 s 93A above.
(From 31.1.01) Failure to register as self-employed (and liable to Class 2 NIC) within three months after the month in which self-employment begins (SI 2001/1004 reg 87).	£100.

B) Corporation tax returns under pay and file and corporation tax self assessment

Offence	Penalty
Pay and file (accounting periods ending before 1 July 1999) Failure to give notice of chargeability to corporation tax within 12 months after end of accounting period (TMA 1970 s 10).	Penalty not exceeding amount of tax unpaid 12 months after end of accounting period (after set-off of income tax credits).
Failure to comply with notice requiring return for corporation tax (TMA 1970 s 94).	(a) If return is delivered within 3 months of due date – £100 (£500 in respect of default for third consecutive period); (b) if return is delivered more than 3 months after due date – £200 (£1,000 in respect of default for third consecutive period); and (c) if return is delivered between 18 months and 2 years after end of return period – an additional penalty of 10% of tax unpaid at end of 18-month period; (d) if return is delivered more than 2 years after end of return period – an additional penalty of 20% of tax unpaid at end of 18-month period.
Fraudulently or negligently delivering incorrect return or accounts or making an incorrect statement in connection with a claim for an allowance, deduction or relief (TMA 1970 s 96).	Penalty not exceeding the difference between the amount payable under the return etc and the amount which would have been payable if the return etc had been correct.

B) Corporation tax returns under pay and file and corporation tax self assessment — continued

Offence	Penalty
Self assessment (accounting periods ending on or after 1 July 1999)	*(For the restriction of penalties where multiple tax-related penalties are payable in respect of the same accounting period see FA 1998 Sch 18 para 90)*
Failure to give notice of chargeability to corporation tax within 12 months after end of accounting period (FA 1998 Sch 18 para 2).	Penalty not exceeding amount of tax payable for that accounting period remaining unpaid 12 months after end of accounting period (taking no account of relief deferred under TA 1988 s 419(4A)).
Failure to deliver a company tax return by the filing date (FA 1998 Sch 18 paras 17, 18).	*Flat-rate penalties* (Unless FA 1998 Sch 18 para 19 (excuse for late delivery of returns) applies) (a) If return is delivered within 3 months of the filing date: £100 (£500 for third successive failure); (b) in any other case: £200 (£1,000 for third successive failure); (the increased penalties under (a) and (b) apply with modifications where the first or second period ends before 1 July 1999 (para 17(4)). *Tax-related penalties* (c) If return is delivered between 18 months (or the filing date, if later) and 2 years after the end of the return period: an additional penalty of 10% of the unpaid tax; (d) if return delivered more than 2 years after the end of the return period: an additional penalty of 20% of the unpaid tax. (In determining the amount of unpaid tax no account is taken of relief deferred under TA 1970 s 419(4A)).
Fraudulently or negligently delivering a company tax return which is incorrect (FA 1998 Sch 18 para 20).	An amount not exceeding the amount of tax understated (taking no account of relief deferred under TA 1988 s 419(4A)).
On discovering that a company tax return delivered by it (neither fraudulently nor negligently) is incorrect, a company does not remedy the error without reasonable delay (FA 1998 Sch 18 para 20).	An amount not exceeding the amount of tax understated (taking no account of relief deferred under TA 1988 s 419(4A)).
Fraudulently or negligently making an incorrect return, statement or declaration in connection with a claim for any tax allowance, deduction or relief, or submitting any incorrect accounts in connection with the ascertainment of the company's tax liability (FA 1998 Sch 18 para 89).	Penalty not exceeding the amount of tax understated (excluding relief deferred under TA 1988 s 419(4A)).

C) PAYE returns

Offence	Penalty
Failure to submit return P9D or P11D (benefits in kind) by due date (6 June following tax year 1995–96; 6 July following subsequent tax years) (TMA 1970 s 98(1)).	(a) An initial penalty not exceeding £300; and (b) a continuing penalty not exceeding £60 for each day on which the failure continues after imposition of the initial penalty.
Fraudulently or negligently submitting incorrect return P9D or P11D (TMA 1970 s 98(2)).	Penalty not exceeding £3,000.
Failure to submit returns P14 (individual end of year summary), P35 (annual return), P38 or P38A (supplementary returns for employees not on P35) by due date (19 May following tax year) (TMA 1970 s 98A).	(a) First 12 months: penalty of £100 for each 50 employees (or part thereof) for each month the failure continues; (b) failures exceeding 12 months: a penalty not exceeding the amount of PAYE or NIC due and unpaid after 19 April following year of assessment. (For late 1995–96 returns, the Revenue will normally limit the amount of the penalty to the total of the tax and NIC that should be reported on the return or to £100, whichever is greater: Revenue Press Release dated 14 June 1996.)
Fraudulently or negligently submitting incorrect form P14, P35, P38 or P38A (TMA 1970 s 98A).	Penalty not exceeding the difference between the amount payable under the return and the amount which would have been payable if the return had been correct.
Failure to submit returns P11D(b) (Class 1A NIC returns) by due date (19 July following tax year, extended for 2000/01 only to 19 September 2001) (SI 2001/1004 reg 81).	(a) First 12 months: penalty of £100 for each 50 employees (or part thereof) for each month the failure continues (but total penalty not to exceed total Class 1A NIC due); (b) failures exceeding 12 months: a penalty not exceeding the amount of Class 1A NIC due and unpaid after 19 July following year of assessment.

D) Inheritance tax returns and information

Offence	Penalty
Failure to deliver an account under IHTA 1984, s 216 or 217. (IHTA 1984 s 245; FA 1999 s 108)	(a) An initial penalty not exceeding £100; (b) further penalty not exceeding £60 (where penalty determined by court or Special Commissioners) for each day on which the failure continues after imposition of initial penalty; and (c) if failure continues after six months following the date on which the account is due, and proceedings have not commenced, a further penalty not exceeding £100.
Failure to make a return under IHTA 1984, s 218 or failure to comply with a notice under s 219.	(a) An initial penalty not exceeding £300; and (b) further penalty not exceeding £60 (where penalty determined by court or Special Commissioners) for each day on which the failure continues after imposition of initial penalty.
Failure to comply with a notice under IHTA 1984, s 219A (1) or (4). (IHTA 1984 s 245A; FA 1999 s 108)	(a) An initial penalty not exceeding £50; and (b) further penalty not exceeding £30 (where penalty determined by court or Special Commissioners) for each day on which the failure continues after imposition of initial penalty.
The taxpayer fraudulently or negligently delivering, furnishing or producing incorrect accounts, information or documents. (IHTA 1984 s 247(1); FA 1999 s 108)	(a) In the case of fraud, a penalty not exceeding the aggregate of £3,000 and the difference between the amount payable according to the information furnished and the amount that would have been payable if the accounts etc had been correct; and (b) in the case of negligence, a penalty not exceeding the aggregate of £1,500 and the difference between the amount payable according to the information furnished and the amount that would have been payable if the accounts etc had been correct.
A person other than the taxpayer fraudulently or negligently delivering, furnishing or producing incorrect accounts, information or documents. (IHTA 1984 s 247(3); FA 1999 s 108)	(a) In the case of fraud, a penalty not exceeding £3,000; and (b) in the case of negligence, a penalty not exceeding £1,500.
Any person assisting in or inducing the delivery, furnishing or production of any account, information or document knowing it to be incorrect. (IHTA 1984 s 247(4); FA 1999 s 108)	A penalty not exceeding £3,000.

E) Special returns of information

Offence	Penalty
Failure to comply with a notice to deliver a return or other document, furnish particulars or make anything available for inspection under any of the provisions listed in column 1 of the table in TMA 1970 s 98. (FA 1999 s 89 extends this to corporation tax payments by instalment.)	(a) An initial penalty not exceeding £300 (£3,000 for failure to comply with TA 1988 s 765A(2)(a) or (b)); and (b) a continuing penalty not exceeding £60 (£600 for failure to comply with TA 1988 s 765A(2)(a) or (b)) for each day on which the failure continues after imposition of the initial penalty.
Failure to comply with requirement to furnish information, give certificates or produce documents or records under any of the provisions listed in column 2 of the table in TMA 1970 s 98. (FA 1999 s 86 extends this to advance pricing agreements.)	(a) An initial penalty not exceeding £300; and (b) a continuing penalty not exceeding £60 for each day on which the failure continues after imposition of the initial penalty.
Fraudulently or negligently delivering any incorrect document, information etc required under any of the provisions listed in column 1 or 2 of the table in TMA 1970 s 98.	Penalty not exceeding £3,000.
(Accounting periods ending after 30 June 1999). Failure of a company to produce documents, etc., for the purposes of an enquiry (FA 1998 Sch 18 para 29).	(a) £50; (b) If failure continues after imposition of penalty under (a), an additional penalty for each day the failure continues, not exceeding: (i) £30 if determined by the Revenue under TMA 1970 s 100; and (ii) £150 if determined by the Commissioners under TMA 1970 s 100C.
Fraudulently or negligently making a false or misleading statement in the preparation of, or application to enter into, any advance pricing agreement (FA 1999 s 86).	Penalty not exceeding £10,000.

F) Other offences by taxpayers, agents etc

Offence	Penalty
Failure to retain records as required by TMA 1970 s 12B(1) (TMA 1970 s 12B(5)).	Penalty not exceeding £3,000.
Falsification of documents (TMA 1970 s 20BB).	On summary conviction, a fine not exceeding the statutory maximum (£5,000); on conviction on indictment, imprisonment for a term not exceeding 2 years or a fine or both.
Failure to produce documents required under TMA 1970 s 19A (power to enquire into self-assessment return, etc) (TMA 1970 s 97AA).	(a) Initial penalty of £50; and (b) further penalty not exceeding £30 (where penalty determined by officer of Board) or £150 (where penalty determined by Commissioners) for each day on which failure continues after imposition of initial penalty.
Offences in connection with the supply of information regarding European Economic Interest Groupings—	
(i) failure to supply information	An initial penalty not exceeding £300 per member of the Grouping at the time of failure and after direction by the Commissioners a continuing penalty not exceeding £60 per member of the Grouping at the end of the day for each day on which the failure continues after notification of the direction.
(ii) fraudulent or negligent delivery of an incorrect return, accounts or statement. (TMA 1970 s 98B).	Not exceeding £3,000 for each member of the Grouping at the time of delivery.
Assisting in the delivery of incorrect returns, accounts or information (TMA 1970 s 99).	Not exceeding £3,000.
Fraudulently or negligently giving a certificate of non-liability to income tax for the purposes of receiving interest gross on a bank or building society account, or failing to comply with an undertaking given in such a certificate (TMA 1970 s 99A).	Not exceeding £3,000.
Refusal to allow a deduction of income tax authorised by the Taxes Acts (TMA 1970 s 106).	£50.
Obstruction of officer of the Board in inspection of property to ascertain its market value (TMA 1970 s 111).	Not exceeding level 1 on the standard scale.
Issue by a company of a certificate of approval for enterprise investment scheme relief fraudulently or negligently or without the authority of the inspector (TA 1988 s 306(6)).	Not exceeding £3,000.
False statement to obtain relief for payments to secure a retirement annuity, a purchased life annuity or under a personal pension scheme (TA 1988 ss 619(7), 653, 658(5)).	Not exceeding £3,000.
Creation or transfer of shares or debentures in a non-resident subsidiary company without the consent of HM Treasury (TA 1988 s 766).	On conviction on indictment— (a) imprisonment for not more than 2 years or a fine, or both; or (b) in the case of a UK company, a fine not exceeding the greater of— (i) £10,000; or (ii) three times the tax payable by the company attributable to income and gains arising in the previous 36 months.
Failure by a Lloyd's syndicate's managing agent to comply with notice requiring return of syndicate's profit or loss (FA 1993 Sch 19 para 2(3), (4)).	£60 for each 50 members of syndicate (or part thereof) for each day the failure continues.
Delivery by a Lloyd's syndicate's managing agent fraudulently or negligently of an incorrect return of syndicate profits (FA 1993 Sch 19 para 2(5)).	Not exceeding £3,000 for each member of the syndicate.

F) Other offences by taxpayers, agents etc — continued

Offence	Penalty
Obstructing, molesting or hindering an officer or other person employed in relation to inland revenue in the execution of his or her duty (Inland Revenue Regulation Act 1890 s 11).	Level 3 on the standard scale.
(Accounting periods ending after 30 June 1999). Deliberately or recklessly failing to pay corporation tax due in respect of total liability of company for accounting period, or fraudulently or negligently making claim for repayment (TMA 1970 s 59E(4); SI 1998/3175 reg 13).	Penalty not exceeding twice amount of interest charged under SI 1998/3175 reg 7.
(Accounting periods ending after 30 June 1999) Failure of a company to keep and preserve records (other than those only required for claims, etc, or dividend vouchers and certificates of income tax deducted where other evidence is available) (FA 1998 Sch 18 para 23).	Penalty not exceeding £3,000.

G) Standard scale penalties under Criminal Justice Act[1]

Level	Amount	
	1.5.84–30.9.92 £	From 1.10.92 £
1	50	200
2	100	500
3	400	1,000
4	1,000	2,500
5 (statutory maximum)	2,000	5,000

[1] Criminal Justice Act 1982 s 37.

Mitigation of penalties

The Board has discretion to mitigate or entirely remit any penalty or to stay or compound any penalty proceedings (TMA 1970 s 102).

Interest on penalties

From 1996–97 penalties under TMA 1970 Parts II (ss 7–12B), IV (ss 28A–43B), VA (ss 59A–59D) and X (ss 93–107) carry interest at the prescribed rate (see p 13): TMA 1970 s 103A. Surcharges on unpaid income tax and capital gains tax carry interest under TMA 1970 s 59C (with effect from 9 March 1998, by virtue of SI 1998/310). As regards corporation tax, the provisions apply for accounting periods ending on or after 1 July 1999.

Stamp duties see page 89.

VAT see page 92.

Time limits for claims and elections

The information in the tables below was originally derived from Tax Digest No 108 "Time limits for claims and elections" (Spring 1992) published by the Institute of Chartered Accountants in England and Wales.

From 1996–97: Whenever possible, a claim or election must be made on the tax return or by an amendment to the return (TMA 1970 s 42 and FA 1998 Sch 18 paras 9, 10, 67 and 79). Exceptions to this general rule are dealt with in TMA 1970 Sch 1A.

Except where another period is expressly prescribed, a claim for relief in respect of income tax and capital gains tax must be made within five years from the 31 January following the year of assessment to which it relates (TMA 1970 s 43(1) as amended). The time limit for claims by companies remains at six years from the end of the accounting period to which it relates (TMA 1970 s 43(1)(b) and, for accounting periods ending after 1 July 1999, FA 1998 Sch 18 para 55).

The tables below set out the main exceptions to the general limits.

Before 1996–97: Except where a longer or shorter period was expressly prescribed, a claim for relief had to be made within six years of the end of the chargeable period to which it related (TMA 1970 s 43(1) as originally enacted).

Income tax only

Claim	Time limit
Claims made under provisions of TA 1988 as amended	
Farming and market gardening: Averaging relief to be available to a person carrying on a trade of farming or market gardening (TA 1988 s 96(8) as amended).	1 year after 31 January next following end of second year which enters into the averaging calculation.
Post-cessation expenditure: Unrelieved qualifying post-cessation expenditure to be set against income (TA 1988 s 109A(1)).	1 year after 31 January following year of assessment in which payment made.
Share options: Tax arising upon the exercise of a share option to be payable by instalments, provided that the option was acquired prior to 6 April 1984 (TA 1988 s 137(1)(d), (3)).	60 days after the end of the year in which the exercise occurs.
Loan benefits: Election by employee for alternative method to be applied in calculating the cash equivalent of the benefit obtained from a loan (TA 1988 s 160, Sch 7 para 5 as amended).	1 year after 31 January next following year of assessment.
Returns: Inspector to be required to issue a return under Schedule E (TA 1988 s 205(4)).	5 years after 31 October next following year of assessment.
Jointly held property: Income from jointly owned property to be assessed on husband and wife in unequal shares (TA 1988 s 282B(2)).	60 days after date of declaration.
Enterprise investment scheme: Relief to be given for the enterprise investment scheme (TA 1988 s 306(1) as amended).	Not earlier than 4 months after the company commences its qualifying activity and no later than fifth anniversary of 31 January next following year of assessment in which shares issued.
Trading losses: Loss sustained in a trade, profession or vocation to be set against other income of the year or the last preceding year. Extended to certain pre-trading expenditure by TA 1988 s 401 (TA 1988 s 380(1) as substituted).	1 year after 31 January next following year of assessment in which loss arose.
Losses of new trade etc: Loss sustained in the first 4 years of a new trade, profession or vocation to be offset against other income arising in the 3 years immediately preceding the year of loss. Extended to certain pre-trading expenditure by TA 1988 s 401 (TA 1988 s 381(1)).	1 year after 31 January next following year of assessment in which loss sustained.
Copyright, assignment: *Certain sums received by an author in respect of the assignment of a copyright to be assessed as if received over a period of up to 3 years (repealed for payments receivable after 5 April 2001, see now TA 1988 Sch 4A below) (TA 1988 s 534(1), (5) as amended).*	*1 year after 31 January next following the latest year of assessment in which payment receivable.*
Copyright, assignment after 10 years: *Spreading claim made under TA 1988 s 535(1) in respect of sums received by author more than 10 years after first publication of the work to be recalculated on the death of the author or the discontinuance of his or her profession (repealed for payments receivable after 5 April 2001, see now TA 1988 Sch 4A below) (TA 1988 s 535(8A)).*	*1 year after 31 January next following year of assessment in which payment receivable.*
Design rights, assignment: *Sums received by a designer for the assignment of rights in a design to be assessed as if received over a period of up to 3 years (repealed for payments receivable after 5 April 2001, see now TA 1988 Sch 4A below) (TA 1988 s 537A(5), (5A) as amended).*	*1 year after 31 January next following the latest year of assessment in which payment receivable.*

Time limits for claims and elections — continued

Claim	Time limit
Loss on disposal of unlisted shares: Loss on disposal by an individual of shares in a qualifying trading company to be offset against other income of the year of loss or the last preceding year (TA 1988 s 574(1) as substituted).	1 year after 31 January next following year of assessment in which loss incurred.
Retirement annuity premiums: Relief to be given in respect of a qualifying premium paid under a retirement annuity contract entered into before 1 July 1988 for the immediately preceding year of assessment (or the year before that if no net relevant earnings in the immediately preceding year) (TA 1988 s 619(4) as amended).	31 January next following year of assessment in which premium paid.
Retirement annuity premiums, carry-forward of unused relief: Unused relief to be available against a qualifying premium paid under a retirement annuity contract entered into before 1 July 1988 where an assessment becomes final and conclusive more than 6 years after the year to which it relates (TA 1988 s 625(3)).	6 months after the date when the assessment becomes final.
Personal pension schemes, carry-back of relief: *Relief to be given in respect of a contribution paid under approved personal pension arrangements for the immediately preceding year of assessment (or the year before that if no net relevant earnings in the immediately preceding year) (repealed for contributions paid after 5 April 2001) (TA 1988 s 641(1), (4) as amended).*	*31 January next following year of assessment in which contributions paid.*
Personal pension schemes, contributions: Contributions paid before 1 February to be treated in whole or part as paid in preceding year of assessment (TA 1988 s 641A)	On or before date of payment of contribution.
Personal pension schemes, carry-forward of relief: *Unused relief to be available for relief against a contribution paid under approved personal pension arrangements where an assessment to tax for a year of assessment becomes final and conclusive more than 6 years after the end of that year (repealed from 2001–02) (TA 1988 s 642(4)).*	*6 months after the date when the assessment for the year in question becomes final and conclusive.*
Maintenance funds for historic buildings: Income arising to trustees of maintenance funds for historic buildings not to be treated as the income of the settlor (TA 1988 s 691(2), (4) as amended).	1 year from 31 January next following year of assessment to which it relates.
Completion of administration: Income of a beneficiary to be adjusted for past years on completion of the administration of a deceased's estate (TA 1988 s 700(1), (3) as amended).	3 years after 31 January next following year of assessment in which the administration is completed.
Creative artists, relief for fluctuation profits: Relevant profits of an individual in two consecutive years to be averaged (TA 1988 Sch 4A).	1 year after 31 January next following later tax year to which it relates (or in which adjustment for other reason is made).
Claims made under provisions of later Finance Acts	
Deduction of trading losses: Unrelieved trading losses to be set against capital gains (FA 1991 s 72, TA 1988 s 380(1)).	12 months from 31 January next following year of assessment in which loss sustained.
Rent a room relief: Relief not to be applied to an individual for a year of assessment (F(No 2)A 1992 Sch 10 para 10).	1 year after 31 January next following year of assessment or such later date as Board may allow.
Rent a room relief: Relief to be applied where the total of all relevant sums for a year exceed the individual's limit (F(No 2)A 1992 Sch 10 paras 11, 12).	1 year after 31 January next following year of assessment or such later date as Board may allow.
Enterprise Incentive Scheme: Notification of grant of options in shares under the Enterprise Incentive Scheme to Inland Revenue (FA 2000 Sch 14 para 2 as amended).	92 days from grant of option where option granted after 11 May 2001 (previously 30 days).

Corporation tax only

Claim	Time limit
Claims made under provisions of TA 1988 as amended	
Carry back of surplus ACT: *Surplus ACT paid to be carried back for offset against corporation tax liabilities for accounting periods beginning within six years prior to the period of payment (TA 1988 s 239(3)) (repealed with respect to accounting periods beginning after 5 April 1999).*	2 years.
Trading losses: Loss sustained by a company in a trade in an accounting period ending after 31 March 1991 to be offset against— (a) profits of that accounting period; (b) profits of the preceding three years for losses arising in accounting periods ending before 2 July 1997 and profits of the preceding one year for losses arising in subsequent accounting periods. Extended to certain pre-trading expenditure by TA 1988 s 401 (TA 1988 s 393A(1) (2A)(10)).	2 years or such further period as Board may allow.
Group relief: Group relief to be given for accounting periods ending after 30 September 1993 and before 1 July 1999. The surrendering company must consent to the claim (TA 1988 s 412, Sch 17A para 2).	2 years after the end of the surrendering company's accounting period or the date on which the relevant assessment becomes final, whichever is later.
Group relief: Group relief to be given for accounting periods ending after 30 June 1999. The surrendering company must consent to the claim (FA 1998 Sch 18 paras 66 to 77)	The last of: (a) 1 year from the filing date of the claimant company's return for the accounting period for which the claim is made; (b) 30 days after the end of an enquiry into the return; (c) if the Revenue amend the return after an enquiry, 30 days after issue of notice of amendment; (d) if an appeal is made against the amendment, 30 days after the determination of the appeal; (or such later time as the Revenue may allow).
Relief for investment companies: Loss on disposal by an investment company of shares in a qualifying trading company to be offset against other income of the period of loss or the preceding accounting period (TA 1988 s 573(2)).	2 years.
Claims made under provisions of later Finance Acts	
Schedule D computation: Adjustment of employer's Schedule D calculation for emoluments paid subsequently, but within 9 months of the end of the employer's period of account (FA 1989 s 43(5)).	2 years from end of period of account.
Non-trading deficit on loan relationship: Relief for non-trading deficits on loan relationships in a company in an accounting period ending after 31 March 1996 to be claimed by: (a) offset against profits of the same period; (b) group relief; (c) offset against post 31 March 1996 profits of earlier accounting periods (as for trading losses above); or (d) offset against non-trading profits for the next accounting period, and so on. (FA 1996, s 83)	2 years or such further period as Board may allow.
Corporate Venturing Scheme: Relief to be given for losses on disposal of shares against income under Corporate Venturing Scheme (FA 2000 Sch 15 para 68).	2 years from end of accounting period in which loss is incurred.

Income tax and corporation tax

Claim	Time limit
Claims made under provisions of TA 1988 as amended	
Gifts to educational establishments: Relief for gifts of plant and machinery to educational establishments (TA 1988 s 84(3), (3A)).	1 year after 31 January next following year of assessment in the basis period of which the gift was made (income tax); 2 years after end of accounting period in which the gift was made (corporation tax).
Herd basis: Herd basis to apply (TA 1988 s 97, Sch 5 para 2 as amended).	1 year after 31 January next following first year of assessment for which profits computed by reference to period in which herd was kept (income tax); 1 year after 31 January next following year of assessment in which fell the end of the first period of account in which herd was kept (partnerships); 2 years after end of first accounting period in which herd was kept (corporation tax).
Valuation of work in progress: Work in progress at date of discontinuance of profession or vocation to be valued at actual cost (TA 1988 s 101(2), (2A)).	1 year after 31 January next following year of assessment in which discontinuance occurred (income tax); 2 years after end of accounting period in which discontinuance occurred (corporation tax).
Post-cessation receipts: Post cessation receipts to be charged as if received on the date of discontinuance or change of basis of computation (TA 1988 s 108 as amended).	1 year after 31 January following end of year of assessment in which sum received.
Furnished holiday lettings: Averaging treatment to be applied in determining the number of days on which holiday accommodation is let (TA 1988 s 504(6), (6A)).	1 year after 31 January next following year of assessment in which accommodation let (income tax); 2 years after end of accounting period in which accommodation let (corporation tax).
Patents (UK residents): UK resident in receipt of a capital sum from the sale of patent rights to be charged to tax for period of receipt (TA 1988 s 524(2), (2A)).	1 year after 31 January next following year of assessment in which sum received (income tax); 2 years after end of accounting period in which sum received (corporation tax).
Patents (non-residents): Non-resident in receipt of a capital sum on the sale of non-UK patent rights to be charged to tax as if the sum was received over a period of 6 years (TA 1988 s 524(4) as amended).	1 year after 31 January next following year of assessment in which sum is paid.
Know-how: Consideration for know-how sold together with a trade or part of a trade not to be treated as a payment for goodwill. Time limit runs from the date of the disposal. Both purchaser and vendor must elect (TA 1988 s 531(3)).	2 years from date of disposal.
Unremittable overseas income: Unremittable overseas income to be excluded from assessment (TA 1988 s 584(2), (6) (as substituted)).	1 year after 31 January next following year of assessment in which income arises (income tax); 2 years after end of accounting period in which income arises (corporation tax).

Capital allowances

Claim	Time limit
Claims made under provisions not included in CAA 2001	
Plant and machinery: Writing down allowance to be available where first year allowance not claimed (CAA 1990 s 25(3) as amended, (3A)). The requirement for notification of expenditure on which allowances may be claimed (FA 1994 s 118) is abolished for periods ending on or after 6 April 1998 (income tax) and 1 April 1998 (corporation tax).	1 year after 31 January next following year of assessment in which ends chargeable period related to incurring of expenditure (income tax);[1] 2 years after end of chargeable period related to incurring of expenditure (corporation tax).

Time limits for claims and elections — continued

Claim	Time limit
Films: Expenditure on production or acquisition of films etc to be reallocated (F(No2)A 1992 s 40B(6)).	1 year after 31 January next following year of assessment in which relevant period ends (income tax); 2 years after end of relevant period (corporation tax).[1]
Claims made under provisions of CAA 2001 **Income tax claims:** Claim for income tax capital allowances made in taxing the trade (CAA 2001 s 3(2), (3)(*a*)).	Claim to be made in return.
Corporation tax claims (accounting periods ending after 30 June 1999): Claims, amended claims and withdrawals of claims in respect of corporation tax capital allowances for accounting periods ending after 30 June 1999 (CAA 2001 s 3(2), (3)(*b*), FA 1998 Sch 18 para 82).	The last of: (a) 1 year after the filing date of the claimant company's return for the accounting period for which the claim is made; (b) 30 days after the end of an enquiry into the return; (c) if the Revenue amend the return after an enquiry, 30 days after issue of notice of amendment; (d) if an appeal is made against the amendment, 30 days after the determination of the appeal; (or such later time as the Revenue may allow).
Corporation tax claims (accounting periods ending before 1 July 1999): Claims, amended claims and withdrawals of claims in respect of corporation tax capital allowances for accounting periods ending after 30 September 1993 and before 1 July 1999 (CAA 1990 s 145A, Sch A1 paras 2, 3). (New provisions apply for self-assessment by companies for accounting periods ending after 30 June 1999, see below.)	The latest of — (a) 2 years after the end of the accounting period; (b) the date on which the company's corporation tax assessment for the period becomes final; and (c) the date on which the determination of the company's losses or the amount available for group relief for the accounting period becomes final.
Short life assets: Plant or machinery to be treated as a short life asset (CAA 2001 s 85(2)).	1 year after 31 January next following year of assessment in which chargeable period in which qualifying expenditure occurred ends (income tax);[1] 2 years after end of chargeable period (corporation tax).
Short life asset transferred to connected person: Transfer of short life asset to a connected person to be treated as taking place at tax written down value (CAA 2001 s 89(6)).	2 years after end of chargeable period in which disposal occurred.
Ships: Single ship pool treatment not to apply to the whole or part of the expenditure (CAA 2001 s 129(2)).	1 year after 31 January next following year of assessment in which chargeable period ends (income tax);[1] 2 years after end of chargeable period (corporation tax).
Ships: Part or all of a first year allowance in respect of expenditure on a ship to be postponed to a later period (CAA 2001 s 130(4)).	1 year after 31 January next following year of assessment in which period of account ends (income tax);[1] 2 years after end of accounting period for which allowance made (corporation tax).
Oilfields: Oilfield abandonment expenditure to be deductible in relation to a ring fence trade (CAA 2001 s 164(2)).	2 years after end of chargeable period related to incurring of expenditure.
Equipment lessors: Plant or machinery which becomes a fixture and is subject to an equipment lease to be treated as belonging to equipment lessor. Election to be made by both lessor and lessee but not permitted if they are connected persons (CAA 2001 s 177(5)).	1 year after 31 January next following year of assessment in which chargeable period ends (income tax);[1] 2 years after end of chargeable period (corporation tax).
Lessee to be treated as owner of fixture: Plant or machinery which has become a fixture on land which is subsequently let to be treated as belonging to lessee. Election to be made by both lessor and lessee but not permitted if they are connected persons (CAA 2001 s 183(2)).	2 years after date on which lease takes effect.

Time limits for claims and elections — continued

Claim	Time limit
Excess corporation tax allowances: Excess of corporation tax capital allowances given by discharge or repayment of tax over the relevant class of income to be set against the profits of that period and the immediately preceding period (CAA 2001 s 260(6)).	2 years.
Connected persons: Succession to a trade between connected persons to be ignored in computing capital allowances (CAA 2001 s 266).	2 years after the date of the succession.
Industrial buildings: Grant of a long lease of a building to be treated as a sale of the relevant interest by the lessor. Both lessor and lessee must elect (CAA 2001 ss 290, 291).	2 years after the date when the lease takes effect.
Agricultural buildings: Cessation of use, demolition or destruction of agricultural buildings or acquisition of relevant interest in capital expenditure on agricultural land and buildings to be treated as a balancing event (CAA 2001 ss 381, 382).	1 year after 31 January next following year of assessment in which chargeable period ends (income tax);[1] 2 years after end of chargeable period (corporation tax).
Connected persons: Disposal and acquisition of property between persons one of which controls the other or which are under common control to be treated as made at the lower of open market value and tax written down value (CAA 2001 s 570(5)).	2 years after the date of the disposal.

[1] For the purposes of income tax, applies from 1997–98 in respect of trades etc set up and commenced before 6 April 1994 and from 1996–97 for trades etc commenced after 5 April 1994: see FA 1996 s 135(3), Sch 21.

Capital gains

Claim	Time limit
Assets of negligible value: Loss to be allowed where the value of an asset has become negligible (TCGA 1992 s 24(2)).	Year for which loss to be allowed, or up to 2 years after the end of that year if the value is still negligible when claim made.
Assets held on 31 March 1982: Events occurring prior to 31 March 1982 to be ignored in computing gains arising after 5 April 1988 (TCGA 1992 s 35 (5), (6) as amended).	1 year after 31 January next following year of assessment in which disposal made (capital gains tax) or 2 years after end of accounting period in which disposal made (corporation tax).
Variation or disclaimer: Variation or disclaimer of the terms of a will or intestacy, made within two years of the death, to be treated as effected by the deceased (TCGA 1992 s 62(6), (7)).	6 months after instrument of variation or disclaimer effected or such longer time as the Board may allow.
Pre-April 1982 share pools: Quoted ordinary (and participating preference) shares and units in certain unit trusts held (or deemed to have been held) at 6 April 1965 to be pooled at their 6 April 1965 values for disposals after 5 April 1985 (31 March 1985 for companies) or 19 March 1968, as the case may be (TCGA 1992 s 109(4), (5), Sch 2 paras 4(2), (11) as amended, 5).	1 year after 31 January next following year of assessment in which first relevant disposal made (capital gains tax); 2 years after end of accounting period in which first relevant disposal made (corporation tax); or such further time as the Board may allow.
Subsidiary company ceasing to be UK resident: Postponement of charge on deemed disposal of assets where a subsidiary company ceases to be resident in the UK (TCGA 1992 s 187(1)).	2 years after date of ceasing to be resident in UK.
Main residence: Determination of main residence for principal private residence exemption (TCGA 1992 s 222(5)(a)).	2 years from the beginning of the period for which a determination requires to be made, ie the date of acquisition of a second or further residence, but provided that an initial notice has been given within the time limit it may subsequently be varied at any time and the notice of variation may have effect from up to 2 years prior to the date on which it is made.
Employee share ownership trusts: Rollover relief on disposal of shares to trustees of qualifying employee share ownership trust (TCGA 1992 s 229(1)).	2 years after date of acquisition of replacement assets.

Time limits for claims and elections — continued

Claim	Time limit
Relief for loans to trades: Losses on certain loans to traders to be allowed as capital losses (TCGA 1992 s 253(3)).	The loss is treated as accruing on the date that the claim is made, or at an earlier date, which is: (a) no more than 2 years before the beginning of the year of assessment in which the claim is made (capital gains tax) or (b) no earlier than the first day of the earliest accounting period ending no more than 2 years before the date of the claim.
Relief for loans to traders (payments by guarantor): Losses arising from payments by guarantor of certain irrecoverable loans to traders to be allowed as capital losses at time of claim or 'earlier time' (TCGA 1992 s 253(4), (4A)).	5 years after 31 January next following year of assessment in which payment made (capital gains tax); 6 years after end of accounting period in which the payment was made (corporation tax: TCGA 1992 s 253(4A), FA 1996 s 135(2): accounting periods ending after 30 June 1999).
Tax paid by instalments: Tax to be paid by instalments where the consideration is payable over a period (TCGA 1992 s 280 as amended).	Date of payment of tax.
Election for valuation at 6 April 1965: Gain on a disposal of an asset held at 6 April 1965 to be computed as if the asset had been acquired on that date. An election once made is irrevocable (TCGA 1992 Sch 2 para 17).	1 year after 31 January next following year of assessment in which disposal made (capital gains tax); 2 years after end of accounting period in which disposal made (corporation tax); or such further time as the Board may by notice allow.
Assets held on 31 March 1982: Halving of postponed charges, or held over or rolled over gains, on disposals of assets acquired after 31 March 1982 (but before 6 April 1988) from a person who acquired (or is deemed to have acquired) them before 31 March 1982 (TCGA 1992 Sch 4 para 9).	1 year after 31 January next following year of assessment in which disposal (or other event) occurred (capital gains tax); 2 years after the end of the accounting period in which the disposal (or other event) occurred, or such longer time as the Board may allow (corporation tax).
Retirement relief: Retirement relief generally. Relief must be claimed unless due by reason of a disposal made by an individual aged 50 or over; reorganisation provisions of TCGA 1992 s 126 *et seq* not to apply; relief to be given in respect of certain capital distributions; spouse's period of ownership to be aggregated with that of person making the disposal (TCGA 1992 Sch 6 as amended paras 2, 5, 12,16). (To be phased out from 6 April 1999 and not available for disposals after 5 April 2003 (FA 1998 s 140).)	1 year after 31 January next following year of assessment.

Inheritance tax

Claim	Time limit
Maintenance funds for historic buildings: Transfer of property to a maintenance fund for historic buildings etc to be exempt (IHTA 1984 s 27 as amended).	2 years after the date of the transfer or such longer period as the Board may allow (transfers of value made after 16 March 1998).
Conditionally exempt transfers of qualifying heritage assets: Transfer of property of national, scientific, historic or artistic etc interest designated as such by the Treasury to be conditionally exempt (IHTA 1984 ss 30, 31 as amended).	2 years after the date of the transfer of value or death or such longer period as the Board may allow (transfers of value or death after 16 March 1998).
Conditional exemption for heritage property leaving discretionary trusts: Qualifying heritage assets leaving discretionary trusts to be conditionally exempt (IHTA 1984 s 78 as amended).	2 years after the date of transfer or other event or such longer period as the Board may allow (transfers of property made and other events occurring after 16 March 1998).
Woodlands: Tax in respect of trees or underwood forming part of the value of a person's estate immediately before death to be deferred (IHTA 1984 ss 125, 126).	2 years after death or such longer period as the Board may allow.
Variations of dispositions on death: Variations or disclaimers of dispositions taking effect on death to be treated as if effected by the deceased (IHTA 1984 s 142).	6 months after the date of the instrument.

Exchanges

Recognised stock exchanges

The following is a list of countries with exchanges which have been designated as recognised stock exchanges under TA 1988 s 841. Unless otherwise specified, any stock exchange (or options exchange) in a country listed below is a recognised stock exchange for the purposes of TA 1988 s 841, provided it is recognised under the law of the country concerned relating to stock exchanges.

Country	*Effective date*
Australia	
Australian Stock Exchange and its stock exchange subsidiaries	22 September 1988
Austria[3]	14 December 1970
Belgium[3]	14 December 1970
Brazil	
Rio De Janeiro Stock Exchange	17 August 1995
São Paulo Stock Exchange	20 December 1995
Canada	
Any stock exchange prescribed for the purposes of the Canadian Income Tax Act	14 December 1970
China	
Hong Kong – Any stock exchange recognised under Section 2A(1) of the Hong Kong Companies Ordinance	6 April 1971
Denmark	
Copenhagen Stock Exchange	22 October 1970
Finland	
Helsinki Stock Exchange	14 December 1970
France[3]	14 December 1970
Germany[3]	16 August 1971
Greece	
Athens Stock Exchange	14 June 1993
Irish Republic[3]	14 December 1970
Italy[3]	3 May 1972
Japan[3]	14 December 1970
Korea	10 October 1994
Luxembourg[3]	29 February 1972
Malaysia	
Kuala Lumpur Stock Exchange	10 October 1994
Mexico	10 October 1994
Netherlands[3]	14 December 1970
New Zealand	22 September 1988
Norway[3]	14 December 1970
Portugal[3]	29 February 1972
Singapore	30 June 1977
South Africa	
Johannesburg Stock Exchange	14 December 1970
Spain[3]	16 August 1971
Sri Lanka	
Colombo Stock Exchange	21 February 1972
Sweden	
Stockholm Stock Exchange	16 July 1985
Switzerland	30 June 1977
Thailand	10 October 1994
United Kingdom	6 April 1965
United States	
Any stock exchange registered with the Securities and Exchange Commission as a national securities exchange[1]	14 December 1970
Nasdaq Stock Market[2]	10 March 1992

[1] The term 'national securities exchange' does not include any local exchanges registered with the Securities and Exchange Commission.

[2] As maintained through the facilities of the National Association of Securities Dealers Inc and its subsidiaries.

[3] Any stock exchange which is a stock exchange within the meaning of the law of the country concerned relating to stock exchanges.

Recognised futures exchanges

The following is a list of exchanges which have been designated as recognised futures exchanges under TCGA 1992 s 288(6). By concession, those exchanges were recognised futures exchanges for the tax year of recognition onwards.

Country	*Tax year of recognition*
Australia	
Sydney Futures Exchange	1988–89
Canada	
Montreal Exchange	1987–88
China	
Hong Kong Futures Exchange	1987–88
Sweden	
OM Stockholm	1991–92
United Kingdom	
International Petroleum Exchange of London	1985–86
London Gold Market	1985–86
London International Financial Futures and Options Exchange (LIFFE)	1991–92
London Metal Exchange	1985–86
London Silver Market	1985–86
OMLX	1991–92
United States	
Chicago Board of Trade	1987–88
Chicago Mercantile Exchange	1986–87
Commodity Exchange (COMEX)	1988–89
Mid America Commodity Exchange	1987–88
New York Board of Trade[1]	—[1]
New York Mercantile Exchange	1986–87
Philadelphia Board of Trade	1986–87

[1] Formed by the merger of Citrus Associate of New York Cotton Exchange (1988–89), Coffee, Sugar and Cocoa Exchange, New York (1987–88) and New York Cotton Exchange (1988–89).

Applications for clearances and approvals

Clearance application	Address
Share exchanges (TCGA 1992 ss 138, 139, 140B, 140D)	Revenue Policy, Capital and Savings, Capital Gains Clearance Section, Sapphire House, 550 Streetsbrook Road, Solihull, West Midlands B91 1QU
Transfer of long term insurance business (TCGA 1992 s 211, TA 1988 s 444A)	Both parties UK-resident: Revenue Policy, Business Tax, Room S16, West Wing, Somerset House, London WC2R 1LB
	At least one party not UK-resident: Revenue Policy, Business Tax, Room S15, West Wing, Somerset House, London WC2R 1LB
Demergers (TA 1988 s 215)	Revenue Policy, Business Tax, Demerger Clearance Unit, Room 101, New Wing, Somerset House, London WC2R 1LB
Company purchase of own shares (TA 1988 s 225)	Revenue Policy, Business Tax, Purchase of Own Shares Clearance Unit (CCU), Room M26, New Wing, Somerset House, London WC2R 1LB
Transactions in securities (TA 1988 s 707)	Revenue Policy, Business Tax, The S703 Compliance Unit (SIS2), 22 Kingsway, London WC2B 6NR
Company migration (FA 1988 s 130)	Revenue Policy, International, Business Tax Group (Company Migrations), Victory House, 30–34 Kingsway, London WC2B 6ES
Advance pricing agreements (FA 1999 ss 85–87)	Revenue Policy, International, Business Tax Group (APAs), Victory House, 30–34 Kingsway, London WC2B 6ES
	For APAs involving oil taxation: Revenue Policy, International, Oil Taxation Office (APAs), Melbourne House, Aldwych, London WC2B 4LL.
Controlled foreign companies (TA 1988 ss 747–756, Schs 24–26)	Revenue Policy, International, Business Tax Group (CFC Clearances), Victory House, 30–34 Kingsway, London WC2B 6ES
Corporate Venturing Schemes (FA 2000 Sch 15)	Revenue Policy, Business Tax, Corporate Venturing Scheme Unit, (CCU), Room M26 New Wing, Somerset House, London WC2R 1LB

Approval application	Address
Pensions (TA 1988 ss 590, 591)	Pension Schemes Office, Yorke House, PO Box 62, Castle Meadow Road, Nottingham NG2 1BG
Employee share schemes (TA 1988 Sch 9)	Revenue Policy, Capital and Savings, Employee Share Schemes, Second Floor, New Wing, Somerset House, London WC2R 1LB
Qualifying life assurance policies (TA 1988 Sch 15)	Revenue Policy, Business Tax (Insurance), Room S11, West Wing, Somerset House, London WC2B 6NR
Professional bodies (relief for subscriptions) (TA 1988 s 201)	Inland Revenue, Personal Taxation Division, Sapphire House, 550 Streetsbrook Road, Solihull, West Midlands B91 1QU

Application for treasury consent	Address
Transactions in shares or debentures (TA 1988 ss 765, 765A)	Revenue Policy, International, Business Tax Group (Treasury Consent), Victory House, 30–34 Kingsway, London WC2B 6ES

Where clearance is sought under more than one of TA 1988 ss 215, 225 and 707 in a single letter, the letter may be sent to just one of the above London addresses for clearances under those sections. Extra copies of the letter should be enclosed for each additional clearance sought.

Inland Revenue explanatory pamphlets

Tax Bulletin: published six times a year. Available on annual subscription or at the Revenue internet site (below): contact Miss Sue Williams, Room 530, 22 Kingsway, London WC2B 6NR (020 7438 7700).

Copies of the pamphlets listed below are obtainable from the offices of HM Inspectors of Taxes, or from Tax Enquiry Centres, with the exception of

IR12: available by subscription (£20 pa) from SR Communications plc, Unit 9, Deptford Trading Estate, Blackhorse Road, London, SE99 7TR (020 7463 8167)

Inheritance tax: CTO: (England and Wales) Ferrers House, PO Box 38, Castle Meadow Road, Nottingham NG2 1BB

(Scotland) Mulberry House, 16 Picardy Place, Edinburgh EH1 3NB

(Northern Ireland) Dorchester House, 52–58 Great Victoria Street, Belfast BT2 7QL

IR76, IR120 (You and the Pensions Schemes Office), PSO1: Pension Schemes Office, Yorke House, PO Box 62, Castle Meadow Road, Nottingham NG2 1BG

IR120: Braille and audio cassette versions must be ordered and will be sent through the post or, together with clear print version, are obtainable from the RNIB on 01345 023153.

The charities publications are available from Customer Services Manager, Charities Division, St. John's House, Merton Road, Bootle, Merseyside L69 9BB; CB series is available from FICO (Scotland), Trinity Park House, South Trinity Road, Edinburgh EH5 3SD.

Digest of DT agreements is available from FICO, Fitz Roy House, PO Box 46, Nottingham NG2 1BD.

Business Economic Notes are obtainable from the Revenue Internet Site or by post from the Inland Revenue Library, Room 28, New Wing, Somerset House, Strand, London WC2R 1LB (price £2.00 per booklet BEN 23-26, £1.50 for earlier booklets – post free) or by calling at the Information Centre (address as above).

The SO series is available from local stamp offices, by phoning 0845 603 0135, or from (England and Wales) The Stamp Office, Room 35, East Block, Barrington Road, Worthing BN12 4SE (01903 508930); (Scotland) Edinburgh Stamp Office, Mulberry House, 16 Picardy Place, Edinburgh EH1 3NF (0131 556 8998); (Northern Ireland) The Stamp Office, Dorchester House, 52-58 Great Victoria Street, Belfast BT2 7QE (02890 505124).

The Collection Series is available from local collection offices. Collection 4 (England and Wales) from Enforcement Office, Durrington Bridge House, Barrington Road, Worthing, West Sussex BN12 4SE; Collection 3 and 4 (Scotland) from Enforcement Section, Elgin House, 20 Haymarket Yards, Edinburgh EH12 5WT; Collection 3 and 4 (N Ireland) from Belfast 2 (Enforcement) 4th Floor, Olivetree House, 23 Fountain Street, Belfast BT1 5ET.

Self-assessment: SAT1 (£7.50) and SAT2 (£5) available from Inland Revenue Library, Room 28, New Wing, Somerset House, Strand, London WC2R 1LB (cheques/po made payable to 'Inland Revenue'). Text also available on 3.5″ disks in 'text only' format (same price).

Self-assessment generally: Orderline 08459 000404; fax 08459 000604; e-mail saorderline.ir@gtnet.gov.uk; PO Box 37, St Austell, Cornwall PL25 5YN. (SA/BK5 from Orderline only.) Information also available on the Internet at: www.inlandrevenue.gov.uk/sa and general advice on the Helpline 0845 9000 444.

Guide to corporation tax self-assessment (£15) available from Inland Revenue Library, Room 28, New Wing, Somerset House, Strand, London WC2R 1LB.

Special Compliance Office (COP8, COP9, IR120): Special Compliance Office, Angel Court, 199 Borough High Street, London SE1 1HZ (020 7234 3708).

The AO series is available from The Adjudicator's Office, Haymarket House, 28 Haymarket, London SW1Y 4SP.

Education Service Pack (free): Beryl St James, External Communications, Inland Revenue, G7 Ground Floor, New Wing, Somerset House, Strand, London WC2R 1LB (020 7438 6796; fax 020 7438 7281). Education service pages are available at the Revenue internet site (below).

Internet: A number of publications are available on the internet at: www.inlandrevenue.gov.uk

Pamphlet	Date	Supp	Title
Catalogue	2000		Catalogue of leaflets and booklets
IR 1	2000		Extra-statutory concessions
IR 6	1994		Double taxation relief for companies
IR 12	2001	(2001)	Practice notes on approval of occupational pension schemes
IR 14/15 (CIS)	1998	(2001)	Construction industry scheme
IR 16	1997		Share acquisitions by directors and employees – explanatory notes
IR 20	1999		Residents and non-residents – liability to tax in the UK
IR 33	2000		Income tax and school leavers
IR 34	1996		Pay As You Earn
IR 37	1999		Appeals against tax, NICs, SSP and SMP
IR 40 (CIS)	2001		Construction industry scheme: conditions for getting a subcontractor's tax certificate
IR 41	2000		Income tax and jobseekers
IR 45	2001		What to do about tax when someone dies
IR 46	2000		Clubs, societies and voluntary associations
IR 56	1999		Employed or self-employed? A guide for tax and national insurance
IR 59	2001		Collection of student loans – a guide for employers
IR 60	1997		Income tax and students
IR 64	2000		Giving to charity by business
IR 65	2000		Giving to charity by individuals
IR 68	1990		Accrued income scheme. Taxing securities on transfer
IR 69	1999		Expenses payments and benefits in kind. How to save yourself work
IR 72	1995		Investigations: the examination of business accounts
IR 73	1994		Inland Revenue investigations: how settlements are negotiated
IR 76	2000		Inland Revenue guidance notes on personal pension schemes

Inland Revenue explanatory pamphlets — continued

Pamphlet	Date Supp	Title
IR 78	2001	Looking to the future: tax reliefs to help you save for retirement
IR 87	1999	Letting and your home. Including the 'Rent a Room' scheme and letting your previous home when you live elsewhere
IR 89	1998	Personal equity plans (PEPs) – a guide for potential investors
IR 90	1999	Tax allowances and reliefs
IR 95	1996	Approved profit-sharing schemes – an outline for employees
IR 96	1996	Approved profit-sharing schemes – explanatory notes
IR 97	1996	Approved SAYE share option schemes – an outline for employees
IR 98	1996	Approved SAYE share option schemes – explanatory notes
IR 101	1996	Approved company share option plans – an outline for employees
IR 102	1996	Approved company share option plans – explanatory notes
IR 109	2000	Employer compliance reviews and negotiations
IR 110	2000	A guide for people with savings
IR 114	1998	TESSA: Tax free interest for taxpayers
IR 115	1992	Tax and childcare
IR 116 (CIS)	1999	Guide for subcontractors with tax certificates
IR 117 (CIS)	1999	Guide for subcontractors with Registration Cards
IR 119	1999	Tax relief for vocational training
IR 120	2000	You and the Inland Revenue (Tax Collection, NICs and Accounts Offices). Versions are available in Bengali, Braille, Chinese, Greek, Gujarati, Hindi, Punjabi, Turkish, Urdu, Vietnamese and Welsh, clear print and audio cassettes
IR 120 (SCO)	2001	You and the Special Compliance Office
IR 120	1998	You and the Pension Scheme Office
IR 120 (EO)	1999	You and the Inland Revenue (Enforcement Office)
IR 120 (CT)	2001	You and the Capital Taxes Office
IR 121	2000	Income tax and pensioners
IR 122	2000	Volunteer drivers
IR 125	2000	Using your own car for work
IR 126	1995	Corporation tax pay and file: a general guide
IR 131	2000	Inland Revenue Statements of Practice
IR 134	2000	Income tax and national insurance contributions on relocation packages
IR 136	1994	Income tax and company vans. A guide for employees and employers
IR 137	1999	The Enterprise Investment Scheme
IR 138	1995	Living or retiring abroad? A guide to UK tax on your UK income and pension
IR 139	1995	Income from abroad? A guide to UK tax on overseas income
IR 140	1999	Non-resident landlords, their agents and tenants
IR 141	2001	Open government
IR 143	2000	IT and redundancy
IR 144	1995	Income tax and incapacity benefit
IR 144	1995	Income tax and incapacity benefit; clear print, audio and braille versions
IR 145	1997	Low interest loans provided by employers
IR 148	2001	Are your workers employed or self-employed? A guide for tax and national insurance for contractors in the construction industry
IR 150	2000	Taxation of rents – a guide to property income
IR 152	1996	Trusts – an introduction
IR 153	1997	Tax exemption for sickness or unemployment insurance payments
IR 155	2001	PAYE settlement agreements
IR 156	1996	Our heritage. Your right to see tax exempt works of art
IR 160	1999	Inland Revenue enquiries under self-assessment
IR 161	1998	Tax relief for employees' business travel. A short guide to the tax treatment of employees' travel expenses from 6 April 1998
IR 162	1999	A better approach to local office enquiry work under self-assessment
IR 166	1998	The euro
IR 167	2000	Charter for Inland Revenue taxpayers
IR 168	2000	How tax credit settlements are negotiated
IR 169	2000	Venture capital trusts (VCTs)—a brief guide
IR 170	1999	Blind person's allowance
IR 171	1999	Income tax: a guide for people with children
IR 172	2001	Income tax and company cars
IR 173	1999	Tax credits: a summary for employers
IR 175	2000	Supplying services through a limited company or partnership
IR 176	2000	Tax, national insurance and green travel
IR 177	2000	All-employee share plan and your entitlement to benefits
IR 178	2000	Giving shares and securities to charity
IR 179	2000	R & D tax credits
IR 2000	2001	The corporate venturing scheme
IR 2001	2001	Trading by charities
IR 2002	2001	The all-employee share ownership plan. A guide for employees
IR 2003	2001	Supplying services. How to calculate the deemed payment
ISA1	1999	The answers on ISAs. Your guide
CB(1)	1993	Setting up a charity in Scotland
CB(1)	1995	A'cur buidheann carthannais air chois an Alba (Gaelic)
480	2001	Expenses and benefits. A tax guide
490	1998	Employee travel. A tax and NICs guide for employers
FEU50	2000	A guide to paying foreign entertainers
DT Digest	2001	Digest of double taxation treaties
PSO1	1995	Occupational pension schemes. A guide for members of tax-approved schemes
PSO2	2001	Personal pension schemes (including stakeholder pension schemes) – a guide for members of tax-approved schemes

Inland Revenue explanatory pamphlets — continued

Pamphlet	Date	Supp	Title
CISFACT 5	1998		The new construction industry scheme. A handy guide
CGT 1	May 2001		Capital gains tax – An introduction
IHT 2	1998		Inheritance tax on lifetime gifts
IHT 3	2001		Inheritance tax – an introduction
IHT 4	2000		Notes on informal calculations of inheritance tax
IHT 8	2001		Alterations to an inheritance following a death. Inheritance tax
IHT 11	2000		Payment of inheritance tax from national savings or British Government Stock
IHT 12	2000		Inheritance tax – when is an excepted estate grant appropriate?
IHT 13	2000		Inheritance tax and penalties
IHT14	2000		Inheritance tax – the personal representatives' responsibilities
IHT15	1996		Inheritance tax – how to calculate the liability
IHT16	2000		Inheritance tax – settled property
IHT17	1996		Inheritance tax – businesses, farms and woodlands
IHT18	1996		Inheritance tax – foreign aspects
SO 1	2000		Stamp duty on buying a freehold house in England, Wales and Northern Ireland
SO 1 (Scotland)	2000		Stamp duty on buying land or buildings in Scotland
SO 2	2000		Stamp Office customer promise and service information
SO 3	2000		If things go wrong ... complaints and lost documents
SO 5	1996		Common stamp duty forms and how to complete them
SO 6	1996		A short history of stamp duties
SO 7	2000		Stamp duty and leases
SO 7 (Scotland)	2000		Stamp duty and leases in Scotland
SO 8	2000		Stamp duty on agreements securing short tenancies
SO 10	2000		Stamp duty interest and penalties
SO 11	1997		Stamp duty and charities
SO 99	2000		Changes to stamp duty from 1st October 1999
CIQRG			Quick reference guide to stamp duty rates
Collection 1		2001	Distraint
Collection 1 (Scotland)		1994	Summary Warrant
Collection 1 (N Ireland)		2000	Distraint
Collection 2		1994	Magistrates' Court proceedings
Collection 2 (Scotland)		1994	Sheriff Court proceedings
Collection 2 (N Ireland)		2000	Magistrates' Court proceedings
Collection 3		1995	County Court proceedings
Collection 3 (Scotland)		1994	Court of Session proceedings
Collection 3 (N Ireland)		2000	High Court proceedings
Collection 4		2001	Bankruptcy and winding up
Collection 4 (Scotland)		2000	Sequestration and winding up
Collection 4 (N Ireland)		2000	Bankruptcy and winding up
COP 1	1999		Mistakes by the Inland Revenue
COP 2	1995		Investigations
COP 3	2000		Reviews of employers' and contractors' records
COP 4	1997		Inspection of schemes operated by financial intermediaries
COP 5	1998		Inspection of charities' records
COP 6	1994		Collection of tax
COP 6 (Sco)	1995		Collection of tax
COP 7	1994		Collection of amounts due from employers and contractors in the construction industry
COP 7 (Sco)	1994		Collection of amounts due from employers and contractors in the construction industry
COP 8	1997		Special Compliance Office Investigations: cases other than suspected serious fraud
COP 9	1997		Special Compliance Office Investigations: cases of suspected serious fraud
COP 10	1999		Information and advice
COP 11	1996		Enquiries into tax returns by local tax offices
COP 14	1999		Enquiries into Company Tax Returns
COP 17	1999		Enquiries into applications for WFTC or DPTC
COP 19	2000		Enquiries by the Inland Revenue
COP 20	2000		How the Inland Revenue handles workers' complaints
COP 22	2001		Orders for the delivery of documents
—	1999		Code of practice on consultation
AO1	2000		How to complain about the Inland Revenue and the Valuation Office Agency
CTSA/BK3	2000		A modern system for corporation tax payments
CTSA/BK4	2000		A general guide to corporation tax self-assessment
CSS/TCO	2000		Inland Revenue Tax Credit Office
CSS/TCO(NI)	2001		Inland Revenue Northern Ireland (Tax Credits)
WFTC/BK1	2000		Your guide to working families' tax credit
DPTC/BK1	2000		Your guide to disabled person's tax credit
CTC/BK1	2000		Help with the cost of childcare
DPTC/BK2	2000		Your guide to the disabled person's tax credit fast-track
CTCR/1	2000		Children's tax credit
WFTC/FS1	2000		Factsheet—working families' tax credit
DPTC/FS1	2000		Factsheet—disabled person's tax credit
CTC/FS1	2000		Factsheet—working families' tax credit, disabled person's tax credit and childcare
WFTC/FF/FS1	2000		Working families' tax credit: a guide for farming families
DPTC/FS2	2000		Factsheet – new disabled person's tax credit fast-track
CTC/FS2	2001		Factsheet – new help with a new child: WFTC and DPTC
WFTC/AP	1999		If you think a tax credit decision is wrong
WFTC/APN1	1999		If you think a tax credit decision is wrong (Northern Ireland)
WFTC/EG	1999		An employer's guide to tax credits WFTC and DPTC
SA/BK3	1995		Self-assessment – a guide to keeping records for the self-employed
SA/BK4	1997		Self-assessment – a general guide to keeping records

Inland Revenue explanatory pamphlets — continued

Pamphlet	Date Supp	Title
SA/BK6	1997	Self-assessment – penalties for late returns
SA/BK7	1997	Self-assessment – surcharges for late payment of tax
SA/BK8	1997	Self-assessment – your guide
SAT 1	1995	Self-assessment: the new current year basis of assessment
SAT 2	1995	Self-assessment: the legal framework
SAT 3	1995	Self-assessment: what it will mean for employers
SV 1	2001	Shares Valuation Division. An introduction
NE 1	2000	First steps as a new employer
NE 3	2000	New and small employers – Support with your payroll
P/SE/1	2001	Thinking of working for yourself?
CWL 2	2001	NI contributions for self-employed people. Class 2 and Class 4
CWL4	2001	Fund-raising events: exemption for charities and other qualifying bodies
CWG 1	2001	Employer's Helpcards
CWG 2	2001	Employer's further guide to PAYE and NICs
—	2000	Education service pack

Business economic notes:

BEN 1	(1990)	Travel agents	BEN 14	(1990)	The pet industry
BEN 2	(1995)	Road haulage	BEN 15	(1990)	Veterinary surgeons
BEN 3	(1990)	The lodging industry	BEN 16	(1990)	Catering—general
BEN 4	(1990)	Hairdressers	BEN 17	(1990)	Catering—restaurants
BEN 5	(1990)	Waste materials reclamation and disposal	BEN 18	(1990)	Catering—fast-foods
			BEN 19	(1993)	Farming—stock valuation for income tax purposes
BEN 6	(1990)	Funeral directors			
BEN 7	(1990)	Dentists	BEN 20	(1994)	Insurance brokers and agents
BEN 8	(1990)	Florists	BEN 21	(1994)	Residential rest and nursing homes
BEN 9	(1988)	Licensed victuallers	BEN 22	(1995)	Dispensing chemists
BEN 10	(1990)	The jewellery trade	BEN 23	(1997)	Driving instructors
BEN 11	(1990)	Electrical retailers	BEN 24	(1997)	Independent fishmongers
BEN 12	(1990)	Antiques and fine art dealers	BEN 25	(1997)	Taxi cabs and private hire vehicles
BEN 13	(1990)	Fish and chip shops	BEN 26	(1997)	Confectioners, tobacconists and newsagents

*Internal guidance booklets and manuals:**

Accounts Office Review Unit (AORU) Manual
Assessed Taxes
Assessment Procedures
Banking Manual
Capital Allowances Instructions
Capital Gains Manual
Claims Manual
Collection Manual
Company Taxation Manual
Complaints Handbook
Compliance and Investigation Operation Manual
COTAX Manual
(CTO) Advanced Instruction Manual (IHT)
(CTO) General Examination Manual (IHT)
Customer Service Manual
Decision Makers Guide (DMG)
Double Taxation Relief Manual
Employee Share Schemes
Employer Compliance Manual
Employers Section Manual
Employment Procedures Manual
Employment Status Manual
Enforcement Manual
Enforcement Manual (Scotland)
Enquiry Handbook
European Economic Interest Groupings
General Insurance Manual
Independent Taxation Manual
Inheritance Tax Double Taxation Conventions
Insolvency Manual
Insolvency Manual (Scotland)
Inspector's Manual
Interest Review Unit Guidelines
International Tax Handbook
Investigation Handbook
Life Assurance Manual
Manufactured Payments Guidance Manuals
Movements Manual (PAYE)
National Audit Group Instructions
Oil Taxation Office PRT Manual
Oil Taxation Office Ring Fence CT Manual
Oil Taxation Office Section 830 Manual
Pay and File Manual (Collection)
PAYE Instructions (Collection)
PAYE Settlement Agreement Handbook
Pension Schemes Office Manual
Personal Contact Manual
Profit Related Pay Manual
Property Income Manual
Recovery Manual
Redress Handbook
Regional Office Manual
Relief
Residence Guide
Schedule D Compliance
Schedule E Manual
Self Assessment Manual
Shares Valuation Division Manual
Small Self Administered Schemes
Stamp Office Manual
Subcontractors in the Construction Industry
Taxation of Rents
Trust Manual

* Copies of the manuals are available on CD-rom, with an updating service, as part of a database, from Butterworths Tolley, 2 Addiscombe Road, Croydon, Surrey CR9 5AF: telephone 020 8686 9141; fax 020 8686 3155. Extracts published in looseleaf format as *Simon's Direct Tax Service*, Binders 12 and 13: prices available on application to the publishers.
All internal guidance manuals are available for inspection free of charge in Inland Revenue Tax Enquiry Centres and a number are now available on the Revenue internet site. The inheritance tax manuals may be inspected free of charge at certain Capital Taxes Offices.

National Insurance Contributions Leaflets see page 88.

Capital gains tax

Annual exemption

Individuals, personal representatives[1] and certain trusts[2]

Exempt amount of net gains	1996-97	1997-98	1998-99	1999-2000	2000-01	2001-02
	£6,300	£6,500	£6,800	£7,100	£7,200	£7,500

[1] Year of death and following 2 years (maximum).
[2] Trusts for mentally disabled persons and those in receipt of attendance allowance or disability living allowance. Exemption divided by number of qualifying settlements created (after 9 March 1981) by one settlor, subject to a minimum of one-tenth.

Trusts[1] generally

Exempt amount of net gains	1996-97	1997-98	1998-99	1999-2000	2000-01	2001-02
	£3,150	£3,250	£3,400	£3,550	£3,600	£3,750

[1] Exemption divided by number of qualifying settlements created (after 6 June 1978) by one settlor, subject to a minimum of one-fifth.

Chattel exemption

	Disposals exemption	Marginal relief: Maximum chargeable gain
1989-90 to 2001-02	£6,000	$^5/_3$ excess over £6,000

Rate of tax

2001-02 and 2000-01	**Individuals:** gains taxed as top slice of income: 10% to starting rate limit, 20% to basic rate limit, 40% above, subject to taper relief in certain cases. **Trusts, personal representatives:** 34%, subject to taper relief in certain cases
1999-2000	**Individuals:** gains taxed as top slice of income: 20% to basic rate limit, 40% above, subject to taper relief in certain cases. **Trusts, personal representatives:** 34%, subject to taper relief in certain cases.
1998-99	**Individuals:** gains taxed at income tax rates (as top slice of income[1]), subject to taper relief in certain cases. **Trusts, personal representatives:** 34%, subject to tapering in certain cases.
1997-98	**Individuals:** gains taxed at income tax rates (as top slice of income[1]) **Trusts, personal representatives:** 23% (34% for trusts charged to rate applicable to trusts)
1996-97	**Individuals:** gains taxed at income tax rates (as top slice of income[1]) **Trusts, personal representatives:** 24% (34% for trusts charged to rate applicable to trusts)

[1] Adjustment is necessary for savings income (including interest from banks and building societies, interest distributions from authorised unit trusts, interest from gilts and other securities including corporate bonds, purchased life annuities, and discounts). Adjustment is also necessary for dividends or other qualifying distributions from a UK-resident company.

Retirement relief (phased out from 6 April 1999)

Disposals after	Minimum age	100% relief on gains up to	50% relief on gains between	Maximum relief
5 April 2003	–	–	–	–
5 April 2002	50	£50,000	£50,000.01–£200,000	£125,000
5 April 2001	50	£100,000	£100,000.01–£400,000	£250,000
5 April 2000	50	£150,000	£150,000.01–£600,000	£375,000
5 April 1999	50	£200,000	£200,000.01–£800,000	£500,000
27 November 1995	50	£250,000	£250,000.01–£1,000,000	£625,000

(% determined by qualifying period. Relief also available where early retirement occurs for reasons of ill-health. Relief given after indexation allowance but before tapering relief.)

Taper relief

Taper relief is available for disposals made after 5 April 1998 (TCGA 1992 s 2A, Sch A1; FA 2000 ss 66, 67). The chargeable gain is reduced according to the length of time for which the asset has been held (counting from 6 April 1998). Non-business assets acquired before 17 March 1998 and business assets acquired before 17 March 1998 and disposed of before 6 April 2000 qualify for an addition of one year to the period for which they are held after 5 April 1998. There is no one-year addition for disposals of business assets after 5 April 2000. The reductions available for gains on business assets are greater than for gains on non-business assets.

Business assets				Non-business assets			
Number of complete yrs after 5.4.98 for which asset held	% of gain chargeable	Equivalent tax rates: Higher rate taxp'r	20% rate taxp'r	Number of complete yrs after 5.4.98 for which asset held	% of gain chargeable	Equivalent tax rates: Higher rate taxp'r	20% rate taxp'r
Disposals after 5 April 2000							
0	100	40	20	0	100	40	20
1	87.5	35	17.5	1	100	40	20
2	75	30	15	2	100	40	20
3	50	20	10	3	95	38	19
4 or more	25	10	5	4	90	36	18
				5	85	34	17
Disposals before 6 April 2000				6	80	32	16
0	100	40	20	7	75	30	15
1	92.5	37	18.5	8	70	28	14
2	85	34	17.0	9	65	26	13
3	77.5	31	15.5	10 or more	60	24	12

Leases

Depreciation table (TCGA 1992 Sch 8 para 1)

Yrs	%	Yrs	%	Yrs	%	Yrs	%	Yrs	%	Yrs	%	Yrs	%
50 (or more)	100	42	96.593	34	91.156	27	83.816	20	72.770	13	56.167	6	31.195
49	99.657	41	96.041	33	90.280	26	82.496	19	70.791	12	53.191	5	26.722
48	99.289	40	95.457	32	89.354	25	81.100	18	68.697	11	50.038	4	21.983
47	98.902	39	94.842	31	88.371	24	79.622	17	66.470	10	46.695	3	16.959
46	98.490	38	94.189	30	87.330	23	78.055	16	64.116	9	43.154	2	11.629
45	98.059	37	93.497	29	86.226	22	76.399	15	61.617	8	39.399	1	5.983
44	97.595	36	92.761	28	85.053	21	74.635	14	58.971	7	35.414	0	0
43	97.107	35	91.981										

Formula: fraction of expenditure disallowed—

$$\frac{\text{Percentage for duration of lease at acquisition or expenditure} - \text{Percentage for duration of lease at disposal}}{\text{Percentage for duration of lease at acquisition or expenditure}}$$

Fractions of years:
Add one-twelfth of the difference between the percentage for the whole year and the next higher percentage for each additional month. Odd days under 14 are not counted; 14 odd days or more count as a month.

Short leases: premiums treated as rent (TA 1988 s 34, TCGA 1992 Sch 8 para 5)
Part of premium for grant of a short lease which is chargeable to income tax under Schedule A—
  $P - (2\% \times (n - 1) \times P)$
Where P = amount of premium
       n = number of complete years which lease has to run when granted

Length of Lease (complete years)	Amount chargeable to CGT %	Income tax Sch A %	Length of Lease (complete years)	Amount chargeable to CGT %	Income tax Sch A %	Length of Lease (complete years)	Amount chargeable to CGT %	Income tax Sch A %
Over 50	100	0	34	66	34	17	32	68
50	98	2	33	64	36	16	30	70
49	96	4	32	62	38	15	28	72
48	94	6	31	60	40	14	26	74
47	92	8	30	58	42	13	24	76
46	90	10	29	56	44	12	22	78
45	88	12	28	54	46	11	20	80
44	86	14	27	52	48	10	18	82
43	84	16	26	50	50	9	16	84
42	82	18	25	48	52	8	14	86
41	80	20	24	46	54	7	12	88
40	78	22	23	44	56	6	10	90
39	76	24	22	42	58	5	8	92
38	74	26	21	40	60	4	6	94
37	72	28	20	38	62	3	4	96
36	70	30	19	36	64	2	2	98
35	68	32	18	34	66	1 or less	0	100

Gilt-edged securities exempt from tax on chargeable gains

The following securities have been specified for the purposes of TCGA 1992 Sch 9 and are exempt from capital gains tax. A similar exemption exists for qualifying corporate bonds issued after 13 March 1984. A 1-year qualifying limit applied to disposals before 2 July 1986. The gain accruing on the disposal of an option or contract to acquire or dispose of gilt-edged securities or qualifying corporate bonds after 1 July 1986 is also exempt from capital gains tax. (Securities redeemed before 31 July 2001 do not appear on this list.)

Readers should note that under the loan relationship provisions of FA 1996 Part IV Chapter II, the definition of 'qualifying corporate bond' for the purposes of corporation tax only has been extended (see TCGA 1992 ss 117, 117A, 117B).

* Repaid at latest date shown unless the Treasury give notice of earlier repayment.

Stocks		Redemption dates	Dividend due dates	
9¾%	Conversion Stock 2001	10 August 2001	10 February	10 August
2½%	Index-Linked Treasury Stock 2001	24 September 2001	24 March	24 September
7%	Treasury Stock 2001	6 November 2001	6 May	6 November
7%	Treasury Stock 2001 'A'			
10%	Conversion Stock 2002	11 April 2002	11 April	11 October
7%	Treasury Stock 2002	7 June 2002	7 June	7 December
9½%	Conversion Stock 2002	14 June 2002	14 June	14 December
9¾%	Treasury Stock 2002	27 August 2002	27 February	27 August
9¾%	Treasury Stock 2002 'A'			
9¾%	Treasury Stock 2002 'B'			
9¾%	Treasury Stock 2002 'C'			
9%	Exchequer Stock 2002	19 November 2002	19 May	19 November
9¾%	Conversion Loan 2003	7 May 2003	7 May	7 November
2½%	Index-Linked Treasury Stock 2003	20 May 2003	20 May	20 November
8%	Treasury Stock 2003	10 June 2003	10 June	10 December
8%	Treasury Stock 2003 'A'			
13¾%	Treasury Stock 2000-03*	25 July 2000/25 July 2003	25 January	25 July
13¾%	Treasury Stock 2000-03 'A'			
10%	Treasury Stock 2003	8 September 2003	8 March	8 September
10%	Treasury Stock 2003 'A'			
10%	Treasury Stock 2003 'B'			
6½%	Treasury Stock 2003	7 December 2003	7 June	7 December
11½%	Treasury Stock 2001-04*	19 March 2001/19 March 2004	19 March	19 September
10%	Treasury Stock 2004	18 May 2004	18 May	18 November
3½%	Funding Stock 1999-2004*	14 July 1999/14 July 2004	14 January	14 July
4⅜%	Index-Linked Treasury Stock 2004	21 October 2004	21 April	21 October
9½%	Conversion Stock 2004	25 October 2004	25 April	25 October
9½%	Conversion Stock 2004 'A'			
6¾%	Treasury Stock 2004	26 November 2004	26 May	26 November
6¾%	Treasury Stock 2004 'A'			
5%	Treasury Loan 2004	7 June 2004	7 June	7 December
9½%	Conversion Stock 2005	18 April 2005	18 April	18 October
9½%	Conversion Stock 2005 'A'			
10½%	Exchequer Stock 2005	20 September 2005	20 March	20 September
12½%	Treasury Stock 2003-05*	21 November 2003/ 21 November 2005	21 May	21 November
12½%	Treasury Stock 2003-05* 'A'			
8½%	Treasury Stock 2005	7 December 2005	7 June	7 December
2%	Index-Linked Treasury Stock 2006	19 July 2006	19 January	19 July
7¾%	Treasury Stock 2006	8 September 2006	8 March	8 September
8%	Treasury Loan 2002-06*	5 October 2002/5 October 2006	5 April	5 October
8%	Treasury Loan 2002-06 'A'			
9¾%	Conversion Stock 2006	15 November 2006	15 May	15 November
7½%	Treasury Stock 2006	7 December 2006	7 June	7 December
11¾%	Treasury Stock 2003-07*	22 January 2003/22 January 2007	22 January	22 July
11¾%	Treasury Stock 2003-07 'A'			
7¼%	Treasury Stock 2007	7 June 2007	7 June	7 December
8½%	Treasury Loan 2007	16 July 2007	16 January	16 July
8½%	Treasury Loan 2007 'A'			
8½%	Treasury Loan 2007 'B'			
8½%	Treasury Loan 2007 'C'			
13½%	Treasury Stock 2004-08*	26 March 2004/26 March 2008	26 March	26 September

Gilt-edged securities — continued

Stocks		Redemption dates	Dividend due dates	
9%	Treasury Loan 2008	13 October 2008	13 April	13 October
9%	Treasury Loan 2008 'A'			
9%	Treasury Loan 2008 'B'			
9%	Treasury Loan 2008 'C'			
9%	Treasury Loan 2008 'D'			
2½%	Index-Linked Treasury Stock 2009	20 May 2009	20 May	20 November
8%	Treasury Stock 2009	25 September 2009	25 March	25 September
8%	Treasury Stock 2009 'A'			
5¾%	Treasury Stock 2009	7 December 2009	7 June	7 December
6¼%	Treasury Stock 2010	25 November 2010	25 May	25 November
9%	Conversion Loan 2011	12 July 2011	12 January	12 July
9%	Conversion Loan 2011 'A'			
9%	Conversion Loan 2011 'B'			
9%	Conversion Loan 2011 'C'			
9%	Conversion Loan 2011 'D'			
2½%	Index-Linked Treasury Stock 2011	23 August 2011	23 February	23 August
9%	Treasury Stock 2012	6 August 2012	6 February	6 August
9%	Treasury Stock 2012 'A'			
5½%	Treasury Stock 2008-12*	10 September 2008/ 10 September 2012	10 March	10 September
2½%	Index-Linked Treasury Stock 2013	16 August 2013	16 February	16 August
8%	Treasury Stock 2013	27 September 2013	27 March	27 September
7¾%	Treasury Loan 2012-15*	26 January 2012/26 January 2015	26 January	26 July
8%	Treasury Stock 2015	7 December 2015	7 June	7 December
8%	Treasury Stock 2015 'A'			
2½%	Treasury Stock 1986-2016*	15 March 1986/15 March 2016	15 March	15 September
2½%	Index-Linked Treasury Stock 2016	26 July 2016	26 January	26 July
2½%	Index-Linked Treasury Stock 2016 'A'			
8¾%	Treasury Stock 2017	25 August 2017	25 February	25 August
8¾%	Treasury Stock 2017 'A'			
12%	Exchequer Stock 2013-17*	12 December 2013/ 12 December 2017	12 June	12 December
2½%	Index-Linked Treasury Stock 2020	16 April 2020	16 April	16 October
8%	Treasury Stock 2021	7 June 2021	7 June	7 December
2½%	Index-Linked Treasury Stock 2024	17 July 2024	17 January	17 July
6%	Treasury Stock 2028	7 December 2028	7 June	7 December
4⅛%	Index-Linked Treasury Stock 2030	22 July 2030	22 January	22 July
4¼%	Treasury Stock 2032	7 June 2032	7 June	7 December
4%	Consolidated Loan	1 February 1957 or after	1 February	1 August
3½%	War Loan	1 December 1952 or after	1 June	1 December
3½%	Conversion Loan	1 April 1961 or after	1 April	1 October
3%	Treasury Stock	5 April 1966 or after	5 April	5 October
2½%	Consolidated Stock	5 April 1923 or after	5 January, 5 July	5 April, 5 October
2½%	Treasury Stock 1975 or after	1 April 1975 or after	1 April	1 October
2½%	Annuities	5 January 1905 or after	5 January, 5 July	5 April, 5 October
2¾%	Annuities	5 January 1905 or after	5 January, 5 July	5 April, 5 October

Reliefs

The following is a summary of the main reliefs and exemptions for the year 2001-02. The legislation should be referred to for conditions and exceptions.

Charities

Gains accruing to charities which are both applicable and applied for charitable purposes	Exempt

Individuals

Annual exemption (see p 36 for earlier years)	£7,500
Chattel exemption (see p 36 for marginal relief)	£6,000
Compensation (injury to person, profession or vocation)	Exempt
Decorations for valour (acquired otherwise than for money or money's worth)	Gain exempt
Enterprise Investment Scheme (see p 75)	Gain on disposal after relevant three year period exempt to extent full relief given on shares
Foreign currency acquired for personal expenditure	Gain exempt
Gifts for public benefit, works of art, historic buildings etc	No chargeable gain/allowable loss
Gilt-edged stock (see p 38)	No chargeable gain/allowable loss
Married persons living together	No chargeable gain/allowable loss on disposals from one to the other
Motor vehicles	Gain exempt
Principal private residence	Gain exempt
If residence is partly let, exemption for the let part is limited to the smaller of—	(1) exemption on owner-occupied part and (2) £40,000
Qualifying corporate bonds	No chargeable gain (for loans made before 17 March 1998, allowable loss in certain cases if all or part of loss is irrecoverable)
Retirement relief (phased-out over 5 years beginning in 1999-2000: see p 36)	£100,000 plus 50% of gains between £100,000 and £400,000
Hold-over relief for gifts	Restricted to: (1) gifts of business assets (including unquoted shares in trading companies and holding companies of trading groups). Relief is not available on the transfer of shares or securities to a company made after 8 November 1999: FA 2000 s 90 (2) gifts of heritage property (3) gifts to heritage maintenance funds (4) gifts to political parties, and (5) gifts which are chargeable transfers for inheritance tax. Where available, transferee's acquisition cost treated as reduced by held-over gain.
Venture capital trusts (see p 76)	Gain on disposal of shares by original investor exempt if company still a venture capital trust. Exemption applies only to shares acquired up to the permitted maximum of £100,000 per year of assessment.

Reliefs — continued
Businesses
Roll-over relief for replacement of business assets

Qualifying assets:
>Buildings and land both occupied and used for the purposes of the trade
>Fixed plant and machinery
>Ships, aircraft and hovercraft
>Satellites, space stations and spacecraft
>Goodwill
>Milk and potato quotas
>Ewe and suckler cow premium quotas
>Fish quotas (from 29 March 1999)
>UK oil licences (from 1 July 1999)

The 'replacement' assets must be acquired within 12 months before or 3 years after the disposal of the old asset. Both assets must be within any of the above classes. Holdover relief is available where the new asset is a depreciating asset (having a predictable useful life not exceeding 60 years).

Personal representatives
Annual exemption

Year of death and following 2 years: (See p 36 for earlier years)	£7,500

Allowable expenses

Expenses allowable for the costs of establishing title in computing chargeable gains on disposal of assets in a deceased person's estate: deaths occurring after 5 April 1993 (SP 8/94). (The Revenue accepts computations based either on the scale or on the actual allowable expenditure incurred.)

Gross value of estate	*Allowable expenditure*
Up to £40,000	1.75% of the probate value of the assets sold by the personal representatives
Between £40,001 and £70,000	£700, to be divided between all the assets of the estate in proportion to the probate values and allowed in those proportions on assets sold by the personal representatives
Between £70,001 and £300,000	1% of the probate value of the assets sold
Between £300,001 and £400,000	£3,000, to be divided between all the assets of the estate in proportion to the probate values and allowed in those proportions on assets sold by the personal representatives
Between £400,001 and £750,000	0.75% of the probate value of the assets sold
Exceeding £75,000	Negotiable according to the facts of the particular case

Trustees
Annual exemption see p 36.

Allowable expenses

Expenses allowable in computing chargeable gains of corporate trustees in the administration of trusts and estates: acquisition, disposals and deemed disposals after 5 April 1993 (SP 8/94). (The Revenue accepts computations based either on the scale or on the actual allowable expenditure incurred.)

Transfers of assets to beneficiaries etc	
(a) Quoted stocks and shares	
(i) One beneficiary	£20 per holding
(ii) More than one beneficiary	£20 per holding, divided equally between the beneficiaries
(b) Unquoted shares	As (a) above, plus any exceptional expenditure
(c) Other assets	As (a) above, plus any exceptional expenditure
Actual disposals and acquisitions	
(a) Quoted stocks and shares	Investment fee as charged by the trustee (where a comprehensive annual management fee is charged, the investment fee is taken to be £0.25 per £100 of the sale or purchase moneys)
(b) Unquoted shares	As (a) above, plus actual valuation costs
(c) Other assets	Investment fee (as (a) above), subject to a maximum of £60, plus actual valuation costs
Deemed disposals by trustees	
(a) Quoted stocks and shares	£6 per holding
(b) Unquoted shares	Actual valuation costs
(c) Other assets	Actual valuation costs

Indexation allowance

For persons subject to capital gains tax, gains on disposals after 5 April 1998 of assets held on that date are indexed up to April 1998 but not beyond. No indexation allowance is available for assets acquired after 31 March 1998. Taper relief is available for disposals after 5 April 1998, see p 37. For persons subject to corporation tax, indexation continues to be available as previously, and there is no taper relief.

The indexation allowance is calculated as follows: allowable expenditure (or MV at 31.3.82) $\times \dfrac{RD - RI}{RI}$

RD = Retail prices index figure for month of disposal
RI = Retail prices index figure for base month (ie the month in which the allowable expenditure was incurred, or March 1982 if later).

The following indexed rise can be used when calculating the allowance—

Month of disposal

Base Month		1996 Apr	May	June	July	Aug	Sept	Oct	Nov	Dec	1997 Jan	Feb	Mar	Apr	May	June	July	Aug	Sept	Oct	Nov	Dec	1998 Jan	Feb	Mar	Apr	May	June	July	Aug	Sept	Oct
1982	Mar	.921	.925	.926	.918	.927	.936	.936	.937	.944	.944	.951	.956	.967	.975	.983	.983	.995	1.005	1.008	1.009	1.014	1.008	1.018	1.024	1.047	1.058	1.057	1.052	1.061	1.069	1.071
	Apr	.883	.887	.888	.881	.889	.898	.898	.899	.905	.905	.913	.918	.929	.936	.944	.944	.956	.966	.968	.969	.974	.968	.978	.984	1.006	1.018	1.016	1.011	1.020	1.029	1.030
	May	.870	.873	.874	.867	.876	.884	.884	.886	.892	.892	.899	.904	.915	.922	.930	.930	.942	.952	.954	.955	.960	.954	.964	.970	.992	1.003	1.002	.997	1.006	1.014	1.015
	June	.864	.868	.869	.862	.870	.879	.879	.880	.886	.886	.894	.899	.910	.917	.924	.924	.936	.946	.949	.950	.955	.949	.958	.965	.987	.998	.996	.991	1.000	1.009	1.010
	July	.864	.867	.869	.861	.870	.878	.878	.880	.886	.886	.893	.898	.909	.916	.924	.924	.936	.946	.948	.949	.954	.948	.958	.964	.986	.997	.996	.991	.999	1.008	1.009
	Aug	.863	.867	.868	.861	.869	.878	.878	.879	.885	.885	.893	.897	.908	.916	.923	.923	.935	.945	.947	.949	.954	.947	.957	.963	.985	.996	.995	.990	.999	1.007	1.009
	Sept	.851	.864	.868	.862	.870	.878	.878	.880	.886	.886	.884	.889	.900	.907	.915	.915	.927	.937	.939	.940	.945	.939	.949	.955	.977	.988	.986	.982	.990	1.000	1.010
	Oct	.855	.859	.860	.853	.861	.870	.870	.871	.877	.877	.874	.889	.900	.907	.915	.915	.927	.937	.939	.940	.945	.939	.949	.955	.977	.988	.986	.982	.990	.999	1.000
	Nov	.846	.850	.851	.844	.852	.861	.861	.862	.868	.868	.875	.880	.891	.898	.905	.905	.917	.927	.930	.931	.936	.930	.939	.945	.967	.978	.977	.972	.980	.989	.990
	Dec	.849	.853	.854	.847	.856	.864	.864	.865	.871	.871	.879	.833	.894	.902	.909	.909	.921	.931	.933	.934	.939	.933	.943	.949	.971	.982	.980	.976	.984	.992	.994
1983	Jan	.847	.851	.852	.845	.853	.862	.862	.863	.869	.869	.876	.881	.892	.899	.907	.907	.919	.928	.931	.932	.937	.931	.940	.946	.968	.979	.978	.973	.982	.990	.991
	Feb	.839	.843	.844	.837	.845	.854	.854	.855	.861	.861	.868	.873	.884	.891	.898	.898	.910	.920	.922	.924	.929	.922	.932	.938	.960	.971	.969	.965	.973	.982	.983
	Mar	.836	.840	.841	.834	.842	.850	.850	.852	.858	.858	.865	.870	.880	.888	.895	.895	.907	.917	.919	.920	.925	.919	.929	.935	.956	.967	.966	.961	.969	.978	.979
	Apr	.811	.814	.815	.808	.816	.825	.825	.826	.832	.832	.839	.844	.854	.862	.869	.869	.881	.890	.892	.894	.898	.892	.902	.908	.929	.940	.939	.934	.942	.951	.952
	May	.803	.807	.808	.801	.809	.817	.817	.818	.824	.824	.821	.836	.847	.854	.861	.861	.873	.882	.884	.886	.890	.884	.894	.900	.921	.932	.931	.926	.934	.942	.944
	June	.799	.802	.803	.796	.805	.813	.813	.814	.820	.820	.827	.832	.842	.849	.856	.856	.868	.878	.880	.881	.886	.880	.889	.895	.917	.927	.926	.921	.929	.938	.939
	July	.789	.793	.794	.787	.795	.803	.803	.804	.810	.810	.817	.822	.839	.846	.846	.846	.858	.868	.870	.871	.876	.870	.879	.885	.906	.917	.916	.911	.919	.927	.929
	Aug	.781	.785	.786	.779	.787	.795	.795	.796	.802	.802	.809	.814	.824	.831	.838	.838	.850	.859	.862	.863	.868	.862	.871	.877	.898	.908	.907	.902	.911	.919	.920
	Sept	.773	.777	.778	.771	.779	.787	.787	.788	.794	.794	.801	.806	.816	.823	.830	.830	.842	.851	.853	.855	.859	.853	.863	.869	.889	.900	.899	.894	.902	.910	.911
	Oct	.767	.770	.772	.765	.773	.781	.781	.782	.788	.788	.795	.799	.810	.817	.824	.824	.835	.845	.847	.848	.853	.847	.856	.862	.883	.893	.892	.887	.895	.904	.905
	Nov	.761	.764	.765	.758	.767	.775	.775	.776	.782	.782	.788	.793	.803	.810	.817	.817	.829	.838	.840	.842	.846	.840	.850	.855	.876	.887	.885	.881	.889	.897	.898
	Dec	.756	.760	.761	.754	.762	.770	.770	.771	.777	.777	.784	.788	.799	.806	.813	.813	.824	.833	.836	.837	.841	.836	.845	.851	.871	.882	.880	.876	.884	.892	.893
1984	Jan	.757	.761	.762	.755	.763	.771	.771	.772	.778	.778	.785	.789	.800	.807	.814	.814	.825	.834	.837	.838	.842	.837	.846	.852	.872	.883	.882	.877	.885	.893	.894
	Feb	.750	.753	.755	.748	.756	.764	.764	.765	.771	.771	.778	.782	.792	.799	.806	.806	.818	.827	.829	.830	.835	.829	.838	.844	.865	.875	.874	.869	.877	.885	.886
	Mar	.744	.748	.749	.742	.750	.758	.758	.759	.765	.765	.772	.776	.787	.794	.800	.800	.812	.821	.823	.824	.829	.823	.832	.838	.859	.869	.868	.863	.871	.879	.880
	Apr	.721	.725	.726	.719	.727	.735	.735	.736	.742	.742	.749	.753	.763	.770	.777	.777	.788	.797	.799	.800	.805	.799	.808	.814	.834	.844	.843	.839	.847	.855	.856
	May	.715	.718	.720	.713	.721	.729	.729	.730	.735	.735	.742	.747	.757	.763	.770	.770	.781	.790	.793	.794	.798	.793	.802	.807	.828	.838	.837	.832	.840	.848	.849
	June	.711	.714	.715	.708	.716	.724	.724	.725	.731	.731	.738	.742	.752	.759	.766	.766	.777	.786	.788	.789	.794	.788	.797	.803	.823	.833	.832	.827	.835	.843	.844
	July	.713	.716	.717	.710	.718	.726	.726	.727	.733	.733	.740	.744	.754	.761	.768	.768	.779	.788	.790	.791	.796	.790	.799	.805	.825	.835	.834	.829	.837	.845	.846
	Aug	.697	.700	.701	.695	.702	.710	.710	.711	.717	.717	.723	.728	.738	.745	.751	.751	.762	.771	.773	.775	.779	.773	.782	.788	.808	.818	.817	.812	.820	.828	.829
	Sept	.693	.697	.698	.691	.699	.707	.707	.708	.713	.713	.720	.724	.734	.741	.748	.748	.759	.768	.770	.771	.776	.770	.779	.784	.804	.814	.813	.809	.817	.824	.825
	Oct	.683	.686	.687	.681	.689	.696	.696	.697	.703	.703	.709	.714	.724	.730	.737	.737	.748	.757	.759	.760	.765	.759	.768	.773	.793	.803	.802	.798	.805	.813	.814
	Nov	.678	.681	.682	.676	.683	.691	.691	.692	.698	.698	.704	.709	.719	.725	.732	.732	.743	.752	.754	.755	.759	.754	.762	.768	.788	.798	.797	.792	.800	.808	.809
	Dec	.679	.683	.684	.677	.685	.692	.692	.694	.699	.699	.705	.710	.720	.727	.733	.733	.744	.753	.755	.756	.761	.755	.764	.769	.789	.799	.798	.794	.801	.809	.810
1985	Jan	.673	.676	.678	.671	.679	.686	.686	.687	.693	.693	.699	.704	.714	.720	.727	.727	.738	.747	.749	.750	.754	.749	.758	.763	.783	.793	.792	.787	.795	.803	.804
	Feb	.660	.663	.664	.658	.665	.673	.673	.674	.679	.679	.686	.690	.700	.707	.713	.713	.724	.733	.735	.736	.740	.735	.744	.749	.769	.778	.777	.773	.781	.788	.789
	Mar	.644	.648	.649	.642	.650	.657	.657	.658	.664	.664	.670	.675	.784	.691	.697	.697	.708	.717	.719	.720	.724	.719	.727	.733	.752	.762	.761	.756	.764	.772	.773
	Apr	.610	.613	.614	.608	.615	.623	.623	.624	.629	.629	.635	.640	.649	.655	.662	.662	.672	.681	.683	.684	.688	.683	.691	.697	.716	.725	.724	.720	.727	.735	.736
	May	.603	.606	.607	.601	.608	.615	.615	.616	.622	.622	.628	.632	.642	.648	.654	.654	.665	.673	.675	.676	.681	.675	.684	.689	.708	.717	.716	.712	.719	.727	.728
	June	.599	.603	.604	.597	.605	.612	.612	.613	.618	.618	.625	.629	.638	.644	.651	.651	.661	.670	.672	.673	.677	.672	.680	.685	.704	.714	.713	.708	.716	.723	.724
	July	.602	.606	.607	.600	.608	.615	.615	.616	.621	.621	.628	.632	.641	.684	.654	.654	.664	.673	.675	.676	.680	.675	.683	.688	.707	.717	.716	.712	.719	.726	.727
	Aug	.598	.601	.602	.596	.603	.611	.611	.612	.617	.617	.623	.627	.637	.643	.649	.649	.660	.668	.670	.671	.676	.670	.679	.684	.703	.712	.711	.707	.714	.722	.723
	Sept	.599	.602	.603	.597	.604	.612	.612	.613	.618	.618	.624	.628	.638	.644	.650	.650	.661	.669	.671	.672	.676	.671	.680	.685	.704	.713	.712	.708	.715	.723	.724
	Oct	.596	.600	.601	.594	.602	.609	.609	.610	.615	.615	.622	.626	.635	.641	.648	.648	.658	.667	.669	.670	.674	.669	.677	.682	.701	.710	.709	.705	.713	.720	.721
	Nov	.591	.594	.595	.589	.596	.603	.603	.604	.610	.610	.616	.620	.630	.636	.642	.642	.652	.661	.663	.664	.668	.663	.671	.676	.695	.705	.704	.699	.707	.714	.715
	Dec	.589	.592	.593	.587	.594	.601	.601	.602	.608	.608	.614	.618	.627	.634	.640	.640	.650	.659	.661	.662	.666	.661	.669	.674	.693	.702	.701	.697	.704	.712	.713

Indexation allowance — continued

Month of disposal

Base Month		1998 Nov	1998 Dec	1999 Jan	1999 Feb	1999 Mar	1999 Apr	1999 May	1999 June	1999 July	1999 Aug	1999 Sept	1999 Oct	1999 Nov	1999 Dec	2000 Jan	2000 Feb	2000 Mar	2000 Apr	2000 May	2000 June	2000 July	2000 Aug	2000 Sept	2000 Oct	2000 Nov	2000 Dec	2001 Jan	2001 Feb	2001 Mar	2001 Apr
1982	Mar	1·069	1·069	1·057	1·061	1·066	1·079	1·085	1·085	1·078	1·083	1·092	1·096	1·098	1·106	1·097	1·108	1·120	1·141	1·149	1·154	1·146	1·146	1·161	1·160	1·166	1·168	1·154	1·165	1·168	1·179
	Apr	1·029	1·029	1·016	1·020	1·025	1·039	1·043	1·043	1·037	1·042	1·051	1·055	1·057	1·064	1·056	1·067	1·078	1·099	1·106	1·111	1·104	1·104	1·119	1·117	1·124	1·125	1·111	1·122	1·125	1·136
	May	1·014	1·014	1·002	1·006	1·010	1·024	1·029	1·029	1·023	1·028	1·036	1·040	1·042	1·050	1·041	1·052	1·063	1·084	1·091	1·096	1·089	1·089	1·104	1·102	1·108	1·110	1·096	1·107	1·110	1·121
	June	1·009	1·009	·996	1·000	1·005	1·018	1·023	1·023	1·017	1·022	1·031	1·034	1·037	1·044	1·035	1·046	1·057	1·078	1·086	1·090	1·083	1·083	1·098	1·097	1·103	1·104	1·090	1·101	1·104	1·115
	July	1·008	1·008	·996	·999	1·003	1·018	1·023	1·023	1·016	1·021	1·030	1·034	1·036	1·043	1·035	1·046	1·057	1·078	1·085	1·090	1·082	1·082	1·097	1·096	1·102	1·103	1·090	1·101	1·103	1·114
	Aug	1·007	1·007	·995	·999	1·004	1·017	1·022	1·022	1·016	1·021	1·029	1·033	1·035	1·043	1·034	1·045	1·056	1·077	1·084	1·089	1·082	1·082	1·096	1·095	1·101	1·103	1·089	1·100	1·103	1·114
	Sept	1·009	1·009	·996	1·000	1·005	1·018	1·023	1·023	1·017	1·022	1·031	1·034	1·037	1·044	1·035	1·046	1·057	1·078	1·086	1·090	1·083	1·083	1·098	1·097	1·103	1·104	1·090	1·101	1·104	1·115
	Oct	·999	·999	·986	·990	·995	1·008	1·013	1·013	1·007	1·012	1·021	1·024	1·027	1·034	1·025	1·036	1·047	1·068	1·075	1·080	1·073	1·073	1·087	1·086	1·092	1·093	1·080	1·091	1·093	1·104
	Nov	·989	·989	·977	·980	·985	·999	1·003	1·003	·997	1·002	1·011	1·014	1·017	1·024	1·015	1·026	1·037	1·058	1·065	1·070	1·063	1·063	1·077	1·076	1·082	1·083	1·070	1·081	1·083	1·094
	Dec	·992	·992	·980	·984	·989	1·002	1·007	1·007	1·001	1·006	1·014	1·018	1·020	1·028	1·019	1·030	1·041	1·062	1·069	1·074	1·066	1·066	1·081	1·080	1·086	1·087	1·074	1·085	1·087	1·098
1983	Jan	·990	·990	·978	·982	·986	1·000	1·005	1·005	·999	1·003	1·012	1·015	1·018	1·025	1·017	1·028	1·038	1·059	1·066	1·071	1·064	1·064	1·078	1·077	1·083	1·084	1·071	1·082	1·084	1·095
	Feb	·982	·982	·969	·973	·978	·991	·996	·996	·990	·995	1·003	1·007	1·009	1·016	1·008	1·019	1·030	1·050	1·057	1·062	1·055	1·055	1·070	1·068	1·074	1·076	1·062	1·073	1·076	1·086
	Mar	·978	·978	·966	·969	·974	·988	·992	·992	·986	·991	1·000	1·003	1·006	1·013	1·004	1·015	1·026	1·046	1·054	1·059	1·051	1·051	1·066	1·065	1·071	1·072	1·059	1·069	1·072	1·083
	Apr	·951	·951	·939	·942	·947	·960	·965	·965	·959	·964	·972	·975	·978	·985	·977	·987	·998	1·018	1·025	1·030	1·023	1·023	1·037	1·036	1·042	1·043	1·030	1·041	1·043	1·054
	May	·942	·942	·931	·934	·939	·952	·957	·957	·951	·955	·964	·967	·970	·977	·968	·979	·990	1·010	1·017	1·022	1·014	1·014	1·029	1·027	1·033	1·035	1·022	1·032	1·035	1·045
	June	·938	·938	·926	·929	·934	·947	·952	·952	·946	·951	·959	·962	·965	·972	·964	·974	·985	1·005	1·012	1·017	1·010	1·010	1·024	1·023	1·028	1·030	1·017	1·027	1·030	1·040
	July	·927	·927	·916	·919	·924	·937	·941	·941	·936	·940	·948	·952	·954	·961	·953	·964	·974	·994	1·001	1·006	·999	·999	1·013	1·012	1·018	1·019	1·006	1·016	1·019	1·029
	Aug	·919	·919	·907	·911	·915	·928	·933	·933	·927	·932	·940	·943	·946	·953	·944	·955	·965	·985	·992	·997	·990	·990	1·004	1·003	1·009	1·010	·997	1·008	1·010	1·020
	Sept	·910	·910	·899	·902	·907	·920	·924	·924	·918	·923	·931	·935	·937	·944	·936	·946	·957	·977	·984	·988	·981	·981	·995	·994	1·000	1·001	·988	·999	1·001	1·011
	Oct	·904	·904	·892	·895	·900	·913	·917	·917	·912	·916	·924	·928	·930	·937	·929	·939	·950	·970	·977	·981	·974	·974	·988	·987	·993	·994	·981	·992	·994	1·004
	Nov	·897	·897	·885	·889	·893	·906	·911	·911	·905	·910	·918	·921	·923	·930	·922	·933	·943	·963	·970	·974	·967	·967	·981	·980	·986	·987	·974	·985	·987	·997
	Dec	·892	·892	·880	·884	·888	·901	·906	·906	·900	·905	·913	·916	·918	·925	·917	·928	·938	·958	·964	·969	·962	·962	·976	·975	·981	·982	·969	·979	·982	·992
1984	Jan	·893	·893	·882	·885	·890	·902	·907	·907	·901	·906	·914	·917	·920	·926	·918	·929	·939	·959	·966	·970	·963	·963	·977	·976	·982	·983	·970	·981	·983	·993
	Feb	·885	·885	·874	·877	·882	·895	·899	·899	·893	·898	·906	·909	·912	·919	·911	·921	·931	·951	·958	·962	·955	·955	·969	·968	·974	·975	·962	·973	·975	·985
	Mar	·879	·879	·868	·871	·876	·888	·893	·893	·887	·892	·900	·903	·906	·912	·904	·915	·925	·944	·951	·956	·949	·949	·963	·962	·967	·968	·956	·966	·968	·979
	Apr	·855	·855	·843	·847	·851	·864	·868	·868	·863	·867	·875	·878	·881	·887	·879	·890	·900	·919	·926	·930	·923	·923	·937	·936	·941	·943	·930	·940	·943	·953
	May	·848	·848	·837	·840	·844	·857	·861	·861	·856	·860	·868	·871	·874	·880	·872	·883	·893	·912	·919	·923	·916	·916	·930	·929	·934	·935	·923	·933	·935	·946
	June	·843	·843	·832	·835	·840	·852	·856	·856	·851	·855	·863	·867	·869	·876	·868	·878	·888	·907	·914	·918	·911	·911	·925	·924	·929	·930	·918	·928	·930	·941
	July	·845	·845	·834	·837	·842	·854	·859	·859	·853	·857	·865	·869	·871	·878	·870	·880	·890	·909	·916	·920	·914	·914	·927	·926	·932	·933	·920	·930	·933	·943
	Aug	·828	·828	·817	·820	·825	·837	·841	·841	·836	·840	·848	·851	·854	·860	·852	·862	·872	·891	·898	·902	·896	·896	·909	·908	·914	·915	·902	·912	·915	·925
	Sept	·824	·824	·813	·817	·821	·833	·838	·838	·832	·837	·844	·848	·850	·857	·849	·859	·869	·888	·894	·899	·892	·892	·905	·904	·910	·911	·899	·909	·911	·921
	Oct	·813	·813	·802	·805	·810	·822	·826	·826	·821	·825	·833	·836	·839	·845	·837	·847	·857	·876	·883	·887	·880	·880	·894	·893	·898	·899	·887	·897	·899	·909
	Nov	·808	·808	·797	·800	·804	·816	·821	·821	·815	·820	·827	·831	·833	·839	·832	·842	·852	·870	·877	·881	·875	·875	·888	·887	·892	·893	·881	·891	·893	·903
	Dec	·809	·809	·798	·801	·806	·818	·822	·822	·817	·821	·829	·832	·834	·841	·833	·843	·853	·872	·878	·883	·876	·876	·889	·888	·894	·895	·883	·893	·895	·905
1985	Jan	·803	·803	·792	·795	·799	·811	·816	·816	·810	·815	·822	·826	·828	·834	·827	·837	·846	·865	·872	·876	·869	·869	·883	·881	·887	·888	·876	·886	·888	·898
	Feb	·788	·788	·777	·781	·785	·797	·801	·801	·796	·800	·808	·811	·813	·820	·812	·822	·832	·850	·857	·861	·854	·854	·868	·866	·872	·873	·861	·871	·873	·883
	Mar	·772	·772	·761	·764	·768	·780	·784	·784	·779	·783	·791	·794	·796	·803	·795	·805	·815	·833	·839	·844	·837	·837	·850	·849	·855	·856	·844	·853	·856	·865
	Apr	·735	·735	·724	·727	·731	·743	·747	·747	·742	·746	·754	·757	·759	·765	·758	·767	·777	·795	·801	·805	·799	·799	·812	·811	·816	·817	·805	·815	·817	·826
	May	·727	·727	·716	·719	·724	·735	·739	·739	·734	·738	·746	·749	·751	·757	·750	·759	·769	·787	·793	·797	·791	·791	·803	·802	·808	·809	·797	·807	·809	·818
	June	·723	·723	·713	·716	·720	·731	·736	·736	·730	·735	·742	·745	·747	·753	·746	·756	·765	·783	·789	·793	·787	·787	·800	·799	·804	·805	·793	·803	·805	·814
	July	·726	·726	·716	·719	·723	·735	·739	·739	·734	·738	·745	·748	·750	·757	·749	·759	·768	·786	·792	·797	·790	·790	·803	·802	·807	·808	·797	·806	·808	·818
	Aug	·722	·722	·711	·714	·719	·730	·734	·734	·729	·733	·741	·744	·746	·752	·745	·754	·764	·781	·788	·792	·786	·786	·798	·797	·802	·803	·792	·801	·803	·813
	Sept	·723	·723	·712	·715	·719	·731	0·735	·735	·730	·734	·741	·745	·747	·753	·746	·755	·765	·782	·787	·793	·787	·787	·799	·798	·803	·804	·793	·802	·804	·814
	Oct	·720	·720	·709	·713	·717	·728	·732	·732	·727	·731	·739	·742	·744	·750	·743	·752	·762	·779	·786	·790	·784	·784	·796	·795	·800	·801	·790	·799	·801	·811
	Nov	·714	·714	·704	·707	·711	·722	·726	·726	·721	·725	·733	·736	·738	·744	·737	·746	·756	·773	·780	·784	·778	·778	·790	·789	·794	·795	·784	·793	·795	·805
	Dec	·712	·712	·701	·704	·709	·720	·724	·724	·719	·723	·730	·734	·736	·742	·735	·744	·753	·771	·777	·781	·775	·775	·788	·787	·792	·793	·781	·791	·793	·802

43

Indexation allowance — continued

Month of disposal

Base month

	1996									1997												1998									
1986	Apr	May	June	July	Aug	Sept	Oct	Nov	Dec	Jan	Feb	Mar	Apr	May	June	July	Aug	Sept	Oct	Nov	Dec	Jan	Feb	Mar	Apr	May	June	July	Aug	Sept	Oct
Jan	·585	·589	·590	·583	·591	·598	·598	·599	·604	·604	·610	·615	·624	·630	·636	·636	·647	·655	·657	·658	·662	·657	·665	·671	·689	·699	·698	·694	·701	·708	·709
Feb	·580	·583	·584	·578	·585	·592	·592	·593	·598	·598	·605	·609	·618	·624	·630	·630	·641	·649	·651	·652	·656	·651	·659	·665	·683	·692	·691	·687	·695	·702	·703
Mar	·578	·581	·582	·576	·583	·590	·590	·591	·596	·596	·602	·607	·616	·622	·628	·628	·639	·647	·649	·650	·654	·649	·657	·662	·681	·690	·689	·685	·692	·700	·701
Apr	·562	·566	·567	·560	·568	·575	·575	·576	·581	·581	·587	·591	·600	·606	·613	·613	·623	·631	·633	·634	·638	·633	·641	·646	·665	·674	·673	·669	·676	·683	·684
May	·560	·563	·564	·558	·565	·572	·572	·573	·578	·578	·584	·588	·597	·604	·610	·610	·620	·628	·630	·631	·635	·630	·638	·643	·662	·671	·670	·666	·673	·680	·681
June	·560	·563	·565	·558	·566	·573	·573	·574	·579	·579	·585	·589	·598	·604	·611	·611	·621	·629	·631	·632	·636	·631	·639	·644	·663	·672	·671	·667	·674	·681	·682
July	·565	·568	·569	·563	·570	·577	·577	·578	·583	·583	·589	·594	·603	·609	·615	·615	·625	·634	·636	·637	·641	·636	·644	·649	·667	·677	·676	·672	·679	·686	·687
Aug	·560	·563	·564	·558	·565	·572	·572	·573	·578	·578	·585	·589	·598	·604	·610	·620	·629	·631	·632	·636	·631	·639	·644	·662	·671	·670	·666	·673	·681	·682	·681
Sept	·552	·555	·556	·550	·557	·565	·565	·556	·571	·571	·577	·581	·590	·596	·602	·602	·612	·621	·623	·624	·628	·623	·631	·636	·654	·663	·662	·658	·665	·672	·673
Oct	·550	·553	·554	·548	·555	·562	·562	·563	·568	·568	·574	·578	·588	·594	·600	·600	·610	·618	·620	·621	·625	·620	·628	·633	·652	·661	·660	·656	·663	·670	·671
Nov	·537	·540	·541	·535	·542	·549	·549	·550	·555	·555	·561	·565	·574	·680	·586	·586	·596	·604	·606	·607	·611	·606	·614	·619	·638	·647	·646	·642	·649	·656	·657
Dec	·532	·535	·536	·530	·537	·544	·544	·545	·550	·550	·556	·556	·569	·575	·581	·581	·591	·599	·601	·602	·606	·601	·609	·614	·632	·641	·640	·636	·643	·650	·651
1987																															
Jan	·526	·529	·530	·524	·531	·538	·538	·539	·544	·544	·550	·554	·563	·569	·575	·575	·585	·593	·595	·596	·600	·595	·603	·608	·626	·635	·634	·630	·637	·644	·645
Feb	·520	·523	·524	·518	·525	·532	·532	·533	·538	·538	·544	·548	·557	·563	·569	·569	·579	·587	·589	·590	·594	·589	·597	·602	·620	·628	·627	·624	·630	·637	·638
Mar	·517	·520	·521	·515	·522	·529	·529	·530	·535	·535	·541	·545	·554	·560	·566	·576	·583	·585	·586	·590	·585	·593	·593	·598	·616	·625	·624	·620	·627	·634	·635
Apr	·499	·502	·503	·497	·504	·511	·511	·512	·517	·517	·523	·527	·535	·541	·547	·547	·557	·565	·567	·568	·572	·567	·575	·580	·597	·606	·605	·601	·608	·615	·616
May	·498	·500	·501	·496	·502	·509	·509	·510	·515	·515	·521	·525	·534	·540	·546	·546	·555	·563	·565	·566	·570	·565	·573	·578	·596	·605	·604	·600	·606	·613	·614
June	·498	·500	·501	·496	·502	·509	·509	·510	·515	·515	·521	·525	·534	·540	·546	·546	·555	·563	·565	·566	·570	·565	·573	·578	·596	·605	·604	·600	·606	·613	·614
July	·499	·502	·503	·497	·504	·511	·511	·512	·517	·517	·523	·527	·535	·541	·547	·547	·557	·565	·567	·568	·572	·567	·575	·580	·597	·606	·605	·601	·608	·615	·616
Aug	·495	·498	·499	·493	·500	·506	·506	·507	·512	·512	·518	·522	·531	·537	·543	·543	·552	·560	·562	·563	·567	·562	·570	·575	·593	·601	·600	·596	·603	·610	·611
Sept	·490	·493	·494	·488	·495	·502	·502	·503	·508	·508	·514	·518	·526	·532	·538	·538	·548	·556	·558	·559	·563	·558	·565	·570	·588	·597	·596	·592	·599	·605	·606
Oct	·483	·486	·487	·481	·488	·495	·495	·496	·500	·500	·506	·510	·519	·525	·531	·531	·540	·548	·550	·551	·555	·550	·558	·563	·580	·589	·588	·584	·591	·598	·599
Nov	·476	·479	·480	·474	·481	·487	·487	·488	·493	·493	·499	·503	·512	·517	·523	·523	·533	·541	·543	·544	·547	·543	·550	·555	·573	·581	·580	·576	·583	·590	·591
Dec	·477	·480	·481	·475	·482	·489	·489	·490	·495	·495	·500	·504	·513	·519	·525	·525	·534	·542	·544	·545	·549	·544	·552	·557	·574	·583	·582	·578	·585	·591	·592
1988																															
Jan	·477	·480	·481	·475	·482	·489	·489	·490	·495	·495	·500	·504	·513	·519	·525	·525	·534	·542	·544	·545	·549	·544	·552	·557	·574	·583	·582	·578	·585	·591	·592
Feb	·472	·474	·475	·470	·476	·483	·483	·484	·489	·489	·495	·499	·507	·513	·519	·519	·528	·536	·538	·539	·543	·538	·546	·551	·568	·577	·576	·572	·579	·585	·586
Mar	·466	·469	·470	·464	·471	·477	·477	·478	·483	·483	·489	·493	·501	·507	·513	·513	·523	·530	·532	·533	·537	·532	540	·545	·562	·571	·570	·566	·573	·579	·580
Apr	·442	·445	·446	·440	·447	·454	·454	·455	·459	·459	·465	·469	·477	·483	·489	·498	·506	·508	·509	·512	·508	·515	·520	·537	·545	·544	·541	·547	·554	·554	·555
May	·437	·440	·441	·435	·442	·448	·448	·449	·454	·454	·460	·463	·472	·477	·483	·493	·492	·500	·502	·503	·507	·502	·509	·514	·531	·540'	·539	·535	·541	·548	·549
June	·432	·434	·435	·430	·436	·443	·443	·444	·448	·448	·454	·458	·466	·472	·477	·477	·487	·494	·496	·497	·501	·496	·504	·508	·525	·534	·533	·529	·536	·542	·543
July	·430	·433	·434	·428	·435	·441	·441	·442	·447	·447	·453	·456	·465	·470	·476	·476	·485	·493	·495	·496	·500	·495	·502	·507	·524	·532	·531	·528	·534	·541	·542
Aug	·414	·417	·418	·412	·419	·425	·425	·426	·431	·431	·437	·440	·449	·454	·460	·460	·469	·476	·478	·479	·483	·478	·486	·490	·507	·515	·514	·511	·517	·524	·525
Sept	·408	·411	·411	·406	·412	·419	·419	·420	·424	·424	·430	·434	·442	·447	·453	·453	·462	·470	·471	·472	·476	·471	·479	·483	·500	·508	·507	·504	·510	·517	·518
Oct	·394	·396	·397	·392	·398	·405	·405	·405	·410	·410	·416	·419	·427	·433	·438	·438	·447	·455	·457	·458	·461	·457	·464	·468	·485	·493	·492	·489	·495	·501	·502
Nov	·387	·390	·391	·385	·392	·398	·398	·399	·404	·404	·409	·413	·421	·426	·432	·432	·441	·448	·450	·451	·455	·450	·457	·462	·478	·486	·485	·482	·488	·495	·495
Dec	·383	·386	·387	·382	·388	·394	·394	·395	·400	·400	·405	·409	·417	·422	·428	·428	·437	·444	·446	·447	·451	·446	·453	·458	·474	·482	·481	·478	·484	·490	·491
1989																															
Jan	·375	·377	·378	·373	·379	·386	·386	·386	·391	·391	·396	·400	·408	·414	·419	·419	·428	·435	·437	·438	·441	·437	·444	·449	·465	·473	·472	·468	·475	·481	·482
Feb	·365	·368	·369	·363	·369	·376	·376	·377	·381	·381	·386	·390	·398	·403	·409	·409	·418	·425	·427	·428	·431	·427	·434	·438	·454	·462	·462	·458	·464	·470	·471
Mar	·359	·362	·362	·357	·363	·370	·370	·370	·375	·375	·380	·384	·392	·397	·402	·402	·411	·419	·420	·421	·425	·420	·427	·432	·448	·456	·455	·451	·458	·464	·465
Apr	·335	·338	·339	·333	·339	·346	·346	·346	·351	·351	·356	·360	·367	·373	·378	·378	·387	·394	·395	·396	·400	·395	·402	·407	·423	·430	·430	·426	·432	·438	·439
May	·327	·330	·330	·325	·321	·337	·337	·338	·343	·343	·348	·351	·359	·364	·370	·370	·378	·385	·387	·388	·391	·387	·394	·398	·414	·422	·421	·417	·423	·430	·430
June	·322	·325	·326	·321	·327	·333	·333	·334	·338	·338	·343	·347	·354	·360	·365	·365	·373	·380	·382	·383	·386	·382	·389	·393	·409	·417	·416	·412	·419	·425	·425
July	·321	·324	·325	·319	·326	·332	·332	·332	·337	·337	·342	·345	·353	·358	·364	·364	·372	·379	·381	·382	·385	·381	·388	·392	·408	·416	·415	·411	·417	·423	·424
Aug	·318	·320	·321	·316	·322	·328	·328	·329	·333	·333	·339	·342	·350	·355	·360	·360	·369	·376	·377	·378	·382	·377	·384	·389	·404	·412	·411	·408	·414	·420	·421
Sept	·309	·311	·312	·307	·313	·319	·319	·320	·324	·324	·329	·333	·340	·346	·351	·351	·359	·366	·368	·369	·372	·368	·375	·379	·395	·402	·401	·398	·404	·410	·411
Oct	·299	·301	·302	·297	·303	·309	·309	·310	·314	·314	·319	·323	·330	·335	·340	·340	·349	·356	·357	·358	·362	·357	·364	·369	·384	·391	·391	·387	·393	·399	·400
Nov	·288	·290	·291	·286	·292	·298	·298	·299	·303	·303	·308	·311	·319	·324	·329	·329	·338	·344	·346	·347	·350	·346	·353	·357	·372	·380	·379	·376	·381	·387	·388
Dec	·285	·287	·288	·283	·289	·295	·295	·295	·300	·300	·305	·308	·316	·321	·326	·326	·334	·341	·343	·343	·347	·343	·349	·354	·369	·376	·375	·372	·378	·384	·385
1990																															
Jan	·277	·279	·280	·275	·281	·287	·287	·288	·292	·292	·297	·300	·308	·313	·318	·318	·326	·333	·335	·336	·339	·335	·341	·346	·361	·368	·367	·364	·370	·376	·377
Feb	·270	·272	·273	·268	·274	·280	·280	·280	·285	·285	·290	·293	·300	·305	·310	·310	·319	·325	·327	·328	·331	·327	·334	·338	·353	·360	·359	·356	·362	·368	·369
Mar	·257	·259	·260	·255	·261	·267	·267	·268	·272	·272	·277	·280	·287	·292	·297	·297	·306	·312	·314	·315	·318	·314	·320	·325	·339	·347	·346	·343	·348	·354	·355
Apr	·220	·222	·223	·218	·224	·229	·229	·230	·234	·234	·239	·242	·249	·254	·259	·259	·267	·273	·275	·276	·279	·275	·281	·285	·300	·307	·306	·303	·309	·314	·315
May	·209	·212	·212	·208	·213	·219	·219	·219	·223	·223	·228	·231	·239	·243	·248	·248	·256	·262	·264	·265	·268	·264	·270	·274	·288	·296	·295	·292	·297	·303	·303
June	·204	·207	·208	·203	·208	·214	·214	·215	·219	·219	·223	·227	·234	·238	·243	·243	·251	·257	·259	·260	·263	·259	·265	·269	·283	·290	·290	·287	·292	·298	·298
July	·203	·206	·207	·202	·207	·213	·213	·214	·218	·218	·222	·226	·233	·237	·242	·242	·250	·256	·258	·259	·262	·258	·264	·268	·282	·289	·289	·285	·291	·297	·297
Aug	·191	·194	·194	·190	·195	·201	·201	·201	·205	·205	·210	·213	·220	·225	·230	·230	·237	·244	·245	·246	·249	·245	·251	·255	·269	·276	·276	·272	·278	·283	·284
Sept	·180	·183	·183	·179	·184	·189	·189	·190	·194	·194	·199	·202	·209	·213	·218	·218	·226	·232	·234	·234	·237	·234	·240	·244	·258	·265	·264	·261	·266	·271	·272
Oct	·171	·173	·174	·170	·175	·180	·180	·181	·185	·185	·190	·193	·200	·204	·209	·209	·216	·223	·224	·225	·228	·224	·230	·234	·248	·255	·254	·251	·256	·262	·262
Nov	·174	·176	·177	·172	·178	·183	·183	·184	·188	·188	·192	·195	·202	·207	·212	·212	·219	·225	·227	·228	·231	·227	·233	·237	·251	·258	·257	·254	·259	·265	·265
Dec	·175	·177	·178	·173	·179	·184	·184	·185	·189	·189	·193	·196	·203	·208	·212	·212	·220	·226	·228	·229	·232	·228	·234	·238	·252	·259	·258	·255	·260	·266	·266

Indexation allowance — continued

Month of disposal

Base month

	1998		1999												2000												2001			
1986	Nov	Dec	Jan	Feb	Mar	Apr	May	June	July	Aug	Sept	Oct	Nov	Dec	Jan	Feb	Mar	Apr	May	June	July	Aug	Sept	Oct	Nov	Dec	Jan	Feb	Mar	Apr
Jan	·708	·708	·698	·701	·705	·716	·721	·721	·715	·720	·727	·730	·732	·738	·731	·740	·750	·767	·774	·778	·771	·771	·784	·783	·788	·789	·778	·787	·789	·798
Feb	·702	·702	·691	·695	·699	·710	·714	·714	·709	·713	·720	·724	·726	·732	·725	·734	·743	·761	·767	·771	·765	·765	·777	·776	·782	·783	·771	·780	·783	·792
Mar	·700	·700	·689	·692	·696	·708	·712	·712	·707	·711	·718	·721	·723	·730	·722	·732	·741	·759	·765	·769	·763	·763	·775	·774	·779	·780	·769	·778	·780	·790
Apr	·683	·683	·673	·676	·680	·691	·696	·696	·690	·695	·702	·705	·707	·713	·706	·715	·724	·742	·748	·752	·746	·746	·758	·757	·762	·763	·752	·761	·763	·772
May	·673	·680	·681	·680	·680	·670	·673	·677	·688	·692	·692	·687	·691	·699	·702	·704	·710	·703	·712	·721	·738	·745	·749	·743	·743	·755	·754	·758	·760	·769
June	·681	·681	·671	·674	·678	·689	·693	·693	·688	·692	·699	·703	·705	·711	·704	·713	·722	·739	·745	·750	·743	·743	·756	·755	·760	·761	·750	·759	·761	·770
July	·686	·686	·676	·679	·683	·694	·698	·698	·693	·697	·704	·707	·709	·716	·708	·718	·727	·744	·750	·755	·748	·748	·761	·760	·765	·766	·755	·764	·766	·775
Aug	·673	·678	·689	·693	·693	·688	·692	·699	·702	·704	·710	·703	·712	·722	·739	·745	·749	·743	·743	·755	·754	·759	·760	·749	·758	·760	·770	·758	·760	·770
Sept	·672	·672	·662	·665	·669	·681	·685	·685	·680	·684	·691	·694	·696	·702	·695	·704	·713	·730	·736	·741	·734	·734	·747	·746	·751	·752	·741	·750	·752	·761
Oct	·670	·670	·660	·663	·667	·678	·682	·682	·677	·681	·688	·691	·693	·699	·692	·701	·710	·728	·734	·738	·732	·732	·744	·743	·748	·749	·738	·747	·749	·758
Nov	·656	·656	·646	·649	·653	·664	·668	·668	·663	·667	·674	·677	·679	·685	·678	·687	·696	·713	·719	·723	·717	·717	·729	·728	·733	·734	·723	·732	·734	·743
Dec	·650	·650	·640	·643	·647	·658	·662	·662	·657	·661	·668	·671	·673	·679	·672	·681	·690	·707	·714	·718	·712	·712	·724	·723	·728	·729	·718	·727	·729	·738
1987																														
Jan	·644	·644	·634	·637	·641	·652	·656	·656	·651	·655	·662	·665	·667	·673	·666	·675	·684	·701	·707	·711	·705	·705	·717	·716	·721	·722	·711	·720	·722	·731
Feb	·637	·637	·627	·630	·634	·645	·649	·649	·644	·648	·655	·658	·660	·666	·659	·668	·677	·694	·700	·704	·698	·698	·710	·709	·714	·715	·704	·713	·715	·724
Mar	·634	·634	·624	·627	·631	·642	·646	·646	·641	·645	·652	·655	·657	·663	·656	·665	·674	·691	·697	·701	·695	·695	·707	·706	·711	·712	·701	·710	·712	·721
Apr	·615	·615	·605	·608	·612	·623	·627	·627	·622	·626	·633	·636	·638	·643	·637	·645	·654	·671	·677	·681	·675	·675	·687	·686	·691	·692	·681	·690	·692	·700
May	·613	·613	·604	·606	·610	·621	·625	·625	·620	·624	·631	·634	·636	·642	·635	·644	·653	·669	·675	·679	·673	·673	·685	·684	·689	·690	·679	·688	·690	·699
June	·613	·613	·604	·606	·610	·621	·625	·625	·620	·624	·631	·634	·636	·642	·635	·644	·653	·669	·675	·679	·673	·673	·685	·684	·689	·690	·679	·688	·690	·699
July	·615	·615	·605	·608	·612	·623	·627	·627	·622	·626	·633	·636	·638	·643	·637	·645	·654	·671	·677	·681	·675	·675	·687	·686	·691	·692	·681	·690	·692	·700
Aug	·610	·610	·600	·603	·607	·618	·622	·622	·617	·621	·628	·631	·633	·639	·632	·641	·649	·666	·672	·676	·670	·670	·682	·681	·686	·687	·676	·685	·687	·695
Sept	·605	·605	·596	·599	·603	·613	·617	·617	·612	·616	·623	·626	·628	·634	·627	·636	·645	·661	·667	·671	·665	·665	·677	·676	·681	·682	·671	·680	·682	·690
Oct	·598	·598	·588	·591	·595	·605	·609	·609	·604	·608	·615	·618	·620	·626	·619	·628	·637	·653	·659	·663	·657	·657	·669	·668	·672	·673	·663	·672	·673	·682
Nov	·590	·590	·580	·583	·587	·598	·602	·602	·597	·601	·607	·610	·612	·618	·611	·620	·629	·645	·651	·655	·649	·649	·661	·660	·664	·665	·655	·663	·665	·674
Dec	·591	·591	·582	·585	·589	·599	·603	·603	·598	·602	·609	·612	·614	·620	·613	·621	·630	·647	·652	·656	·651	·651	·662	·661	·666	·667	·656	·665	·667	·676
1988																														
Jan	·591	·591	·582	·585	·589	·599	·603	·603	·598	·602	·609	·612	·614	·620	·613	·621	·630	·647	·652	·656	·651	·651	·662	·661	·666	·667	·656	·665	·667	·676
Feb	·585	·585	·576	·579	·582	·593	·597	·597	·592	·596	·603	·606	·608	·613	·607	·615	·624	·640	·646	·650	·644	·644	·656	·655	·660	·661	·650	·659	·661	·669
Mar	·579	·579	·570	·573	·576	·587	·591	·591	·586	·590	·597	·599	·601	·607	·600	·609	·618	·634	·640	·644	·638	·638	·649	·648	·653	·654	·644	·652	·654	·663
Apr	·554	·554	·544	·547	·551	·561	·565	·565	·560	·564	·571	·574	·576	·581	·575	·583	·592	·608	·613	·617	·612	·612	·623	·622	·627	·628	·617	·626	·628	·636
May	·548	·548	·548	·541	·545	·556	·559	·559	·555	·558	·565	·568	·570	·575	·569	·577	·586	·602	·607	·611	·605	·605	·617	·616	·621	·621	·611	·620	·621	·630
June	·542	·542	·533	·536	·539	·550	·553	·553	·549	·553	·559	·562	·564	·569	·563	·571	·580	·596	·601	·605	·599	·599	·611	·610	·614	·615	·605	·614	·615	·624
July	·541	·541	·531	·534	·538	·548	·552	·552	·547	·551	·558	·560	·562	·568	·561	·570	·578	·594	·600	·604	·598	·598	·609	·608	·613	·614	·604	·612	·614	·622
Aug	·524	·524	·514	·517	·521	·531	·535	·535	·530	·534	·540	·543	·545	·551	·544	·552	·561	·576	·582	·586	·580	·580	·591	·590	·595	·596	·586	·594	·596	·604
Sept	·517	·517	·507	·510	·514	·524	·528	·528	·523	·527	·533	·536	·538	·543	·537	·545	·554	·569	·575	·578	·573	·573	·584	·583	·588	·589	·578	·587	·589	·597
Oct	·501	·501	·492	·495	·499	·509	·512	·512	·508	·511	·518	·521	·522	·528	·521	·530	·538	·553	·559	·563	·557	·557	·568	·567	·572	·573	·563	·571	·573	·581
Nov	·495	·495	·485	·488	·492	·502	·505	·505	·501	·505	·511	·514	·515	·521	·515	·523	·531	·546	·552	·555	·550	·550	·561	·560	·565	·565	·555	·564	·565	·574
Dec	·490	·490	·481	·484	·488	·498	·501	·501	·497	·500	·507	·510	·511	·517	·510	·519	·527	·542	·548	·551	·546	·546	·557	·556	·560	·561	·551	·559	·561	·569
1989																														
Jan	·481	·481	·472	·475	·478	·488	·492	·492	·487	·491	·497	·500	·502	·507	·501	·509	·517	·532	·538	·541	·536	·536	·547	·546	·550	·551	·541	·550	·551	·559
Feb	·470	·470	·462	·464	·468	·478	·481	·481	·477	·480	·487	·489	·491	·496	·490	·498	·506	·521	·527	·530	·525	·525	·536	·535	·539	·540	·530	·538	·540	·548
Mar	·464	·464	·455	·458	·461	·471	·475	·475	·470	·474	·480	·483	·484	·490	·484	·492	·500	·515	·520	·524	·518	·518	·529	·528	·533	·533	·524	·532	·533	·541
Apr	·438	·438	·430	·432	·436	·445	·449	·449	·444	·448	·454	·457	·458	·464	·458	·465	·473	·488	·493	·497	·492	·492	·502	·501	·506	·507	·497	·505	·507	·514
May	·430	·430	·421	·423	·427	·437	·440	·440	·436	·439	·445	·448	·450	·455	·449	·457	·464	·479	·484	·488	·483	·483	·493	·492	·497	·497	·488	·496	·497	·505
June	·425	·425	·416	·419	·422	·432	·435	·435	·431	·434	·440	·443	·445	·450	·444	·451	·459	·474	·479	·483	·477	·477	·488	·487	·491	·492	·483	·490	·492	·500
July	·423	·423	·415	·417	·421	·430	·434	·434	·429	·433	·439	·442	·443	·448	·442	·450	·458	·473	·478	·481	·476	·476	·487	·486	·490	·491	·481	·489	·491	·499
Aug	·420	·420	·411	·414	·417	·427	·430	·430	·426	·429	·435	·438	·440	·445	·439	·446	·454	·469	·474	·478	·472	·472	·483	·482	·486	·487	·478	·485	·487	·495
Sept	·410	·410	·401	·404	·407	·417	·420	·420	·416	·419	·425	·428	·430	·435	·429	·437	·444	·459	·464	·467	·462	·462	·473	·472	·476	·477	·467	·475	·477	·485
Oct	·399	·399	·391	·393	·397	·406	·409	·409	·405	·409	·414	·417	·419	·424	·418	·426	·433	·448	·453	·456	·451	·451	·461	·460	·465	·466	·456	·464	·466	·473
Nov	·387	·387	·379	·381	·385	·394	·397	·397	·393	·397	·403	·405	·407	·412	·406	·414	·421	·435	·441	·444	·439	·439	·449	·448	·452	·453	·444	·451	·453	·461
Dec	·384	·384	·375	·378	·381	·391	·394	·394	·390	·393	·399	·402	·403	·408	·402	·410	·418	·432	·437	·440	·435	·435	·445	·444	·449	·449	·440	·448	·449	·457
1990																														
Jan	·376	·376	·367	·370	·373	·382	·386	·386	·382	·385	·391	·393	·395	·400	·394	·402	·409	·423	·428	·432	·427	·427	·437	·436	·440	·441	·432	·439	·441	·449
Feb	·368	·368	·359	·362	·365	·374	·378	·378	·374	·377	·383	·385	·387	·392	·386	·394	·401	·415	·420	·423	·418	·418	·428	·428	·432	·433	·423	·431	·433	·440
Mar	·354	·354	·346	·348	·352	·361	·364	·364	·360	·363	·369	·371	·373	·378	·372	·380	·387	·401	·406	·409	·404	·404	·414	·414	·418	·418	·409	·417	·418	·426
Apr	·314	·314	·306	·309	·312	·321	·324	·324	·320	·323	·329	·331	·333	·337	·332	·339	·346	·360	·365	·368	·363	·363	·373	·372	·376	·376	·368	·375	·376	·384
May	·303	·303	·295	·297	·300	·309	·312	·312	·308	·311	·317	·319	·321	·326	·320	·327	·334	·348	·353	·356	·351	·351	·361	·360	·364	·365	·356	·363	·365	·372
June	·298	·298	·290	·292	·295	·304	·307	·307	·303	·306	·312	·314	·316	·320	·315	·322	·329	·343	·347	·350	·346	·346	·355	·354	·358	·359	·350	·358	·359	·366
July	·297	·297	·289	·291	·294	·303	·306	·306	·302	·305	·311	·313	·315	·319	·314	·321	·328	·341	·346	·349	·345	·345	·354	·353	·357	·358	·349	·356	·358	·365
Aug	·283	·283	·276	·278	·281	·290	·293	·293	·289	·292	·297	·300	·301	·306	·301	·308	·315	·328	·333	·336	·331	·331	·340	·340	·343	·344	·336	·343	·344	·351
Sept	·271	·271	·264	·266	·269	·278	·281	·281	·277	·280	·285	·288	·289	·294	·288	·295	·302	·316	·320	·323	·319	·319	·328	·327	·331	·332	·323	·330	·332	·339
Oct	·262	·262	·254	·256	·259	·268	·271	·271	·267	·270	·276	·278	·279	·284	·279	·285	·292	·305	·310	·313	·309	·309	·318	·317	·321	·322	·313	·320	·322	·328
Nov	·265	·265	·257	·259	·262	·271	·274	·274	·270	·273	·278	·281	·282	·287	·282	·288	·295	·308	·313	·316	·312	·312	·321	·320	·324	·325	·316	·323	·325	·332
Dec	·266	·266	·258	·260	·263	·272	·275	·275	·271	·274	·279	·282	·283	·288	·283	·289	·296	·309	·314	·317	·313	·313	·322	·321	·325	·326	·317	·324	·326	·333

Indexation allowance — continued

Month of disposal

Base month

	1996									1997												1998									
1991	Apr	May	June	July	Aug	Sept	Oct	Nov	Dec	Jan	Feb	Mar	Apr	May	June	July	Aug	Sept	Oct	Nov	Dec	Jan	Feb	Mar	Apr	May	June	July	Aug	Sept	Oct
Jan	·172	·174	·175	·171	·176	·181	·181	·182	·186	·186	·190	·194	·200	·205	·210	·210	·217	·224	·225	·226	·229	·225	·231	·235	·249	·256	·255	·252	·257	·263	·263
Feb	·166	·168	·169	·164	·170	·175	·175	·176	·180	·180	·184	·187	·194	·199	·203	·203	·211	·217	·218	·219	·222	·218	·225	·228	·242	·249	·248	·245	·251	·256	·257
Mar	·161	·164	·160	·165	·170	·170	·170	·171	·175	·175	·180	·183	·189	·194	·199	·199	·206	·212	·214	·215	·218	·214	·220	·224	·237	·244	·244	·240	·246	·251	·252
Apr	·147	·149	·150	·145	·150	·156	·156	·156	·160	·160	·165	·168	·174	·179	·183	·183	·191	·197	·198	·199	·202	·198	·204	·208	·222	·228	·228	·225	·230	·235	·236
May	·143	·145	·146	·142	·147	·152	·152	·153	·157	·157	·161	·164	·171	·175	·180	·180	·187	·193	·195	·196	·199	·195	·201	·204	·218	·225	·224	·221	·226	·231	·232
June	·138	·140	·141	·136	·142	·147	·147	·148	·151	·151	·156	·159	·166	·170	·174	·174	·182	·188	·189	·190	·193	·189	·195	·199	·213	·219	·218	·216	·221	·226	·227
July	·141	·143	·143	·139	·144	·149	·149	·150	·154	·154	·158	·161	·168	·173	·177	·177	·185	·191	·192	·193	·196	·192	·198	·202	·215	·222	·221	·218	·223	·229	·229
Aug	·138	·140	·141	·136	·142	·147	·147	·148	·151	·151	·156	·159	·166	·170	·174	·174	·182	·188	·189	·190	·193	·189	·195	·199	·213	·219	·218	·216	·221	·226	·227
Sept	·134	·136	·137	·132	·137	·143	·143	·143	·147	·147	·152	·155	·161	·166	·170	·170	·178	·184	·185	·186	·189	·185	·191	·195	·208	·215	·214	·211	·216	·221	·222
Oct	·130	·132	·132	·128	·133	·138	·138	·139	·143	·143	·147	·150	·157	·161	·166	·166	·173	·179	·181	·181	·184	·181	·187	·190	·204	·210	·209	·207	·212	·217	·218
Nov	·125	·128	·128	·124	·129	·134	·134	·135	·139	·139	·143	·146	·153	·157	·162	·162	·169	·175	·176	·177	·180	·176	·182	·186	·199	·206	·205	·202	·207	·212	·213
Dec	·125	·127	·127	·123	·128	·133	·133	·134	·138	·138	·142	·145	·152	·156	·161	·161	·168	·174	·175	·176	·179	·175	·181	·185	·198	·205	·204	·201	·206	·211	·212
1992																															
Jan	·125	·128	·128	·124	·129	·134	·134	·135	·139	139	·143	·146	·153	·157	·162	·162	·169	·175	·176	·177	·180	·176	·182	·186	·199	·206	·205	·202	·207	·212	·213
Feb	·120	·122	·123	·118	·123	·128	·128	·129	·133	·133	·140	·147	·151	·156	·156	·156	·163	·169	·170	·171	·174	·170	·176	·180	·193	·200	·199	·196	·201	·206	·207
Mar	·116	·119	·119	·115	·120	·125	·125	·126	·129	·129	·134	·137	·143	·148	·152	·152	·159	·165	·167	·168	·170	·167	·173	·176	·189	·196	·195	·192	·198	·203	·203
Apr	·099	·102	·102	·098	·103	·108	·108	·109	·112	·112	·117	·120	·126	·130	·135	·135	·142	·148	·149	·150	·153	·149	·155	·159	·171	·178	·177	·174	·179	·184	·185
May	·095	·098	·098	·094	·099	·104	·104	·105	·108	·108	·113	·116	·122	·126	·131	·131	·138	·144	·145	·146	·149	·145	·151	·154	·167	·174	·173	·170	·175	·180	·181
June	·095	·098	·098	·094	·099	·104	·104	·105	·108	·108	·113	·122	·126	·131	·131	·131	·138	·144	·145	·146	·149	·145	·151	·154	·167	·174	·173	·170	·175	·180	·181
July	·099	·102	·102	·098	·103	·108	·108	·109	·112	·112	·117	·120	·126	·130	·135	·135	·142	·148	·149	·150	·153	·149	·155	·159	·171	·178	·177	·174	·179	·184	·185
Aug	·099	·101	·102	·097	·102	·107	·107	·108	·112	·112	·116	·119	·125	·130	·134	·134	·141	·147	·148	·149	·152	·148	·154	·158	·171	·177	·176	·174	·179	·184	·184
Sept	·095	·097	·098	·093	·098	·103	·103	·104	·108	·108	·112	·115	·121	·126	·130	·130	·137	·143	·144	·145	·148	·144	·150	·154	·166	·173	·172	·169	·174	·179	·180
Oct	·091	·093	·094	·089	·094	·099	·099	·100	·104	·104	·108	·111	·117	·122	·126	·126	·133	·139	·140	·141	·144	·140	·146	·149	·162	·169	·168	·165	·170	·175	·176
Nov	·092	·094	·095	·091	·096	·101	·101	·102	·105	·105	·110	·112	·119	·123	·127	·127	·135	·140	·142	·142	·145	·142	·147	·151	·164	·170	·170	·167	·172	·177	·178
Dec	·096	·098	·099	·095	·100	·105	·105	·106	·109	·109	·114	·116	·123	·127	·131	·131	·139	·144	·146	·147	·149	·146	·152	·155	·168	·175	·174	·171	·176	·181	·182
1993																															
Jan	·107	·109	·109	·105	·110	·115	·115	·116	·120	·120	·124	·127	·133	·138	·142	·142	·149	·155	·157	·157	·160	·157	·162	·166	·179	·186	·185	·182	·187	·192	·193
Feb	·099	·102	·102	·098	·103	·108	·108	·109	·112	·112	·117	·120	·126	·130	·135	·135	·142	·148	·149	·150	·153	·149	·155	·159	·171	·178	·177	·174	·179	·184	·185
Mar	·095	·098	·098	·094	·099	·104	·104	·105	·108	·108	·113	·116	·122	·126	·131	·131	·138	·144	·145	·146	·149	·145	·151	·154	·167	·174	·173	·170	·175	·180	·181
Apr	·085	·087	·088	·084	·089	·094	·094	·095	·098	·098	·102	·105	·112	·116	·120	·120	·127	·133	·134	·135	·138	·134	·140	·144	·156	·163	·162	·159	·164	·169	·170
May	·082	·084	·084	·080	·085	·090	·090	·091	·094	·094	·099	·101	·108	·112	·116	·116	·123	·129	·130	·131	·134	·130	·136	·140	·152	·159	·158	·155	·160	·165	·166
June	·082	·084	·085	·081	·086	·091	·091	·091	·095	·095	·099	·102	·109	·113	·117	·117	·124	·130	·131	·132	·135	·131	·137	·140	·153	·160	·159	·156	·161	·166	·167
July	·085	·087	·087	·083	·088	·093	·093	·094	·097	·097	·102	·104	·111	·115	·119	·119	·127	·132	·134	·134	·137	·134	·139	·143	·156	·162	·161	·158	·168	·169	·168
Aug	·080	·082	·083	·079	·084	·088	·088	·089	·093	·093	·097	·100	·106	·110	·115	·115	·122	·127	·129	·130	·132	·129	·134	·138	·151	·157	·156	·154	·159	·163	·164
Sept	·075	·078	·078	·074	·079	·084	·084	·085	·088	·088	·092	·095	·101	·106	·110	·110	·117	·123	·124	·125	·128	·124	·130	·133	·146	·152	·152	·149	·154	·159	·159
Oct	·076	·078	·079	·075	·080	·085	·085	·085	·089	·089	·093	·096	·102	·106	·111	·111	·118	·123	·125	·126	·128	·125	·130	·134	·147	·153	·152	·150	·154	·159	·160
Nov	·078	·080	·081	·076	·081	·086	·086	·087	·090	·090	·095	·097	·104	·108	·112	·112	·119	·125	·126	·127	·130	·126	·132	·136	·148	·155	·154	·151	·156	·161	·162
Dec	·075	·078	·078	·074	·079	·084	·084	·085	·088	·088	·092	·095	·101	·106	·110	·110	·117	·123	·124	·125	·128	·124	·130	·133	·146	·152	·152	·149	·154	·159	·159
1994																															
Jan	·080	·082	·083	·079	·084	·088	·088	·089	·093	·093	·097	·100	·106	·110	·115	·115	·122	·127	·129	·130	·132	·129	·134	·138	·151	·157	·156	·154	·159	·163	·164
Feb	·074	·076	·077	·072	·077	·082	·082	·083	·087	·087	·091	·094	·100	·104	·108	·108	·115	·121	·122	·123	·126	·122	·128	·132	·144	·151	·150	·147	·152	·157	·158
Mar	·071	·073	·074	·069	·074	·079	·079	·080	·084	·084	·088	·091	·097	·101	·105	·105	·112	·118	·119	·120	·123	·119	·125	·128	·141	·147	·147	·144	·149	·154	·154
Apr	·058	·060	·061	·057	·062	·067	·067	·067	·071	·071	·075	·078	·084	·088	·092	·092	·099	·105	·106	·107	·110	·106	·112	·115	·128	·134	·133	·130	·135	·140	·141
May	·055	·057	·057	·053	·058	·063	·063	·064	·067	·067	·071	·074	·080	·084	·088	·088	·095	·101	·102	·103	·106	·102	·108	·111	·124	·130	·129	·126	·131	·136	·137
June	·055	·057	·057	·053	·058	·063	·063	·064	·067	·067	·071	·074	·080	·084	·088	·088	·095	·101	·102	·103	·106	·102	·108	·111	·124	·130	·129	·126	·131	·136	·137
July	·060	·062	·063	·058	·063	·068	·068	·069	·072	·072	·076	·079	·085	·090	·094	·094	·101	·106	·108	·108	·111	·108	·113	·117	·129	·135	·135	·132	·137	·142	·142
Aug	·055	·057	·057	·053	·058	·063	·063	·064	·067	·067	·071	·074	·080	·084	·088	·088	·095	·101	·102	·103	·106	·102	·108	·111	·124	·130	·129	·126	·131	·136	·137
Sept	·052	·054	·055	·051	·056	·061	·061	·061	·065	·065	·069	·072	·078	·082	·086	·086	·093	·099	·100	·101	·103	·100	·106	·109	·121	·128	·127	·124	·129	·134	·134
Oct	·051	·053	·054	·050	·054	·059	·059	·060	·063	·063	·067	·070	·076	·081	·085	·085	·092	·097	·098	·099	·102	·098	·104	·107	·120	·126	·125	·123	·127	·132	·133
Nov	·050	·052	·053	·049	·054	·058	·058	·059	·063	·063	·067	·070	·076	·080	·084	·084	·091	·096	·098	·098	·101	·098	·103	·107	·119	·125	·125	·122	·127	·131	·132
Dec	·045	·047	·048	·044	·049	·053	·053	·054	·058	·058	·062	·064	·071	·075	·079	·079	·086	·091	·092	·093	·096	·092	·098	·101	·114	·120	·119	·116	·121	·126	·127
1995																															
Jan	·045	·047	·048	·044	·049	·053	·053	·054	·058	·058	·062	·064	·071	·075	·079	·079	·086	·091	·092	·093	·096	·092	·098	·101	·114	·120	·119	·116	·121	·126	·127
Feb	·039	·041	·042	·037	·042	·047	·047	·048	·051	·051	·055	·058	·064	·068	·072	·072	·079	·084	·086	·086	·089	·086	·091	·095	·107	·113	·112	·110	·114	·119	·120
Mar	·035	·037	·037	·033	·038	·043	·043	·043	·047	·047	·051	·054	·060	·064	·068	·068	·075	·080	·081	·082	·085	·081	·087	·090	·102	·108	·108	·105	·110	·115	·115
Apr	·024	·026	·027	·023	·028	·032	·032	·033	·036	·036	·040	·043	·049	·053	·057	·057	·064	·069	·070	·071	·074	·070	·076	·079	·091	·097	·097	·094	·099	·103	·104
May	·020	·022	·023	·019	·023	·028	·028	·029	·032	·032	·036	·039	·045	·049	·053	·053	·059	·065	·066	·067	·070	·066	·072	·075	·087	·093	·092	·090	·094	·099	·100
June	·019	·021	·021	·017	·022	·027	·027	·027	·031	·031	·035	·037	·043	·047	·051	·051	·058	·063	·065	·065	·068	·065	·070	·073	·085	·091	·091	·088	·093	·097	·098
July	·023	·025	·026	·022	·027	·032	·032	·032	·036	·036	·040	·042	·048	·052	·056	·056	·063	·068	·070	·070	·073	·070	·075	·078	·091	·097	·096	·093	·098	·103	·103
Aug	·018	·020	·021	·017	·021	·026	·026	·027	·030	·030	·034	·037	·043	·047	·051	·051	·057	·063	·064	·065	·067	·064	·069	·073	·085	·091	·090	·087	·092	·097	·097
Sept	·013	·015	·016	·012	·017	·021	·021	·022	·025	·025	·029	·032	·038	·042	·046	·046	·052	·058	·059	·060	·062	·059	·064	·068	·080	·086	·085	·082	·087	·092	·092
Oct	·019	·021	·021	·017	·022	·027	·027	·027	·031	·031	·035	·037	·043	·047	·051	·051	·058	·063	·065	·065	·068	·065	·070	·073	·085	·091	·091	·088	·093	·097	·098
Nov	·019	·021	·021	·017	·022	·027	·027	·027	·031	·031	·035	·037	·043	·047	·051	·051	·058	·063	·065	·065	·068	·065	·070	·073	·085	·091	·091	·088	·093	·097	·098
Dec	·013	·015	·015	·011	·016	·021	·021	·021	·025	·025	·029	·031	·037	·041	·045	·045	·052	·057	·058	·059	·062	·058	·064	·067	·079	·085	·084	·082	·086	·091	·092

Indexation allowance — continued

Month of disposal

Base month	1998		1999												2000												2001			
1991	Nov	Dec	Jan	Feb	Mar	Apr	May	June	July	Aug	Sept	Oct	Nov	Dec	Jan	Feb	Mar	Apr	May	June	July	Aug	Sept	Oct	Nov	Dec	Jan	Feb	Mar	Apr
Jan	·263	·263	·255	·257	·260	·269	·272	·272	·268	·271	·276	·279	·280	·285	·280	·286	·293	·306	·311	·314	·310	·310	·319	·318	·322	·323	·314	·321	·323	·329
Feb	·256	·256	·248	·251	·254	·262	·265	·265	·261	·264	·270	·272	·273	·278	·273	·280	·286	·299	·304	·307	·303	·303	·312	·311	·315	·316	·307	·314	·316	·322
Mar	·251	·251	·244	·246	·249	·257	·260	·260	·256	·260	·265	·267	·269	·273	·268	·275	·282	·295	·299	·302	·298	·298	·307	·306	·310	·311	·302	·309	·311	·317
Apr	·235	·235	·228	·230	·233	·241	·244	·244	·240	·243	·249	·251	·252	·257	·252	·258	·265	·278	·282	·285	·281	·281	·290	·289	·293	·294	·285	·292	·294	·301
May	·231	·231	·224	·226	·229	·237	·240	·240	·237	·240	·245	·247	·249	·253	·248	·255	·261	·274	·279	·282	·277	·277	·286	·285	·289	·290	·282	·288	·290	·297
June	·226	·226	·218	·221	·224	·232	·235	·235	·231	·234	·239	·242	·243	·248	·242	·249	·256	·268	·273	·276	·271	·271	·280	·280	·283	·284	·276	·283	·284	·291
July	·229	·229	·221	·223	·226	·235	·238	·238	·234	·237	·242	·244	·246	·250	·245	·252	·259	·271	·276	·279	·274	·274	·283	·283	·286	·287	·279	·286	·287	·294
Aug	·226	·226	·218	·221	·224	·232	·235	·235	·231	·234	·239	·242	·243	·248	·242	·249	·256	·268	·273	·276	·271	·271	·280	·280	·283	·284	·276	·283	·284	·291
Sept	·221	·221	·214	·216	·219	·227	·230	·230	·227	·230	·235	·237	·238	·243	·238	·244	·251	·264	·268	·271	·267	·267	·276	·275	·279	·279	·271	·278	·279	·286
Oct	·217	·217	·209	·212	·215	·223	·226	·226	·222	·225	·230	·232	·234	·238	·233	·240	·246	·259	·264	·266	·262	·262	·271	·270	·274	·275	·266	·273	·275	·281
Nov	·212	·212	·205	·207	·210	·218	·221	·221	·218	·221	·226	·228	·229	·234	·229	·235	·242	·254	·259	·262	·257	·257	·266	·265	·269	·270	·262	·268	·270	·277
Dec	·211	·211	·204	·206	·209	·217	·220	·220	·217	·220	·225	·227	·228	·233	·228	·234	·241	·254	·258	·261	·256	·256	·265	·265	·268	·269	·261	·268	·269	·276
1992																														
Jan	·212	·212	·205	·207	·210	·218	·221	·221	·218	·221	·226	·228	·229	·234	·229	·235	·242	·254	·259	·262	·257	·257	·266	·265	·269	·270	·262	·268	·270	·277
Feb	·206	·206	·199	·201	·204	·212	·215	·215	·211	·214	·219	·222	·223	·227	·222	·229	·236	·248	·252	·255	·251	·251	·260	·259	·263	·263	·255	·262	·263	·270
Mar	·203	·203	·195	·198	·200	·208	·211	·211	·208	·211	·216	·218	·219	·224	·219	·225	·232	·244	·249	·252	·247	·247	·256	·255	·259	·260	·252	·258	·260	·266
Apr	·184	·184	·177	·179	·182	·190	·193	·193	·189	·192	·197	·200	·201	·205	·200	·207	·213	·226	·230	·233	·228	·228	·237	·236	·240	·241	·233	·239	·241	·247
May	·180	·180	·173	·175	·178	·186	·189	·189	·185	·188	·193	·195	·197	·201	·196	·202	·209	·221	·225	·228	·224	·224	·233	·232	·235	·236	·228	·235	·236	·243
June	·180	·180	·173	·175	·178	·186	·189	·189	·185	·188	·193	·195	·197	·201	·196	·202	·209	·221	·225	·228	·224	·224	·233	·232	·235	·236	·228	·235	·236	·243
July	·184	·184	·177	·179	·182	·190	·193	·193	·189	·192	·197	·200	·201	·205	·200	·207	·213	·226	·230	·233	·228	·228	·237	·236	·240	·241	·233	·239	·241	·247
Aug	·184	·184	·176	·179	·181	·189	·192	·192	·189	·192	·197	·199	·200	·204	·199	·206	·212	·225	·229	·232	·228	·228	·236	·235	·239	·240	·232	·238	·240	·246
Sept	·179	·179	·172	·174	·177	·185	·188	·188	·184	·187	·192	·194	·196	·200	·195	·202	·208	·220	·225	·227	·223	·223	·232	·231	·235	·235	·227	·234	·235	·242
Oct	·175	·175	·168	·170	·173	·181	·184	·184	·180	·183	·188	·190	·192	·196	·191	·197	·204	·216	·220	·223	·219	·219	·227	·227	·230	·231	·223	·229	·231	·237
Nov	·177	·177	·170	·172	·175	·183	·185	·185	·182	·185	·190	·192	·193	·198	·193	·199	·205	·218	·222	·225	·220	·220	·229	·228	·232	·233	·225	·231	·233	·239
Dec	·181	·181	·174	·176	·179	·187	·190	·190	·186	·189	·194	·196	·198	·202	·197	·203	·210	·222	·226	·229	·225	·225	·233	·233	·236	·237	·229	·236	·237	·244
1993																														
Jan	·192	·192	·185	·187	·190	·198	·201	·201	·197	·200	·205	·207	·209	·213	·208	·215	·221	·234	·238	·241	·236	·236	·245	·244	·248	·249	·241	·247	·249	·255
Feb	·184	·184	·177	·179	·182	·190	·193	·193	·189	·192	·197	·200	·201	·205	·200	·207	·213	·226	·230	·233	·228	·228	·237	·236	·240	·241	·233	·239	·241	·247
Mar	·180	·180	·173	·175	·178	·186	·189	·189	·185	·188	·193	·195	·197	·201	·196	·202	·209	·221	·225	·228	·224	·224	·233	·232	·235	·236	·228	·235	·236	·243
Apr	·169	·169	·162	·164	·167	·175	·178	·178	·174	·177	·182	·184	·186	·190	·185	·191	·198	·210	·214	·217	·213	·213	·221	·220	·224	·225	·217	·223	·225	·231
May	·166	·165	·165	·160	·163	·171	·174	·174	·170	·173	·178	·180	·181	·186	·181	·187	·193	·206	·210	·213	·208	·208	·217	·216	·220	·220	·213	·219	·220	·227
June	·166	·166	·159	·161	·164	·172	·174	·174	·171	·174	·179	·181	·182	·187	·182	·188	·194	·206	·211	·213	·209	·209	·218	·217	·221	·221	·213	·220	·221	·228
July	·169	·168	·168	·163	·166	·174	·177	·177	·173	·176	·181	·183	·185	·189	·184	·190	·197	·209	·213	·216	·212	·212	·220	·220	·223	·224	·216	·222	·224	·230
Aug	·163	·163	·156	·159	·161	·169	·172	·172	·168	·171	·176	·178	·180	·184	·179	·185	·192	·204	·208	·211	·207	·207	·215	·214	·218	·219	·211	·217	·219	·225
Sept	·159	·159	·152	·154	·156	·164	·167	·167	·163	·166	·171	·173	·175	·179	·174	·180	·187	·199	·203	·206	·202	·202	·210	·209	·213	·214	·206	·212	·214	·220
Oct	·159	·159	·152	·154	·157	·165	·168	·168	·164	·167	·172	·174	·176	·180	·175	·181	·188	·200	·204	·207	·202	·202	·211	·210	·214	·214	·207	·213	·214	·221
Nov	·161	·161	·154	·156	·159	·167	·169	·169	·166	·169	·174	·176	·177	·181	·177	·183	·189	·201	·206	·208	·204	·204	·213	·212	·215	·216	·208	·215	·216	·222
Dec	·159	·159	·152	·154	·156	·164	·167	·167	·163	·166	·171	·173	·175	·179	·174	·180	·187	·199	·203	·206	·202	·202	·210	·209	·213	·214	·206	·212	·214	·220
1994																														
Jan	·163	·163	·156	·159	·161	·169	·172	·172	·168	·171	·176	·178	·180	·184	·179	·185	·192	·204	·208	·211	·207	·207	·215	·214	·218	·219	·211	·217	·219	·225
Feb	·157	·157	·150	·152	·155	·163	·165	·165	·162	·165	·170	·172	·173	·177	·172	·179	·185	·197	·201	·204	·200	·200	·208	·208	·211	·212	·204	·210	·212	·218
Mar	·154	·154	·147	·149	·152	·159	·162	·162	·159	·161	·166	·168	·170	·174	·169	·175	·182	·194	·198	·201	·196	·196	·205	·204	·208	·208	·201	·207	·208	·215
Apr	·140	·140	·133	·135	·138	·146	·148	·148	·145	·148	·153	·155	·156	·160	·155	·162	·168	·180	·184	·187	·182	·182	·191	·190	·193	·194	·187	·193	·194	·200
May	·136	·136	·129	·131	·134	·142	·144	·144	·141	·144	·149	·151	·152	·156	·151	·158	·164	·176	·180	·182	·178	·178	·187	·186	·189	·190	·182	·189	·190	·196
June	·136	·136	·129	·131	·134	·142	·144	·144	·141	·144	·149	·151	·152	·156	·151	·158	·164	·176	·180	·182	·178	·178	·187	·186	·189	·190	·182	·189	·190	·196
July	·142	·142	·135	·137	·140	·147	·150	·150	·147	·149	·154	·156	·158	·162	·157	·163	·169	·181	·185	·188	·184	·184	·192	·192	·195	·196	·188	·194	·196	·202
Aug	·136	·136	·129	·131	·134	·142	·144	·144	·141	·144	·149	·151	·152	·156	·151	·158	·164	·176	·180	·182	·178	·178	·187	·186	·189	·190	·182	·189	·190	·196
Sept	·134	·134	·127	·129	·132	·139	·142	·142	·139	·141	·146	·148	·150	·154	·149	·155	·161	·173	·177	·180	·176	·176	·184	·183	·187	·188	·180	·186	·188	·194
Oct	·132	·132	·125	·127	·130	·138	·140	·140	·137	·140	·145	·147	·148	·152	·147	·154	·160	·171	·176	·178	·174	·174	·183	·182	·185	·186	·178	·185	·186	·192
Nov	·131	·131	·125	·127	·129	·137	·140	·140	·136	·139	·144	·146	·147	·151	·147	·153	·159	·171	·175	·178	·173	·173	·182	·181	·184	·185	·178	·184	·185	·191
Dec	·126	·126	·119	·121	·124	·132	·134	·134	·131	·134	·138	·140	·142	·146	·141	·147	·153	·165	·169	·172	·168	·168	·176	·175	·179	·179	·172	·178	·179	·186
1995																														
Jan	·126	·126	·119	·121	·124	·132	·134	·134	·131	·134	·138	·140	·142	·146	·141	·147	·153	·165	·169	·172	·168	·168	·176	·175	·179	·179	·172	·178	·179	·186
Feb	·119	·119	·112	·114	·117	·125	·127	·127	·124	·127	·131	·133	·135	·139	·134	·140	·146	·158	·162	·165	·161	·161	·169	·168	·172	·172	·165	·171	·172	·178
Mar	·115	·115	·108	·110	·113	·120	·123	·123	·119	·122	·127	·129	·130	·134	·129	·136	·142	·153	·157	·160	·156	·156	·164	·163	·167	·167	·160	·166	·167	·174
Apr	·103	·103	·097	·099	·101	·109	·111	·111	·108	·111	·115	·117	·119	·123	·118	·124	·130	·142	·146	·148	·144	·144	·152	·152	·155	·156	·148	·154	·156	·162
May	·099	·099	·092	·094	·097	·104	·107	·107	·104	·106	·111	·113	·114	·118	·114	·120	·126	·137	·141	·144	·140	·140	·148	·147	·150	·151	·144	·150	·151	·157
June	·097	·097	·091	·093	·095	·103	·105	·105	·102	·105	·109	·111	·113	·117	·112	·118	·124	·136	·140	·142	·138	·138	·146	·146	·149	·150	·142	·148	·150	·156
July	·103	·103	·096	·098	·101	·108	·111	·111	·107	·110	·115	·117	·118	·122	·117	·123	·129	·141	·145	·148	·144	·144	·152	·151	·154	·155	·148	·154	·155	·161
Aug	·097	·097	·090	·092	·095	·102	·105	·105	·101	·104	·109	·111	·112	·116	·111	·117	·123	·135	·139	·141	·137	·137	·145	·145	·148	·149	·141	·147	·149	·155
Sept	·092	·092	·085	·087	·090	·097	·100	·100	·096	·099	·104	·106	·107	·111	·106	·112	·118	·129	·133	·136	·132	·132	·140	·139	·143	·143	·136	·142	·143	·149
Oct	·097	·097	·091	·093	·095	·103	·105	·105	·102	·105	·109	·111	·113	·117	·112	·118	·124	·136	·140	·142	·138	·138	·146	·146	·149	·150	·142	·148	·150	·156
Nov	·097	·091	·091	·093	·095	·103	·105	·105	·102	·105	·109	·111	·113	·117	·112	·118	·124	·136	·140	·142	·138	·138	·146	·146	·149	·150	·142	·148	·150	·156
Dec	·091	·091	·084	·086	·089	·096	·099	·099	·096	·098	·103	·105	·106	·110	·106	·111	·117	·129	·133	·135	·131	·131	·139	·139	·142	·143	·135	·141	·143	·149

Indexation allowance — continued

Month of disposal

Base month		1996									1997												1998									
		Apr	May	June	July	Aug	Sept	Oct	Nov	Dec	Jan	Feb	Mar	Apr	May	June	July	Aug	Sept	Oct	Nov	Dec	Jan	Feb	Mar	Apr	May	June	July	Aug	Sept	Oct
1996	Jan	·016	·018	·019	·015	·019	·024	·024	·025	·028	·028	·032	·035	·041	·045	·049	·049	·055	·061	·062	·063	·065	·062	·067	·071	·083	·089	·088	·085	·090	·095	·095
	Feb	·011	·013	·014	·010	·015	·019	·019	·020	·023	·023	·027	·030	·036	·040	·044	·044	·050	·056	·057	·058	·060	·057	·062	·066	·078	·083	·083	·080	·085	·089	·090
	Mar	·007	·009	·010	·006	·011	·015	·015	·016	·019	·019	·023	·026	·032	·036	·040	·040	·046	·051	·053	·053	·056	·053	·058	·061	·073	·079	·079	·076	·081	·085	·086
	Apr	—	·002	·003	·000	·003	·008	·008	·009	·012	·012	·016	·018	·024	·028	·032	·032	·039	·044	·045	·046	·048	·045	·050	·054	·066	·071	·071	·068	·073	·077	·078
	May	—	—	·001	·000	·001	·006	·006	·007	·010	·010	·014	·016	·022	·026	·030	·030	·037	·042	·043	·044	·046	·043	·048	·052	·063	·069	·069	·066	·071	·075	·076
	June	—	—	—	·000	·001	·005	·005	·006	·009	·009	·013	·016	·022	·025	·029	·029	·036	·041	·042	·043	·046	·042	·048	·051	·063	·069	·068	·065	·070	·075	·075
	July	—	—	—	—	·005	·009	·009	·010	·013	·013	·017	·020	·026	·030	·033	·033	·040	·045	·047	·047	·050	·047	·052	·055	·067	·073	·072	·070	·074	·079	·079
	Aug	—	—	—	—	—	·005	·005	·005	·008	·008	·012	·015	·021	·025	·029	·029	·035	·040	·042	·042	·045	·042	·047	·050	·062	·068	·067	·065	·069	·074	·074
	Sept	—	—	—	—	—	—	·000	·001	·004	·004	·008	·010	·016	·020	·024	·024	·031	·036	·037	·038	·040	·037	·042	·046	·057	·063	·062	·060	·064	·069	·070
	Oct	—	—	—	—	—	—	—	·001	·004	·004	·008	·010	·016	·020	·024	·024	·031	·036	·037	·038	·040	·037	·042	·046	·057	·063	·062	·060	·064	·069	·070
	Nov	—	—	—	—	—	—	—	—	·003	·003	·007	·010	·016	·019	·023	·023	·030	·035	·036	·037	·040	·036	·042	·045	·057	·062	·062	·059	·064	·068	·069
	Dec	—	—	—	—	—	—	—	—	—	·000	·004	·006	·012	·016	·020	·020	·027	·032	·033	·034	·036	·033	·038	·041	·053	·059	·058	·056	·060	·065	·065
1997	Jan	—	—	—	—	—	—	—	—	—	—	·004	·006	·012	·016	·020	·020	·027	·032	·033	·034	·036	·033	·038	·041	·053	·059	·058	·056	·060	·065	·065
	Feb	—	—	—	—	—	—	—	—	—	—	—	·003	·008	·012	·016	·016	·023	·028	·029	·030	·032	·029	·034	·037	·049	·055	·054	·052	·056	·061	·061
	Mar	—	—	—	—	—	—	—	—	—	—	—	—	·006	·010	·014	·014	·020	·025	·025	·027	·030	·026	·032	·035	·046	·052	·051	·049	·053	·058	·059
	Apr	—	—	—	—	—	—	—	—	—	—	—	—	—	·004	·008	·008	·014	·019	·020	·021	·024	·020	·026	·029	·040	·046	·045	·043	·047	·052	·052
	May	—	—	—	—	—	—	—	—	—	—	—	—	—	—	·004	·004	·010	·015	·017	·017	·020	·017	·022	·025	·036	·042	·041	·039	·043	·048	·043
	June	—	—	—	—	—	—	—	—	—	—	—	—	—	—	—	·000	·006	·011	·013	·013	·016	·013	·018	·021	·032	·038	·037	·035	·039	·044	·044
	July	—	—	—	—	—	—	—	—	—	—	—	—	—	—	—	—	·006	·011	·013	·013	·016	·013	·018	·021	·032	·038	·037	·035	·039	·044	·044
	Aug	—	—	—	—	—	—	—	—	—	—	—	—	—	—	—	—	—	·005	·006	·007	·009	·006	·011	·015	·026	·032	·031	·028	·033	·037	·038
	Sept	—	—	—	—	—	—	—	—	—	—	—	—	—	—	—	—	—	—	·001	·002	·004	·001	·006	·009	·021	·026	·026	·023	·028	·032	·033
	Oct	—	—	—	—	—	—	—	—	—	—	—	—	—	—	—	—	—	—	—	·001	·003	·000	·005	·008	·019	·025	·024	·022	·026	·031	·031
	Nov	—	—	—	—	—	—	—	—	—	—	—	—	—	—	—	—	—	—	—	—	·003	·000	·004	·008	·019	·024	·024	·021	·026	·030	·031
	Dec	—	—	—	—	—	—	—	—	—	—	—	—	—	—	—	—	—	—	—	—	—	·000	·002	·005	·016	·022	·021	·019	·023	·028	·028
1998	Jan	—	—	—	—	—	—	—	—	—	—	—	—	—	—	—	—	—	—	—	—	—	—	·005	·008	·019	·025	·024	·022	·026	·031	·031
	Feb	—	—	—	—	—	—	—	—	—	—	—	—	—	—	—	—	—	—	—	—	—	—	—	·003	·014	·020	·019	·017	·021	·026	·026
	Mar	—	—	—	—	—	—	—	—	—	—	—	—	—	—	—	—	—	—	—	—	—	—	—	—	·011	·017	·016	·014	·018	·022	·023
	Apr	—	—	—	—	—	—	—	—	—	—	—	—	—	—	—	—	—	—	—	—	—	—	—	—	—	·006	·005	·002	·007	·011	·012
	May	—	—	—	—	—	—	—	—	—	—	—	—	—	—	—	—	—	—	—	—	—	—	—	—	—	—	·000	·000	·001	·006	·006
	June	—	—	—	—	—	—	—	—	—	—	—	—	—	—	—	—	—	—	—	—	—	—	—	—	—	—	—	·000	·002	·006	·007
	July	—	—	—	—	—	—	—	—	—	—	—	—	—	—	—	—	—	—	—	—	—	—	—	—	—	—	—	—	·004	·009	·009
	Aug	—	—	—	—	—	—	—	—	—	—	—	—	—	—	—	—	—	—	—	—	—	—	—	—	—	—	—	—	—	·004	·005
	Sept	—	—	—	—	—	—	—	—	—	—	—	—	—	—	—	—	—	—	—	—	—	—	—	—	—	—	—	—	—	—	·001
	Oct	—	—	—	—	—	—	—	—	—	—	—	—	—	—	—	—	—	—	—	—	—	—	—	—	—	—	—	—	—	—	—
	Nov	—	—	—	—	—	—	—	—	—	—	—	—	—	—	—	—	—	—	—	—	—	—	—	—	—	—	—	—	—	—	—
	Dec	—	—	—	—	—	—	—	—	—	—	—	—	—	—	—	—	—	—	—	—	—	—	—	—	—	—	—	—	—	—	—
1999	Jan	—	—	—	—	—	—	—	—	—	—	—	—	—	—	—	—	—	—	—	—	—	—	—	—	—	—	—	—	—	—	—
	Feb	—	—	—	—	—	—	—	—	—	—	—	—	—	—	—	—	—	—	—	—	—	—	—	—	—	—	—	—	—	—	—
	Mar	—	—	—	—	—	—	—	—	—	—	—	—	—	—	—	—	—	—	—	—	—	—	—	—	—	—	—	—	—	—	—
	Apr	—	—	—	—	—	—	—	—	—	—	—	—	—	—	—	—	—	—	—	—	—	—	—	—	—	—	—	—	—	—	—
	May	—	—	—	—	—	—	—	—	—	—	—	—	—	—	—	—	—	—	—	—	—	—	—	—	—	—	—	—	—	—	—
	June	—	—	—	—	—	—	—	—	—	—	—	—	—	—	—	—	—	—	—	—	—	—	—	—	—	—	—	—	—	—	—
	July	—	—	—	—	—	—	—	—	—	—	—	—	—	—	—	—	—	—	—	—	—	—	—	—	—	—	—	—	—	—	—
	Aug	—	—	—	—	—	—	—	—	—	—	—	—	—	—	—	—	—	—	—	—	—	—	—	—	—	—	—	—	—	—	—
	Sept	—	—	—	—	—	—	—	—	—	—	—	—	—	—	—	—	—	—	—	—	—	—	—	—	—	—	—	—	—	—	—
	Oct	—	—	—	—	—	—	—	—	—	—	—	—	—	—	—	—	—	—	—	—	—	—	—	—	—	—	—	—	—	—	—
	Nov	—	—	—	—	—	—	—	—	—	—	—	—	—	—	—	—	—	—	—	—	—	—	—	—	—	—	—	—	—	—	—
	Dec	—	—	—	—	—	—	—	—	—	—	—	—	—	—	—	—	—	—	—	—	—	—	—	—	—	—	—	—	—	—	—

Indexation allowance — continued

Month of disposal

Base month	1998		1999												2000												2001			
1996	Nov	Dec	Jan	Feb	Mar	Apr	May	June	July	Aug	Sept	Oct	Nov	Dec	Jan	Feb	Mar	Apr	May	June	July	Aug	Sept	Oct	Nov	Dec	Jan	Feb	Mar	Apr
Jan	·095	·095	·088	·090	·093	·100	·103	·103	·099	·102	·107	·109	·110	·114	·109	·115	·121	·132	·136	·139	·135	·135	·143	·142	·146	·146	·139	·145	·146	·152
Feb	·089	·089	·083	·085	·087	·095	·097	·097	·094	·097	·101	·103	·105	·109	·104	·110	·116	·127	·131	·134	·130	·130	·138	·137	·140	·141	·134	·140	·141	·147
Mar	·085	·085	·079	·081	·087	·090	·093	·093	·090	·092	·097	·099	·100	·104	·100	·106	·112	·123	·127	·129	·125	·125	·133	·133	·136	·137	·129	·135	·137	·143
Apr	·077	·077	·071	·073	·075	·083	·085	·085	·082	·085	·089	·091	·092	·096	·092	·098	·104	·115	·119	·121	·117	·117	·125	·125	·128	·128	·121	·127	·128	·134
May	·075	·075	·069	·071	·073	·080	·083	·083	·080	·082	·087	·089	·090	·094	·090	·095	·101	·112	·116	·119	·115	·115	·123	·122	·126	·126	·119	·125	·126	·132
June	·075	·075	·068	·070	·073	·080	·082	·082	·079	·082	·086	·088	·090	·093	·089	·095	·101	·112	·116	·118	·114	·114	·122	·122	·125	·125	·118	·124	·125	·131
July	·079	·079	·072	·074	·077	·084	·087	·087	·083	·086	·091	·093	·094	·098	·093	·099	·105	·116	·120	·123	·119	·119	·127	·126	·129	·130	·123	·129	·130	·136
Aug	·074	·074	·067	·069	·072	·079	·082	·082	·078	·081	·086	·088	·089	·093	·088	·094	·100	·111	·115	·118	·114	·114	·121	·121	·124	·125	·118	·123	·125	·131
Sept	·069	·069	·062	·064	·067	·074	·077	·077	·073	·076	·081	·083	·084	·088	·083	·089	·095	·106	·110	·112	·109	·109	·116	·116	·119	·120	·112	·118	·120	·125
Oct	·069	·069	·062	·064	·067	·074	·077	·077	·073	·076	·081	·083	·084	·088	·083	·089	·095	·106	·110	·112	·109	·109	·116	·116	·119	·120	·112	·118	·120	·125
Nov	·068	·068	·062	·064	·066	·073	·076	·076	·073	·075	·080	·082	·083	·087	·083	·088	·094	·105	·109	·112	·108	·108	·116	·115	·118	·119	·112	·118	·119	·125
Dec	·065	·065	·058	·060	·063	·070	·073	·073	·069	·072	·076	·078	·080	·084	·079	·085	·091	·102	·106	·108	·104	·104	·112	·111	·115	·115	·108	·114	·115	·121
1997																														
Jan	·065	·065	·058	·060	·063	·070	·073	·073	·069	·072	·076	·078	·080	·084	·079	·085	·091	·102	·106	·108	·104	·104	·112	·111	·115	·115	·108	·114	·115	·121
Feb	·061	·061	·054	·056	·059	·066	·068	·068	·065	·068	·072	·074	·075	·079	·075	·081	·086	·097	·101	·104	·100	·100	·108	·107	·110	·111	·104	·110	·111	·117
Mar	·058	·058	·051	·053	·056	·063	·066	·066	·062	·065	·069	·071	·073	·077	·072	·078	·084	·095	·098	·101	·097	·097	·105	·104	·107	·108	·101	·107	·108	·114
Apr	·052	·052	·045	·047	·050	·057	·060	·060	·056	·059	·063	·065	·067	·070	·066	·072	·077	·088	·092	·095	·091	·091	·099	·098	·101	·102	·095	·100	·102	·107
May	·048	·048	·041	·043	·046	·053	·055	·055	·052	·055	·059	·061	·062	·066	·062	·068	·073	·084	·088	·091	·087	·087	·094	·094	·097	·098	·091	·096	·098	·103
June	·044	·044	·037	·039	·042	·049	·051	·051	·048	·051	·055	·057	·058	·062	·058	·063	·069	·080	·084	·086	·083	·083	·090	·090	·093	·093	·086	·092	·093	·099
July	·044	·044	·037	·039	·042	·049	·051	·051	·048	·051	·055	·057	·058	·062	·058	·063	·069	·080	·084	·086	·083	·083	·090	·090	·093	·093	·086	·092	·093	·099
Aug	·037	·037	·031	·033	·035	·042	·045	·045	·042	·044	·049	·050	·052	·056	·051	·057	·062	·073	·077	·079	·076	·076	·083	·083	·086	·086	·079	·085	·086	·092
Sept	·032	·032	·026	·028	·030	·037	·040	·040	·036	·039	·043	·045	·046	·050	·046	·051	·057	·068	·072	·074	·070	·070	·078	·077	·080	·081	·074	·080	·081	·087
Oct	·031	·031	·024	·026	·029	·036	·038	·038	·035	·038	·042	·044	·045	·049	·045	·050	·056	·066	·070	·073	·069	·069	·076	·076	·079	·080	·073	·078	·080	·085
Nov	·030	·030	·024	·026	·028	·035	·038	·038	·034	·037	·041	·043	·044	·048	·044	·049	·055	·066	·070	·072	·068	·068	·076	·075	·078	·079	·072	·078	·079	·085
Dec	·028	·028	·021	·023	·026	·032	·035	·035	·032	·034	·039	·041	·042	·046	·041	·047	·053	·063	·067	·069	·066	·066	·073	·073	·076	·076	·069	·075	·076	·082
1998																														
Jan	·031	·031	·024	·026	·029	·036	·038	·038	·035	·038	·042	·044	·045	·049	·045	·050	·056	·066	·070	·073	·069	·069	·076	·076	·079	·080	·073	·078	·080	·085
Feb	·026	·026	·019	·021	·024	·031	·033	·033	·030	·032	·037	·039	·040	·044	·039	·045	·051	·061	·065	·067	·064	·064	·071	·070	·074	·074	·067	·073	·074	·080
Mar	·022	·022	·016	·018	·021	·027	·030	·030	·027	·029	·034	·035	·037	·040	·036	·042	·047	·058	·062	·064	·060	·060	·068	·067	·070	·071	·064	·070	·071	·076
Apr	·011	·011	·005	·007	·009	·016	·018	·018	·015	·018	·022	·024	·025	·029	·025	·030	·036	·046	·050	·052	·049	·049	·056	·055	·058	·059	·052	·058	·059	·065
May	·006	·006	·000	·001	·004	·010	·013	·013	·010	·012	·017	·018	·020	·023	·019	·024	·030	·040	·044	·046	·043	·043	·050	·050	·053	·053	·046	·052	·053	·059
June	·006	·006	·000	·002	·004	·011	·013	·013	·010	·013	·017	·019	·020	·024	·020	·025	·031	·041	·045	·047	·043	·043	·051	·050	·053	·054	·047	·053	·054	·059
July	·009	·009	·002	·004	·007	·013	·016	·016	·013	·015	·020	·021	·023	·026	·022	·028	·033	·044	·047	·050	·046	·046	·053	·053	·056	·056	·050	·055	·056	·062
Aug	·004	·004	·000	·000	·002	·009	·012	·012	·009	·011	·015	·017	·018	·022	·018	·023	·029	·039	·043	·045	·042	·042	·049	·048	·051	·052	·045	·051	·052	·057
Sept	·000	·000	·000	·000	·000	·005	·007	·007	·004	·007	·011	·013	·014	·018	·013	·019	·024	·035	·038	·041	·037	·037	·044	·044	·047	·047	·041	·046	·047	·053
Oct	·000	·000	·000	·000	·000	·004	·007	·007	·004	·006	·010	·012	·013	·017	·013	·018	·024	·034	·038	·040	·036	·036	·044	·043	·046	·047	·040	·046	·047	·052
Nov	–	·000	·000	·000	·000	·005	·007	·007	·004	·007	·011	·013	·014	·018	·013	·019	·024	·035	·038	·041	·037	·037	·044	·044	·047	·047	·041	·046	·047	·053
Dec	–	–	·000	·000	·000	·005	·007	·007	·004	·007	·011	·013	·014	·018	·013	·019	·024	·035	·038	·041	·037	·037	·044	·044	·047	·047	·041	·046	·047	·053
1999																														
Jan	–	–	–	·002	·004	·011	·013	·013	·010	·013	·017	·019	·020	·024	·020	·025	·031	·041	·045	·047	·043	·043	·051	·050	·053	·054	·047	·053	·054	·059
Feb	–	–	–	–	·002	·009	·012	·012	·009	·011	·015	·017	·018	·022	·018	·023	·029	·039	·043	·045	·042	·042	·049	·048	·051	·052	·045	·051	·052	·057
Mar	–	–	–	–	–	·007	·009	·009	·006	·009	·013	·015	·016	·020	·015	·021	·026	·037	·040	·043	·039	·039	·046	·046	·049	·049	·043	·048	·049	·055
Apr	–	–	–	–	–	–	·002	·002	·000	·002	·006	·008	·009	·013	·008	·014	·019	·030	·033	·036	·032	·032	·039	·039	·042	·042	·036	·041	·042	·048
May	–	–	–	–	–	–	–	·000	·000	·000	·004	·005	·007	·010	·006	·011	·017	·027	·031	·033	·030	·030	·037	·036	·039	·040	·033	·039	·040	·045
June	–	–	–	–	–	–	–	–	·000	·000	·004	·005	·007	·010	·006	·011	·017	·027	·031	·033	·030	·030	·037	·036	·039	·040	·033	·039	·040	·045
July	–	–	–	–	–	–	–	–	–	·002	·007	·008	·010	·013	·009	·015	·020	·030	·034	·036	·033	·033	·040	·039	·042	·043	·036	·042	·043	·048
Aug	–	–	–	–	–	–	–	–	–	–	·004	·006	·007	·011	·007	·012	·018	·028	·031	·034	·030	·030	·037	·037	·040	·040	·034	·039	·040	·046
Sept	–	–	–	–	–	–	–	–	–	–	–	·002	·003	·007	·002	·008	·013	·023	·027	·029	·026	·026	·033	·032	·035	·036	·029	·035	·036	·042
Oct	–	–	–	–	–	–	–	–	–	–	–	–	·001	·005	·001	·006	·011	·022	·025	·028	·024	·024	·031	·031	·034	·034	·028	·033	·034	·040
Nov	–	–	–	–	–	–	–	–	–	–	–	–	–	·004	·000	·005	·010	·020	·024	·026	·023	·023	·030	·029	·032	·033	·026	·032	·033	·038
Dec	–	–	–	–	–	–	–	–	–	–	–	–	–	–	·000	·001	·007	·017	·020	·023	·019	·019	·026	·026	·029	·029	·023	·028	·029	·035
2000																														
Jan	–	–	–	–	–	–	–	–	–	–	–	–	–	–	–	·005	·011	·021	·025	·027	·023	·023	·031	·030	·033	·034	·027	·032	·034	·039
Feb	–	–	–	–	–	–	–	–	–	–	–	–	–	–	–	–	·005	·016	·019	·021	·018	·018	·025	·024	·027	·028	·021	·027	·028	·033
Mar	–	–	–	–	–	–	–	–	–	–	–	–	–	–	–	–	–	·010	·014	·016	·012	·012	·020	·019	·022	·023	·016	·021	·023	·028
Apr	–	–	–	–	–	–	–	–	–	–	–	–	–	–	–	–	–	–	·004	·006	·002	·002	·009	·009	·012	·012	·006	·011	·012	·018
May	–	–	–	–	–	–	–	–	–	–	–	–	–	–	–	–	–	–	–	·002	·000	·000	·006	·005	·008	·009	·002	·008	·009	·014
June	–	–	–	–	–	–	–	–	–	–	–	–	–	–	–	–	–	–	–	–	·000	·000	·004	·003	·006	·006	·000	·005	·006	·012
July	–	–	–	–	–	–	–	–	–	–	–	–	–	–	–	–	–	–	–	–	–	·000	·007	·006	·009	·010	·004	·009	·010	·015
Aug	–	–	–	–	–	–	–	–	–	–	–	–	–	–	–	–	–	–	–	–	–	–	·007	·006	·009	·010	·004	·009	·010	·015
Sept	–	–	–	–	–	–	–	–	–	–	–	–	–	–	–	–	–	–	–	–	–	–	–	·000	·002	·003	·000	·002	·003	·008
Oct	–	–	–	–	–	–	–	–	–	–	–	–	–	–	–	–	–	–	–	–	–	–	–	–	·003	·003	·000	·002	·003	·009
Nov	–	–	–	–	–	–	–	–	–	–	–	–	–	–	–	–	–	–	–	–	–	–	–	–	–	·001	·000	·000	·001	·006
Dec	–	–	–	–	–	–	–	–	–	–	–	–	–	–	–	–	–	–	–	–	–	–	–	–	–	–	·000	·000	·000	·005
2001																														
Jan	–	–	–	–	–	–	–	–	–	–	–	–	–	–	–	–	–	–	–	–	–	–	–	–	–	–	–	·005	·006	·012
Feb	–	–	–	–	–	–	–	–	–	–	–	–	–	–	–	–	–	–	–	–	–	–	–	–	–	–	–	–	·001	·006
Mar	–	–	–	–	–	–	–	–	–	–	–	–	–	–	–	–	–	–	–	–	–	–	–	–	–	–	–	–	–	·005

Retail prices index

	Jan	Feb	Mar	Apr	May	June	July	Aug	Sept	Oct	Nov	Dec
1947	–	–	–	–	–	7·33	7·40	7·33	7·40	7·40	7·55	7·63
1948	7·63	7·78	7·78	8·33	8·33	8·49	8·33	8·33	8·33	8·33	8·41	8·41
1949	8·41	8·41	8·41	8·41	8·57	8·57	8·57	8·57	8·65	8·65	8·65	8·73
1950	8·73	8·73	8·73	8·81	8·81	8·81	8·81	8·73	8·81	8·89	8·97	8·97
1951	9·03	9·11	9·19	9·35	9·59	9·67	9·72	9·80	9·88	9·96	9·96	10·04
1952	10·20	10·28	10·28	10·44	10·44	10·65	10·65	10·04	9·96	10·11	10·11	10·11
1953	10·11	10·19	10·67	10·34	10·27	10·34	10·34	10·27	10·27	10·27	10·27	10·27
1954	10·27	10·27	10·34	10·42	10·34	10·42	10·62	10·57	10·49	10·57	10·62	10·62
1955	10·70	10·70	10·70	10·77	10·77	11·00	11·00	10·93	11·00	11·15	11·28	11·28
1956	11·25	11·25	11·38	11·56	11·53	11·51	11·48	11·51	11·48	11·56	11·58	11·63
1957	11·74	11·74	11·71	11·76	11·76	11·89	11·99	11·96	11·94	12·04	12·12	12·17
1958	12·17	12·09	12·19	12·32	12·29	12·40	12·19	12·19	12·19	12·29	12·34	12·40
1959	12·42	12·40	12·40	12·32	12·27	12·29	12·27	12·29	12·22	12·29	12·37	12·40
1960	12·37	12·37	12·34	12·40	12·40	12·47	12·50	12·42	12·42	12·52	12·60	12·62
1961	12·62	12·62	12·67	12·75	12·78	12·90	12·90	13·00	13·00	13·00	13·16	13·18
1962	13·21	13·23	13·28	13·46	13·51	13·59	13·54	13·43	13·41	13·41	13·46	13·51
1963	13·56	13·69	13·71	13·74	13·74	13·74	13·66	13·61	13·66	13·71	13·74	13·76
1964	13·84	13·84	13·89	14·02	14·14	14·20	14·20	14·25	14·25	14·27	14·37	14·42
1965	14·47	14·47	14·52	14·80	14·85	14·90	14·90	14·93	14·93	14·96	15·01	15·08
1966	15·11	15·11	15·13	15·34	15·44	15·49	15·41	15·51	15·49	15·51	15·61	15·64
1967	15·67	15·67	15·67	15·79	15·79	15·84	15·74	15·72	15·69	15·86	15·92	16·02
1968	16·07	16·15	16·20	16·50	16·50	16·58	16·58	16·60	16·63	16·70	16·76	16·96
1969	17·06	17·16	17·21	17·41	17·39	17·47	17·47	17·41	17·47	17·59	17·64	17·77
1970	17·90	18·00	18·10	18·38	18·43	18·48	18·63	18·61	18·71	18·91	19·04	19·16
1971	19·42	19·54	19·70	20·13	20·25	20·38	20·51	20·53	20·56	20·66	20·79	20·89
1972	21·01	21·12	21·19	21·39	21·50	21·62	21·70	21·88	22·00	22·31	22·38	22·48
1973	22·64	22·79	22·92	23·35	23·52	23·65	23·75	23·83	24·03	24·51	24·69	24·87
1974	25·35	25·78	26·01	26·89	27·28	27·55	27·81	27·83	28·14	28·69	29·20	29·63
1975	30·39	30·90	31·51	32·72	34·09	34·75	35·11	35·31	35·61	36·12	36·55	37·01
1976	37·49	37·97	38·17	38·91	39·34	39·54	39·62	40·18	40·71	41·44	42·03	42·59
1977	43·70	44·24	44·56	45·70	46·06	46·54	46·59	46·82	47·07	47·28	47·50	47·76
1978	48·04	48·31	48·62	49·33	49·61	49·99	50·22	50·54	50·75	50·98	51·33	51·76
1979	52·52	52·95	53·38	54·30	54·73	55·67	58·07	58·53	59·11	59·72	60·25	60·68
1980	62·18	63·07	63·93	66·11	66·72	67·35	67·91	68·06	68·49	68·92	69·48	69·86
1981	70·29	70·93	71·99	74·07	74·55	74·98	75·31	75·87	76·30	76·98	77·78	78·28
1982	78·73	78·76	79·44	81·04	81·62	81·85	81·88	81·90	81·85	82·26	82·66	82·51
1983	82·61	82·97	83·12	84·28	84·64	84·84	85·30	85·68	86·06	86·36	86·67	86·89
1984	86·84	87·20	87·48	88·64	88·97	89·20	89·10	89·94	90·11	90·67	90·95	90·87
1985	91·20	91·94	92·80	94·78	95·21	95·41	95·23	95·49	95·44	95·59	95·92	96·05
1986	96·25	96·60	96·73	97·67	97·85	97·79	97·52	97·82	98·30	98·45	99·29	99·62
1987	100·00	100·40	100·60	101·80	101·90	101·90	101·80	102·10	102·40	102·90	103·40	103·30
1988	103·30	103·70	104·10	105·80	106·20	106·60	106·70	107·90	108·40	109·50	110·00	110·30
1989	111·00	111·80	112·30	114·30	115·00	115·40	115·50	115·80	116·60	117·50	118·50	118·80
1990	119·50	120·20	121·40	125·10	126·20	126·70	126·80	128·10	129·30	130·30	130·00	129·90
1991	130·20	130·90	131·40	133·10	133·50	134·10	133·80	134·10	134·60	135·10	135·60	135·70
1992	135·60	136·30	136·70	138·80	139·30	139·30	138·80	138·90	139·40	139·90	139·70	139·20
1993	137·90	138·80	139·30	140·60	141·10	141·00	140·70	141·30	141·90	141·80	141·60	141·90
1994	141·30	142·10	142·50	144·20	144·70	144·70	144·00	144·70	145·00	145·20	145·30	146·00
1995	146·00	146·90	147·50	149·00	149·60	149·80	149·10	149·90	150·60	149·80	149·80	150·70
1996	150·20	150·90	151·50	152·60	152·90	153·00	152·40	153·10	153·80	153·80	153·90	154·40
1997	154·40	155·00	155·40	156·30	156·90	157·50	157·50	158·50	159·30	159·50	159·60	160·00
1998	159·50	160·30	160·80	162·60	163·50	163·40	163·00	163·70	164·40	164·50	164·40	164·40
1999	163·40	163·70	164·10	165·20	165·60	165·60	165·10	165·50	166·20	166·50	166·70	167·30
2000	166·60	167·50	168·40	170·10	170·70	171·10	170·50	170·50	171·70	171·60	172·10	172·20
2001	171·10	172·00	172·20	173·10	174·20	174·40						

Corporation tax

Rates of corporation tax and advance corporation tax

Financial year	1992	1993	1994	1995	1996	1997	1998	1999	2000	2001
Corporation tax (full rate)	33%	33%	33%	33%	33%	31%	31%	30%	30%	30%
Advance corporation tax: from 6 April	$\frac{1}{3}$	$\frac{9}{31}$	$\frac{1}{4}$	$\frac{1}{4}$	$\frac{1}{4}$	$\frac{1}{4}$	$\frac{1}{4}$	—*	—*	—*
Tax credit: from 6 April	25%	20%†	20%†	20%†	20%†	20%†	20%†	10%†	10%†	10%†

The full rate of corporation tax will remain at 30% for the financial year beginning on 1 April 2002 (FA 2001 s 54).
* Advance corporation tax is abolished from 6 April 1999. ACT remains at ¼ for distributions on 1 April to 5 April 1999.
† Individual shareholders not subject to tax at the higher rate will have no further tax to pay.
  In the case of charities, the reduced tax credit was phased in over four years, 1993–94 to 1996–97.

Starting and small companies rates (TA 1988 ss 13, 13AA)

Financial year:	1995	1996	1997	1998	1999	2000	2001
Starting rate	—	—	—	—	—	10%	10%
first relevant amount*	—	—	—	—	—	£10,000	£10,000
second relevant amount*	—	—	—	—	—	£50,000	£50,000
marginal relief fraction	—	—	—	—	—	$\frac{1}{40}$	$\frac{1}{40}$
Small companies rate	25%	24%	21%	21%	20%	20%	20%
lower relevant amount*	£300,000	£300,000	£300,000	£300,000	£300,000	£300,000	£300,000
upper relevant amount*	£1,500,000	£1,500,000	£1,500,000	£1,500,000	£1,500,000	£1,500,000	£1,500,000
marginal relief fraction	$\frac{1}{50}$	$\frac{9}{400}$	$\frac{1}{40}$	$\frac{1}{40}$	$\frac{1}{40}$	$\frac{1}{40}$	$\frac{1}{40}$

* Reduced proportionally for accounting periods of less than 12 months. Associated companies: divide limits by total number of associated companies (including the company in question).
1) The starting and the small companies rate apply to *basic profits* ("I") where *profits* ("P") do not exceed the first (in the case of the starting rate) and lower (small companies rate) relevant amounts.
2) Where *profits* ("P") exceed the first or lower relevant amounts but not the second or upper relevant amounts, corporation tax on *basic profits* ("I") is reduced by—

$$(\text{second or upper relevant amount} - P) \times \frac{I}{P} \times \text{fraction}$$

For the purposes of 1) and 2) above—
P = profits as finally computed for corporation tax purposes *plus* franked investment income *excluding* franked investment income from UK companies in the same group or from UK companies owned by a consortium of which the recipient is a member (TA 1988 s 13(7) amended by FA 1998 Sch 3 para 7 for distributions made after 5 April 1999).
I = profits on which corporation tax is actually borne (income plus chargeable gains).

Capital gains

A company's chargeable gains are taxed without adjustment (other than indexation for post-1982 gains) at the rate of corporation tax applying to the company's other profits. The taper relief regime and the freezing of indexation allowance for individuals, trustees and personal representatives does not extend to companies.

Close investment-holding companies

Charged at full rate of corporation tax (see above).

Corporate venturing scheme (FA 2000 s 63, Schs 15, 16; FA 2001 s 64, Sch 16)

	1.4.00–6.3.01	7.3.01 onwards
Rate of corporation tax relief	20%	20%
Minimum percentage of investee company's ordinary share capital held by individuals	20%	20%
Investing company's maximum stake in investee company	30%	30%
Minimum investment period	3 years	3 years
Minimum percentage of invested money employed in qualifying business within 12 months	100%	80%

Companies can obtain corporation tax relief on amounts invested in new ordinary unquoted shares in small higher-risk trading companies.

Research and development expenditure

From **1 April 2000** (FA 2000 ss 68, 69, Schs 19, 20)

Rate of corporation tax relief	150%
Minimum threshold on spending	£25,000
Maximum turnover limit	£25 million

Companies not yet in profit or which have not yet started to trade can claim the relief up front.
See also the 100% capital allowance for research and development, p 54
Research into specified diseases: extra 50% relief to be introduced in Finance Bill 2002 (2001) SWTI 447.

Capital allowances

Rates

Agricultural and forestry land

	Expenditure incurred after		% Rate
Initial allowance		11 April 1978	20
		31 March 1986	Nil
		31 October 1992[1]	20
		31 October 1993	Nil
Writing-down allowance		5 April 1946	10
		31 March 1986	4

Note:

[1] Buildings or works constructed under a contract entered into between 1 November 1992 and 31 October 1993, and brought into use for the purposes of the farming trade by 31 December 1994.

Dredging

	Expenditure incurred after	% Rate
Initial allowance	16 January 1966	15
	31 March 1986	Nil
Writing-down allowance	5 November 1962	4

Industrial buildings and structures

	Expenditure[1] incurred after		% Rate
Initial allowance		12 November 1974[2]	50
		10 March 1981[2-6]	75
		13 March 1984[2/4-8]	50
		31 March 1985[2/5-8]	25
		31 March 1986[2/5-8]	Nil
		31 October 1992[2/5/10]	20
		31 October 1993[5/11]	Nil
Writing-down allowance		5 November 1962[9]	4

Notes:

[1] The amount qualifying for allowance is the price paid for the relevant interest *minus* (i) the value of the land element and (ii) any value attributable to elements over and above those which would feature in a normal commercial lease negotiated in the open market: FA 1995 s 100 confirming previous practice.

[2] Qualifying hotels: expenditure incurred after 11 April 1978 and before 1 April 1986, or between 1 November 1992 and 31 October 1993 – 20% initial allowance. No initial allowance after 31 March 1986 except under certain pre-14 March 1984 contracts and as above.

[3] Small industrial workshops: expenditure incurred after 26 March 1980 and before 27 March 1983 – 100% initial allowance.

[4] Very small workshops: expenditure incurred after 26 March 1980 and before 27 March 1985 – 100% initial allowance.

[5] Enterprise zones: expenditure incurred not more than 10 years after the site was first included in the zone – 100% initial allowance. (See p 54 for list of enterprise zones.)

[6] Rates and transitional relief apply also to dwelling houses let on assured tenancies: 10 March 1982 – 31 March 1987.

[7] Expenditure qualifying for a regional development grant (where a written offer of financial assistance was made between 1 April 1980–13 March 1984) – 75%.

[8] Payments made after 13 March 1984 but before 1 April 1987 under a contract agreed before 14 March 1984 – 75%.

[9] Small industrial workshops: expenditure incurred after 26 March 1980 and before 27 March 1983 – 25% writing-down allowance.

Very small workshops: expenditure incurred after 26 March 1980 and before 27 March 1985 – 25% writing-down allowance.

Enterprise zones: expenditure incurred not more than 10 years after the site was first included in the zone (including qualifying hotels in an enterprise zone) – 25% writing-down allowance.

Qualifying hotels (other than in an enterprise zone) – 4% writing-down allowance.

Toll roads: for accounting periods or basis periods ending after 5 April 1991 – 4% writing-down allowance for expenditure on construction of toll roads.

[10] Building constructed under, or bought unused under, a contract entered into after 31 October 1992 and before 1 November 1993, and brought into use in qualifying trade by 31 December 1994. Balance of relief by 4% pa writing-down allowance. All or part of the initial allowance may be disclaimed. See FA 1993 s 113.

[11] 100% allowance for expenditure incurred after 10 May 2001 on renovating or converting vacant or storage space above commercial properties to provide low-value flats for rent (CAA 2001, ss 393A–393W; FA 2001, s 67, Sch 19).

Know-how

Writing-down allowance

Expenditure incurred after 31 March 1986: annual 25% writing-down allowance (reducing balance basis).

Rates — continued

Plant and machinery		
	Expenditure incurred after	% Rate
First-year allowance (FYA)	31 October 1993[1]	Nil
	1 July 1997 (and before 2 July 1998)[2]	50
	11 May 1998 (Northern Ireland)[4]	100
	1 July 1998[3]	40
	31 March 2000 (ICT)[6]	100
	31 March 2001 (energy-saving)[7]	100
Writing-down allowance (WDA)	26 October 1970	25
FYA: long-life assets[5]	25 November 1996	Nil
	1 July 1997 (and before 2 July 1998)[2]	12
	1 July 1998	Nil
WDA: long-life assets[5]	25 November 1996	6

Notes:

[1] First-year allowances available universally had been generally abolished for expenditure after 31 March 1986 but were reintroduced temporarily for expenditure in the 12 months to 31 October 1993. Thereafter, first-year allowances have been specifically targeted as below.

[2] Qualifying expenditure incurred by *qualifying businesses* during the year ended 1 July 1998 attracts a first-year allowance of 50% rather than the normal writing-down allowance of 25%. This does not apply to certain expenditure including that on plant and machinery for leasing, motor cars, ships or railway assets. For qualifying long-life asset expenditure incurred in that year (see note 5 below), the rate of the first-year allowance is restricted to 12%. After the first year, allowances revert to the normal writing-down rate of 25%/6%. Qualifying businesses are, broadly, those which satisfy any two of the following conditions: (a) turnover £11,200,000 or less (b) assets £5,600,000 or less (c) not more than 250 employees (CAA 1990 ss 22(3C)(6B), 22A).

[3] The conditions for relief for qualifying expenditure incurred by *qualifying businesses* after 1 July 1998 are similar to those outlined in footnote 2 above, but long-life assets do not qualify (see footnote 5 below) (CAA 2001 ss 44, 46-49).

[4] Northern Ireland. Qualifying expenditure on plant and machinery for use in Northern Ireland incurred before 12 May 2002 by *qualifying businesses* attracts a first-year allowance of 100% rather than the normal 25% writing-down allowance. The conditions for relief are similar to those outlined in footnote 2 above, but long-life assets and goods vehicles used in freight haulage businesses do not qualify (CAA 2001 ss 40-43, 46).

[5] On reducing balance basis. Applies to plant or machinery with an expected working life, when new, of 25 years or more. Applies where expenditure on long-life assets in a year is £100,000 or more (in the case of companies the de minimis limit is £100,000 divided by one plus the number of associated companies). Transitional provisions apply to maintain a 25% allowance for expenditure incurred before 1 January 2001 under a contract entered into before 26 November 1996 and to expenditure on second-hand plant or machinery if old rules applied to vendor. It does not apply to plant or machinery in a building used wholly or mainly as, or for purposes ancillary to, a dwelling-house, retail shop, showroom, hotel or office, cars, or sea-going ships and railway assets acquired before 1 January 2011 (CAA 2001 ss 90-104, Sch 3 para 20).

[6] ICT (information and communications technology). *Small businesses* buying computers or investing in e-commerce and new information technology before 1 April 2003 are able to write off in the first year 100% of the investment. Small businesses are, broadly, those which satisfy any two of the following conditions: (a) turnover £2,800,000 or less (b) assets £1,400,000 or less (c) not more than 50 employees (CAA 2001 ss 45, 46).

[7] Energy-saving plant and machinery: 100% first-year allowances are available for investment by *any* business in designated energy-saving plant and machinery in accordance with the Government's Energy Technology Product List (CAA 2001 ss 45A–45C; FA 2001 s 65, Sch 17; SI 2001/2541).

Cars: Threshold for restriction on capital allowances for expenditure on business cars £12,000 for cars leased or purchased after 10 March 1992 (CAA 2001 ss 74, 75). The requirement that expenditure on cars costing £12,000 or less goes into a separate pool is removed from the start of the chargeable period which includes 1 April 2000 (corporation tax) or 6 April 2000 (income tax) or the start of the chargeable period which includes 1 (or 6) April 2001 at the option of the taxpayer (CAA 1990 s 41; FA 2000 s 74).

Leased assets: First-year allowances are not available for expenditure after 31 October 1993 on the provision of leased plant or machinery. Writing-down allowances are available, but at the reduced rate of 10% where leasing is to non-UK residents.

Films: From 10 March 1992, pre-production expenditure on films produced with sufficient EC content is relieved as it occurs. 100% write-off is available for expenditure incurred after 1 July 1997 and before 2 July 2005 on a qualifying British film completed after 1 July 1997. See F(No 2)A 1992 ss 41, 42; F(No 2)A 1997 s 48; FA 2001 s 72; Statement of Practice SP1/98.

Rates — continued

Mineral extraction

Expenditure incurred after		% Rate
Initial allowance	16 January 1966	40
	31 March 1986	Nil

Amount of writing-down allowance
Expenditure incurred before 1 April 1986—

Greater of: 1) $\dfrac{A}{A+B}$ × residue of expenditure

       where A = output from source in chargeable period or its basis period,
         and B = total potential future output of source, estimated as at the end of that chargeable period or its basis period.
       2) 5% residue of expenditure for full year.

Expenditure incurred after 31 March 1986: annual writing-down allowance on reducing balance basis—10% for certain pre-trading expenditure and expenditure on the acquisition of a mineral asset, otherwise 25%.

Note: Transitional provisions for expenditure incurred before 31 March 1987 under contract entered into before 16 July 1985.

Patent rights

Writing-down allowance
Expenditure incurred before 1 April 1986 spread equally over 17 years or, if less
    (a) the period for which the rights are acquired, or
    (b) 17 years less the number of complete years from the commencement of the patent to the acquisition.

Expenditure incurred after 31 March 1986: annual 25% writing-down allowance (reducing balance basis).

Research and development (formerly scientific research)*

Expenditure incurred after		% Rate
Allowance in year 1	5 November 1962	100

Note: Land and houses are excluded from 1 April 1985.
*See also corporation tax relief, p 51.

Enterprise zones

The following areas have been designated as enterprise zones. The designation applies for 10 years from the commencement date. Previous enterprise zones, the designation of which has lapsed, are not shown.

Area	*Commencement date*
Lanarkshire (Hamilton)	1 February 1993
Lanarkshire (Motherwell)	1 February 1993
Lanarkshire (Monklands)	1 February 1993
Dearne Valley	3 November 1995
East Midlands (North East Derbyshire)	3 November 1995
East Midlands (Bassetlaw)	16 November 1995
East Midlands (Ashfield)	21 November 1995
East Durham	29 November 1995
Tyne Riverside (North Tyneside)	19 February 1996
Tyne Riverside (North Tyneside and South Tyneside)	21 October 1996

Time limits for capital allowances claims see p 25.

Income tax

Starting, basic and higher rates and rate applicable to trusts

Band of taxable income £	Band £	Rate %	Tax £	Cumulative tax £
2001–02				
0–1,880	1,880	10	188.00	188.00
1,881–29,400	27,520	22	6,054.40	6,242.40
over 29,400	—	40	—	—
2000–01				
0–1,520	1,520	10	152.00	152.00
1,521–28,400	26,880	22	5,913.60	6,065.60
over 28,400	—	40	—	—
1999–2000				
0–1,500	1,500	10	150	150
1,501–28,000	26,500	23	6,095	6,245
over 28,000	—	40	—	—
1998–99				
0–4,300	4,300	20	860	860
4,301–27,100	22,800	23	5,244	6,104
over 27,100	—	40	—	—
1997–98				
0–4,100	4,100	20	820	820
4,101–26,100	22,000	23	5,060	5,880
over 26,100	—	40	—	—
1996–97				
0–3,900	3,900	20	780	780
3,901–25,500	21,600	24	5,184	5,964
over 25,500	—	40	—	—
1995–96				
0–3,200	3,200	20	640	640
3,201–24,300	21,100	25	5,275	5,915
over 24,300	—	40	—	—

Taxation of savings: From 6 April 1999, savings income is chargeable at the rates of 10% (if within the starting rate band), 20% and/or 40% (TA 1988 s1A; FA 2000 s 32). From 6 April 1996 to 5 April 1999, savings income was chargeable at the rates of 20% and 40%.

Savings income includes interest from banks and building societies, interest distributions from authorised unit trusts, interest on gilts and other securities including corporate bonds, purchased life annuities and discounts.

Where income does not exceed the basic rate limit, there will be no further tax to pay on savings income from which the 20% tax rate has been deducted, and any tax over-deducted is repayable. Higher rate taxpayers are liable to pay tax at 40% on that part of their savings income falling above the higher rate limit.

From 6 April 1999, savings income is generally treated as the second top slice of income behind dividends.

Non-taxpayers may apply to have interest paid without deduction of tax where their total income is expected to be covered by personal allowances. Taxpayers who are entitled to a refund of tax deducted from interest can claim the refund using form R40. The Revenue have launched a *Taxback* website page to simplify repayments: www.inlandrevenue.gov.uk/taxback

Taxation of dividends: UK and foreign dividends (except those foreign dividends taxed under the remittance basis) form the top slice of taxable income. From 6 April 1999, special rates apply to dividend income following the reduction of the tax credit to 10%. Where income does not exceed the basic rate limit the rate is 10% so that the liability is met by the tax credit. Higher rate taxpayers are liable to pay tax at 32.5% on that part of their dividend income falling above the basic rate limit. For 1993–94 to 1998–99 inclusive, dividend income was chargeable at the 20% and 40% rates as for savings income above.
See FA 1999 s 22; TA 1988 s 1A.

Rate applicable to trusts: 1996–97 onwards: 34%, 1993–94 to 1995–96: 35%.

Schedule F trust rate: 1999–2000 onwards: 25%.

Construction industry sub-contractors rate of deduction at source: 2000–01 onwards: 18%, 1999-2000 and before: basic rate of tax.

Table of income tax reliefs

	2001-02	2000-01
Personal allowance (under 65)	£4,535	£4,385
Married couple's allowance[2] (from 6 April 2000 available only where either spouse is aged 65 or over at 5 April 2000, see Age allowance below) Monthly reduction in year of marriage	— —	— —
Children's tax credit[1]	£520	—
Age allowance Abatement of relief by £1 for every £2 income over.. Personal allowance (under 75)... Not beneficial if individual's total income exceeds .... Married couple's allowance (elder spouse under 75) either spouse born before 6 April 1935.................................. Minimum married couple's allowance where income exceeds limit[2] .... Not beneficial if husband: under 65 and his total income exceeds .... 65-74 and his total income exceeds............................ Personal allowance (75 and over).. Not beneficial if individual's total income exceeds .... Married couple's allowance[2] (either spouse 75 or over).. Minimum married couple's allowance where income exceeds limit[2] .... Not beneficial if husband: under 65 and his total income exceeds .... 65-74 and his total income exceeds............................ 75 or over and his total income exceeds....................	£17,600 £5,990 £20,510 £5,365 £2,070 £24,190 £27,100 £6,260 £21,050 £5,435 £2,070 £24,330 £27,240 £27,780	£17,000 £5,790 £19,810 £5,185 £2,000 £23,370 £26,180 £6,050 £20,330 £5,255 £2,000 £23,510 £26,320 £26,840
Widow's bereavement allowance[2] (available only where the death occurred before 6 April 2000 and the wife had not remarried before that date)	—	£2,000
Additional relief for children[2]	—	—
Blind person (each)	£1,450	£1,400
Mortgage interest relief Limit on amount available for relief.. Relief restricted to	— —	— —
Life assurance relief For contracts made before 14 March 1984 *only*, given by deduction	12·5%	12·5%
NI Class 2 Small earnings exception	£3,955	£3,825
NI Class 4 *Band* *Maximum payable*	£4,535–£29,900 £25,365 @ 7% £1,775·55	£4,385–£27,820 £23,435 @ 7% £1,640·45
Starting rate (before 1999–2000, lower rate) of tax Band	10% £1,880	10% £1,520
Basic rate of tax Band	22% £27,520	22% £26,880

[1] The relief is withdrawn at the rate of £1 for every £15 of income chargeable to income tax at the higher rate.
[2] Relief is restricted to 10% of figure quoted from 1999–2000 and 15% from 1995–96 to 1998–99 and is given as a reduction in tax liability.

1999-2000	1998-99	1997-98	1996-97	1995-96
£4,335	£4,195	£4,045	£3,765	£3,525[3]
£1,970 £164·16	£1,900 £158·33	£1,830 £152·50	£1,790 £149·17	£1,720 £143·33
—	—	—	—	—
£16,800 £5,720	£16,200 £5,410	£15,600 £5,220	£15,200 £4,910	£14,600 £4,630
£19,570	£18,630	£17,950	£17,490	£16,810
£5,125	£3,305	£3,185	£3,115	£2,995
£1,970	£1,900	£1,830	£1,790	£1,720
£23,110 £25,880 £5,980	£19,010 £21,440 £5,600	£18,310 £20,660 £5,400	£17,850 £20,140 £5,090	£17,150 £19,360 £4,800
£20,090	£19,010	£18,310	£17,850	£17,150
£5,195	£3,345	£3,225	£3,155	£3,035
£1,970	£1,900	£1,830	£1,790	£1,720
£23,250 £26,020 £26,540	£19,090 £21,520 £21,900	£18,390 £20,740 £21,100	£17,930 £20,220 £20,580	—[4] £19,440 £19,780
£1,970	£1,900	£1,830	£1,790	£1,720
£1,970	£1,900	£1,830	£1,790	£1,720
£1,380	£1,330	£1,280	£1,250	£1,200
£30,000 10%	£30,000 10%	£30,000 15%	£30,000 15%	£30,000 15%
12·5%	12·5%	12·5%	12·5%	12·5%
£3,770	£3,590	£3,480	£3,430	£3,260
£7,530-£26,000 £18,470 @ 6% £1,108·20	£7,310-£25,220 £17,910 @ 6% £1,074·60	£7,010-£24,180 £17,170 @ 6% £1,030·20	£6,860-£23,660 £16,800 @ 6% £1,008	£6,640-£22,880 £16,240 @ 7·3% £1,185·52[5]
10% £1,500	20% £4,300	20% £4,100	20% £3,900	20% £3,200
23% £26,500	23% £22,800	23% £22,000	24% £21,600	25% £21,100

[3] Transitional relief: a married man under 65 may in certain circumstances claim a £3,540 personal allowance if his wife was 75 or over on 5 April 1990 (subject to abatement if his total income exceeds £14,600 in 1995-96).

[4] Varies depending on personal allowance: see above and note[3].

[5] Before 6 April 1996 50% of class 4 contribution paid is deductible from total income.

Car benefits

PRIVATE USE

Basic cash equivalent 1999–2000 to 2001–02*

List price of car plus extra qualifying accessories[1] *less* capital contributions[2] by employee[3,4].

Multiplied by –

35% where business mileage is under 2,500[5] miles.
25% where business mileage is at least 2,500[5] but less than 18,000[5] miles.
15% where business mileage is 18,000[5] miles or more[6].

Adjustments

1. Reduce cash equivalent by –
¼ where car is 4 years old or more at end of year of assessment.
2. Reduce adjusted cash equivalent in **1** proportionately where car is not available throughout year of assessment.
3. Reduce adjusted cash equivalent in **2** by amount of payments by employee for private use.

Basic cash equivalent 1994–95 to 1998–99*

35% x (list price of car plus extra qualifying accessories[1] *less* capital contributions[2] by employee[3])[4].

Adjustments

1. Reduce *basic cash equivalent* by –
1/3 where business mileage is at least 2,500[5] but less than 18,000[5] miles
2/3 where business mileage is 18,000[5] miles or more[6].
2. Reduce *adjusted cash equivalent* in **1** by –
1/3 where car is 4 years old or more at end of year of assessment.
3. Reduce *adjusted cash equivalent* in **2** proportionately where car is not available throughout year of assessment.
4. Reduce *adjusted cash equivalent* in **3** by amount of payments by employee for private use.

---

[1] Excluding an accessory provided after car was made available if it was provided before 1 August 1993 or its list price was less than £100. From 6 April 1995 accessories designed for use only by disabled people are also excluded. From 1998–99 where a car is manufactured so as to be capable of running on road fuel gas, its price is proportionately reduced by so much of that price as is reasonably attributable to it being manufactured in that way. Where a new car is converted to run on road fuel gas, the equipment is not regarded as an accessory.
[2] Up to £5,000.
[3] List price as adjusted capped at £80,000.
[4] Classic cars (aged 15 years or more and with a market value of £15,000 or more at end of year of assessment): substitute market value at end of year of assessment if this is higher than adjusted list price. £80,000 cap and reduction for capital contributions apply.
[5] Mileage figures are reduced proportionately where car is not available for whole year.
[6] For second and subsequent cars there is no reduction if business mileage is under 18,000 miles; **from 1999-2000** reduce basic cash equivalent to 25% if business mileage is 18,000 miles or more (from 1994-95 to 1998-99 the basic cash equivalent was reduced by 1/3).

From 6 April 2002: The existing income tax charge based on 35% of the car's price (subject to certain reductions) is to be abolished. It will be replaced by a charge on a percentage of the car's price graduated according to the level of the car's carbon dioxide emissions measured in grams per kilometre (g/km) and rounded down to the nearest 5 g/km: FA 2000 s 59, Sch 11. The following table shows how it is proposed that cars will be taxed in the first three years from 2002–03:

CO_2 emissions in grams per kilometre			Percentage of car's price taxed	CO_2 emissions in grams per kilometre			Percentage of car's price taxed
2002–03	2003–04	2004–05		2002–03	2003–04	2004–05	
165	155	145	15[1]	220	210	200	26[1]
170	160	150	16[1]	225	215	205	27[1]
175	165	155	17[1]	230	220	210	28[1]
180	170	160	18[1]	235	225	215	29[1]
185	175	165	19[1]	240	230	220	30[1]
190	180	170	20[1]	245	235	225	31[1]
195	185	175	21[1]	250	240	230	32[1]
200	190	180	22[1]	255	245	235	33[2]
205	195	185	23[1]	260	250	240	34[3]
210	200	190	24[1]	265	255	245	35[4]
215	205	195	25[1]				

Supplement if car runs solely on diesel:
[1]Add 3%. [2]Add 2%. [3]Add 1%. [4]Maximum charge and so no diesel supplement.
The benefit will be reduced for employee contributions up to £5,000 and where the car is unavailable for part of the year. Further details are available on the internet at www.inlandrevenue.gov.uk/cars.
*This formula is also used to calculate the national insurance contributions payable by employers on the benefit of cars they provide for the private use of their employees, see p 87.

Car benefits — continued

FUEL		(For VAT on fuel, see p 94)
2001-02		
Cylinder capacity: (non-diesel cars)	1,400 cc or less Over 1,400 cc up to 2,000 cc Over 2,000 cc	£1,930 £2,460 £3,620
Cylinder capacity: (diesel cars)	2,000 cc or less Over 2,000 cc	£2,460 £3,620
No internal combustion engine		£3,620
2000-01		
Cylinder capacity: (non-diesel cars)	1,400 cc or less Over 1,400 cc up to 2,000 cc Over 2,000 cc	£1,700 £2,170 £3,200
Cylinder capacity: (diesel cars)	2,000 cc or less Over 2,000 cc	£2,170 £3,200
No internal combustion engine		£3,200
1999-2000		
Cylinder capacity: (non-diesel cars)	1,400 cc or less Over 1,400 cc up to 2,000 cc Over 2,000 cc	£1,210 £1,540 £2,270
Cylinder capacity: (diesel cars)	2,000 cc or less Over 2,000 cc	£1,540 £2,270
No internal combustion engine		£2,270
1998-99		
Cylinder capacity: (non-diesel cars)	1,400 cc or less Over 1,400 cc up to 2,000 cc Over 2,000 cc	£1,010 £1,280 £1,890
Cylinder capacity: (diesel cars)	2,000 cc or less Over 2,000 cc	£1,280 £1,890
No internal combustion engine		£1,890
1997-98		
Cylinder capacity: (non-diesel cars)	1,400 cc or less Over 1,400 cc up to 2,000 cc Over 2,000 cc	£800 £1,010 £1,490
Cylinder capacity: (diesel cars)	2,000 cc or less Over 2,000 cc	£740 £940
No internal combustion engine		£1,490
1996-97		
Cylinder capacity: (non-diesel cars)	1,400 cc or less Over 1,400 cc up to 2,000 cc Over 2,000 cc	£710 £890 £1,320
Cylinder capacity: (diesel cars)	2,000 cc or less Over 2,000 cc	£640 £820
No internal combustion engine		£1,320
1995-96:		
Cylinder capacity: (non-diesel cars)	1,400 cc or less Over 1,400 cc up to 2,000 cc Over 2,000 cc	£670 £850 £1,260
Cylinder capacity: (diesel cars)	2,000 cc or less Over 2,000 cc	£605 £780
No internal combustion engine		£1,260

Fuel benefit reduced to *nil* if the employee is required to make good whole cost of private fuel.

Note: This table is also used to calculate the national insurance contributions payable by employers on the benefit of free fuel they provide for the private use of employees, see p 87.

Car benefits — continued

	VANS: PRIVATE USE INCLUDING FUEL	
	Under 4 years old[1]	4 years old or more[1]
1993-94 onwards: Vehicle design weight:		
up to 3.5 tonnes	£500	£350
over 3.5 tonnes	—	—
[1] At the end of the relevant year of assessment.		

Fixed profit car scheme: tax-free allowances for business travel[1]

Business mileage	Engine size Up to 1,000cc	1,001–1,500cc	1,501–2,000cc	Over 2,000cc	One rate[2]
2001-02					
Up to 4,000 miles	40p	40p	45p	63p	—
Excess over 4,000 miles	25p	25p	25p	36p	—
1997-98 to 2000-01:[3,4]					
Up to 4,000 miles	28p	35p	45p	63p	40p
Excess over 4,000 miles	17p	20p	25p	36p	22·5p
1996-97:[3]					
Up to 4,000 miles	27p	34p	43p	61p	38.5p
Excess over 4,000 miles	16p	19p	23p	33p	21p
1995-96:[3]					
Up to 4,000 miles	27p	34p	43p	60p	38.5p
Excess over 4,000 miles	15p	19p	23p	32p	21p

[1] From 1996–97, employees using their own car may claim these rates as a tax-free allowance or as a deduction whether or not their employer operates the scheme (1995) SWTI 1879.
[2] Where the same rate of mileage allowance is paid irrespective of the engine size, a fixed rate based on the average of the two middle bands is used.
[3] Subject to transitional relief.
[4] The rates remain unchanged for 1998-99 to 2000-01 (IR Press Release of 8 December 1997 (1997) SWTI 1583, 7 December 1998 (1998) SWTI 1692 and 14 December 1999 (2000) SWTI 7).

Pedal cycles: From 6 April 1999, employees using their bicycle for business cycling are allowed to receive a tax-free mileage rate of up to 12p per mile. Where the employee is not paid by the employer for business cycling, the employee is able to claim tax relief on 12p per business mile (or on the balance up to 12p per mile if the employer pays less than this rate (1999) SWTI 430, (2000) SWTI 7).

Motorcycles: From 6 April 2000, employees using their motorcycle for business travel are allowed to receive a tax-free mileage allowance at up to 24p per mile. Where the employee is not paid by the employer for using the motorcycle, the employee is able to claim tax relief on 24p per business mile (or on the balance up to 24p per mile if the employer pays less than this rate (2000) SWTI 7).

A new system will be introduced from 6 April 2002 (see TA 1988 ss 197 AD–197 AH, Sch 12AA). Except in the case of the rate applying in respect of passengers, if the employer pays less than the statutory rate, the employee can claim tax relief on the difference.

2002-03	
Cars and vans	**Rate per mile**
Annual business mileage up to 10,000 miles	40p
Each additional mile over 10,000 miles	25p
Each passenger making same business trip	5p
Motor cycles	24p
Bicycles	20p

Bus services

From 6 April 1999 onwards: No taxable benefit in respect of the provision of works buses with a seating capacity of 12 or more, provided to employees (or their children) to travel to and from work (TA 1988 s 197AA; FA 1999 s 48). The maximum seating capacity is reduced to 9 from 2002–03 onwards where the vehicle was originally constructed to carry that number of seats (FA 2001 s 60).

Cycles and cyclist's safety equipment

From 6 April 1999 onwards: No taxable benefit in respect of the provision to employees of bicycles or cycling safety equipment for travel to and from work (TA 1988 s 197AC; FA 1999 s 50).

Parking facilities

No taxable benefit for work place provision of car parking spaces, or, from 6 April 1999, parking for bicycles or motorcycles (TA 1988 ss 141, 142, 155, 197A; FA 1999 s 49).

Mobile telephones

6 April 1999 onwards: no taxable benefit

Cash equivalent of benefit from 6 April 1991 to 5 April 1999   £200

Expensive cars: restricted allowances

Writing-down allowances
(CAA 2001 ss 74, 75)

Expenditure incurred after 10 March 1992
Cars costing more than £12,000 and bought outright, on hire purchase or by way of a lease with option to purchase: writing-down allowance limited to £3,000 per annum.

Expenditure incurred before 11 March 1992
Cars costing more than £8,000 and bought outright, on hire purchase or by way of a lease with option to purchase: writing-down allowance limited to £2,000 per annum.

Restriction on deduction for hire charge
(TA 1988 ss 578A, 578B)

Contracts made after 10 March 1992
If a car with a retail price when new of more than £12,000 is acquired under a rental lease the maximum allowable deduction in computing Schedule D Case I or II profits is —

$$\frac{£12,000 + P}{2P} \times R$$

P = retail price of car when new
R = annual rental

Working families' and disabled person's tax credits

The Working Families' Tax Credit (WFTC) and the Disabled Person's Tax Credit (DPTC) were introduced in October 1999 to replace Family Credit and Disability Working Allowance. The tax credits have been payable to working families depending on their circumstances from 5 October 1999 and from April 2000, are administered by employers and paid through the PAYE system. The credits do not form part of taxable income and normally last for 26 weeks.

Working families' tax credit[1]	Weekly 9.4.01 onwards £	Weekly 11.4.00–8.4.01 £
Adult credit – basic	54.00/59.00	53.15
– working 30 hours	11.45	11.25
Child credit – under 16	26.00	21.25/25.60
– 16–18	26.75	26.35
Disabled child tax credit	30.00	22.25
Enhanced disability tax credit – lone parent/couple	16.00	—
– child[2]	41.05	—
Childcare credit (70% of eligible costs) – 1 child (max)	100.00/135.00	100.00
– 2 or more children (max)	150.00/200.00	150.00
Earnings at which credit is reduced by 55%	92.90	91.45
Capital – upper limit	8,000	8,000
– amount disregarded	3,000	3,000

Disabled person's tax credit[1]	Weekly 9.4.01 onwards £	Weekly 11.4.00–8.4.01 £
Adult credit – single	56.05/61.05	55.15
– couples/lone parents	86.25/91.25	84.90
– working 30 hours	11.45	11.25
Child credit – under 16	26.00	21.25/25.60
– 16–18	26.75	26.35
Disabled child tax credit	30.00	22.25
Enhanced disability tax credit – lone parent/couple	16.00	—
– single person	11.05	—
– child[2]	41.05	—
Childcare credit (70% of eligible costs) – 1 child (max)	100.00/135.00	100.00
– 2 or more children (max)	150.00/200.00	150.00
Earnings at which credit is reduced by 55% – single	72.25	71.10
– couples/lone parents	92.90	91.45
Capital – upper limit	16,000	16,000
– amount disregarded	3,000	3,000

[1] Higher rates apply from June 2001 and June 2000 respectively.
[2] Includes the disabled child tax credit for relevant awards starting from April 2001.

Flat rate expenses

For most classes of industry flat rate allowances for the upkeep of tools and special clothing have been agreed between the Revenue and the trade unions concerned. Alternatively, the individual employee may claim as a deduction his or her actual expenses (Concession A1). Rates for healthcare and fire service employees have been introduced (see (1999) SWTI 353). They were added to Concession A1 in the 2000 edition of IR1.

Industry code	Industry	Occupation	Deduction from 1995–96
10	Agriculture	All workers	70
100	Aluminium	(a) Continual casting operators, process operators, de-dimplers, driers, drill punchers, dross unloaders, firemen, furnace operators and their helpers, leaders, mouldmen, pourers, remelt department labourers, roll flatteners	130
		(b) Cable hands, case makers, labourers, mates, truck drivers and measurers, storekeepers	60
		(c) Apprentices	45
		(d) All other workers	100
330	Banks	Uniformed bank employees	40
90	Brass and Copper	All workers	100
270	Building	(a) Joiners and carpenters	105
		(b) Cement works and roofing felt and asphalt labourers	55
		(c) Labourers and navvies	40
		(d) All other workers	85
250	Building Materials	(a) Stone-masons	85
		(b) Tilemakers and labourers	40
		(c) All other workers	55
190	Clothing	(a) Lacemakers, hosiery bleachers, dyers, scourers and knitters, knitwear bleachers and dyers	45
		(b) All other workers	30
150	Constructional Engineering	(a) Blacksmiths and their strikers, burners, caulkers, chippers, drillers, erectors, fitters, holders up, markers off, platers, riggers, riveters, rivet heaters, scaffolders, sheeters, template workers, turners, welders	115
		(b) Banksmen, labourers, shop-helpers, slewers, straighteners	60
		(c) Apprentices and storekeepers	45
		(d) All other workers	75
170	Electrical and Electricity Supply	(a) Those workers incurring laundry costs only (generally CEGB employees)	25
		(b) All other workers	90
110	Engineering	(a) Pattern makers	120
		(b) Labourers, supervisory and unskilled workers	60
		(c) Apprentices and storekeepers	45
		(d) Motor mechanics in garage repair shops	100
		(e) All other workers	100
Not known	Fire service (see above)	Uniformed fire fighters and fire officers	60
220	Food	All workers	40
20	Forestry	All workers	70
240	Glass	All workers	60
Not known	Healthcare (see above)	(a) Ambulance staff on active service	110
		(b) Nurses and midwives, chiropodists, dental nurses, occupational, speech and other therapists, phlebotomists, physiotherapists, radiographers	70
		(c) Plaster room orderlies, hospital porters, ward clerks, sterile supply workers, hospital domestics, hospital catering staff	60
		(d) Laboratory staff, pharmacists, pharmacy assistants	45
		(e) Uniformed ancillary staff maintenance workers, grounds staff, drivers, parking attendants and security guards, receptionists and other uniformed staff	45
280	Heating	(a) Pipe fitters and plumbers	100
		(b) Coverers, laggers, domestic glaziers, heating engineers and their mates	90
		(c) All gas workers, all other workers	70
50	Iron Mining	(a) Fillers, miners and underground workers	100
		(b) All other workers	75
70	Iron and Steel	(a) Day labourers, general labourers, stockmen, time keepers, warehouse staff and weighmen	60
		(b) Apprentices	45
		(c) All other workers	120

Flat rate expenses — continued

Industry code	Industry	Occupation	Deduction from 1995–96
210	Leather	(a) Curriers (wet workers), fellmongering workers, tanning operatives (wet) (b) All other workers	55 40
140	Particular Engineering	(a) Pattern makers (b) All chainmakers; cleaners, galvanisers, tinners and wire drawers in the wire drawing industry; tool-makers in the lock making industry (c) Apprentices and storekeepers (d) All other workers	120 100 45 60
355	Police Force	Uniformed police officers (ranks up to and including Chief Inspector)	55
160	Precious Metals	All workers	70
230	Printing	(a) Letterpress Section Electrical engineers (rotary presses), electrotypers, ink and roller makers, machine minders (rotary), maintenance engineers (rotary presses) and stereotypers (b) Bench hands (P & B), compositors (Lp), readers (Lp), T & E Section wire room operators, warehousemen (Ppr box) (c) All other workers	105 30 70
320	Prisons	Uniformed prison officers	55
300	Public Service	(i) Dock and Inland Waterways (a) Dockers, dredger drivers, hopper steerers (b) All other workers (ii) Public Transport (a) Garage hands (including cleaners) (b) Conductors and drivers	 55 40 55 40
60	Quarrying	All workers	70
290	Railways	(See the appropriate category for craftsmen, e.g. engineers, vehicle builders etc.) All other workers	70
30	Seamen	(a) Carpenters (Seamen) Passenger liners (b) Carpenters (Seamen) Cargo vessels, tankers, coasters and ferries (c) Other seamen Passenger liners (d) Other seamen Cargo vessels, tankers, coasters and ferries	165 130 nil nil
120	Shipyards	(a) Blacksmiths and their strikers, boilermakers, burners, carpenters, caulkers, drillers, furnacemen (platers), holders up, fitters, platers, plumbers, riveters, sheet iron workers, shipwrights, tubers, welders (b) Labourers (c) Apprentices and storekeepers (d) All other workers	115 60 45 75
200	Textile Prints	All workers	60
180	Textiles	(a) Carders, carding engineers, overlookers (all), technicians in spinning mills (b) All other workers	85 60
130	Vehicles	(a) Builders, railway wagon etc. repairers, and railway wagon lifters (b) Railway vehicle painters and letterers, railway wagon etc. builders' and repairers' assistants (c) All other workers	105 60 40
260	Wood & Furniture	(a) Carpenters, cabinet makers, joiners, wood carvers and woodcutting machinists (b) Artificial limb makers (other than in wood), organ builders and packing case makers (c) Coopers not providing own tools, labourers, polishers and upholsterers (d) All other workers	115 90 45 75

1) 'Industry code' is an industry identification term used for Inland Revenue computer purposes.
2) The expressions 'all workers' and 'all other workers' refer only to manual workers who have to bear the cost of upkeep of tools and special clothing. They do not extend to other employees such as office staff.

Loan benefits and official rate of interest

A director, or an employee earning £8,500 or more a year, who receives a loan by reason of his or her employment may be charged to tax on the cash equivalent of the benefit for the year (TA 1988 s 160, Sch 7).

From 6 April 1994, there is no charge to tax if either:
(a) all the beneficial loans provided by reason of the employment; or
(b) all the beneficial loans, excluding loans qualifying for tax relief, do not exceed £5,000.

The cash equivalent is calculated using the difference between the interest paid (if any) and the official rate of interest.

In January 2000 it was announced that the official rate of interest will be set, in advance, for the whole of the following tax year (although this policy may be changed if typical mortgage rates fall sharply during the year). Under this policy, the official rate of interest is set to remain at 6.25% for 1999-00, 2000-01 and 2001-02: (2000) SWTI 95, (2001) SWTI 192.

The official rate of interest is set out below.

Date	Rate
From 6 March 1999	6.25%
6 August 1997–5 March 1999	7.25%
6 November 1996–5 August 1997	6.75%
6 June 1996–5 November 1996	7%
6 February 1996–5 June 1996	7.25%
6 October 1995–5 February 1996	7.75%
6 November 1994–5 October 1995	8%
6 January 1994–5 November 1994	7·5%
6 March 1993–5 January 1994	7·75%
6 January 1993–5 March 1993	8·25%
6 December 1992–5 January 1993	9%
6 November 1992–5 December 1992	9·75%
6 June 1992–5 November 1992	10·5%
6 March 1992–5 June 1992	10·75%
6 October 1991–5 March 1992	11·25%
6 August 1991–5 October 1991	11·75%
6 July 1991–5 August 1991	12·25%
6 May 1991–5 July 1991	12·75%
6 April 1991–5 May 1991	13·5%
6 March 1991–5 April 1991	14·5%
6 November 1990–5 March 1991	15·5%
6 November 1989–5 November 1990	16·5%
6 July 1989–5 November 1989	15·5%
6 January 1989–5 July 1989	14·5%
6 October 1988–5 January 1989	13·5%
6 August 1988–5 October 1988	12%
6 May 1988–5 August 1988	9·5%
6 December 1987–5 May 1988	10·5%
6 September 1987–5 December 1987	11·5%
6 June 1987–5 September 1987	10·5%
6 April 1987–5 June 1987	11·5%
6 October 1982–5 April 1987	12%

	1993–94	1994–95	1995–96	1996–97	1997–98	1998–99
Average official rate of interest	7·688%	7·7%	7·79%	6·93%	7·08%	7·16%

Note
From 6 April 1994, loans made on commercial terms by employers who lend predominantly to the general public are generally exempt.

Foreign currency loans

Currency	Date	Rate
Swiss franc	From 6 July 1994	5·5%
	6 June 1994 – 5 July 1994	5·7%
Japanese yen	From 6 June 1994	3·9%

Loans of computer equipment

From 6 April 1999 onwards: No taxable benefit in respect of loan to employees (provided loans are not restricted to directors or senior staff) of computer equipment for private home use, the value of the equipment and related expenses not to exceed £2,500 (TA 1988 s 156A).

Relocation expenses and benefits
Qualifying removal benefits and expenses[1]

Date of move	Limit
After 5 April 1993	£8,000

[1] The statutory relief covers the following expenses and benefits (TA 1988 Sch 11A) —
  (a) *disposal expenses and benefits* (legal and advertising expenses in connection with the disposal of accommodation, penalty for redeeming a mortgage, auctioneers' and estate agents' fees, disconnection of public utilities, rent, maintenance and insurance costs while the property is unoccupied);
  (b) *acquisition expenses and benefits* (legal expenses in connection with the acquisition of an interest in a new main residence, loan fees, mortgage indemnity insurance costs, survey and land registry fees, stamp duty, connection of public utilities). (NB: similar expenses and benefits are covered in respect of abortive acquisitions, if the property would have been the employee's new residence but the acquisition does not proceed either for reasons outside the employee's control or because he or she reasonably declines to proceed);
  (c) *transportation of domestic belongings* (including insurance costs);
  (d) *travelling and subsistence expenses and benefits* (for temporary visits to new residence before relocation; travel from old residence to new place of work or from new residence to old place of work where date of move and relocation of work do not coincide; subsistence and travel costs of child under 19 relocating before or after parents for educational reasons; benefit of a car or van for use in connection with the relocation where it is not otherwise available for private use);
  (e) *bridging loan expenses and beneficial bridging loans* (relief is given on any charge to interest at the official rate on a beneficial loan to the extent that the aggregate value of other qualifying benefits and expenses falls short of the maximum exempt amount);
  (f) *duplicate expenses and benefits in respect of new residence* (replacement domestic items).

Approved employee share schemes
Inland Revenue share schemes web page: www.inlandrevenue.gov.uk/shareschemes

All-employee share ownership plans
(TCGA 1992 s 236A, Sch 7C; FA 2000 ss 47, 48 Schs 8, 9) Applications for approval of Employee Share Ownership Plans can be made from 28 July 2000.

Free share plan

	Annual maximum
2000-01 onwards	£3,000

Partnership share plan

	Monthly maximum
2000-01 onwards	£125

Matching shares

2000-01 onwards	Maximum number of shares given by employer to employee for each partnership share bought	2

Reliefs
Where the conditions of the scheme are complied with–
  (a) Free share plans: employers can give shares to employees free of income tax and national insurance contributions. (Some or all of these shares may be awarded for reaching performance targets.)
  (b) Partnership share plans: employees may allocate part of their pre-tax salary to buy shares in their employing company without income tax or national insurance contributions being payable.
  (c) Generally, all shares held in a plan for five years, will be free of income tax and national insurance contributions.
  (d) No capital gains tax is payable on the withdrawal of shares from the plan and they are deemed to be acquired at their market value at that time.
  (e) There is no stamp duty charge when the employee buys shares from trustees of the plan (FA 2000 Sch 8 para 116A; FA 2001 s 95).
  (f) If shares are taken out of a plan within between three and five years, income tax and national insurance contributions will be payable on the lower of their initial value and their value on leaving the plan.
  (g) Dividends paid on the shares are tax free (up to a £1,500 annual limit) provided they are used to acquire additional shares in the company.
  (h) The costs of the plan will be deductible from profits for tax purposes.

Main conditions for relief
1 There is a limit on the value of the shares that can be purchased or allocated under the scheme.
2 Free and matching shares must normally be kept in the plan for at least three years. (Employees can take partnership shares out of the plan at any time.)
3 Shares must be taken out of the plan when the employee ceases to be employed by the company. (Some employees may lose their free and matching shares if they leave within three years of getting the shares.)

Enterprise management incentives
FA 2000 s 62, Sch 14; FA 2001 s 62, Sch 14

With effect from 28 July 2000, independent trading companies with gross assets not exceeding £15 million may grant share options then worth up to £100,000 to an eligible employee without income tax or NIC consequences (except to the extent that the option is to acquire shares at less than their market value). The total value of shares in respect of which unexercised qualifying options exist must not exceed £3 million. (For options granted before 11 May 2001 the number of employees who could hold options at any one time was limited to 15, giving an overall limit of £1.5 million.) Capital gains tax will be payable when the shares are sold, but business assets taper relief (see p 37) will be available and will begin to run from the date on which the options are granted.

Company share option plans
(TA 1988 ss 185, 187 and Sch 9; FA 1996 s 114 and Sch 16)
Limit on value of shares under option held by employee at any one time

From 29 April 1996	£30,000

Reliefs
Where the conditions of the scheme are complied with, no Schedule E charge arises on the employee in respect of –
  (a) the grant of an option to acquire shares;
  (b) the exercise of the option; or
  (c) any increase in the value of the shares.

Capital gains tax is chargeable on disposal of the shares: the CGT base cost is the consideration given by the employee for both the shares and the option.

Approved employee share schemes — continued

Main conditions for relief
1. There is a limit (see above) on the value of shares under option held by an employee at any one time (the value being that of the shares at the time the options are granted).
2. Options must be granted at a share price not manifestly less than the market value at the date of the grant.
3. The scheme shares must be fully paid up, not redeemable and not subject to special restrictions.
4. Only full time directors or qualifying employees may participate in the scheme.
5. Options must be exercised between 3 and 10 years after the grant, and not less than 3 years after the last exercise by the participator of an option (under the same or another approved company share option plan).

Approved savings related share option schemes
(TA 1988 ss 185, 187, Sch 9)

Monthly contributions to SAYE scheme

	Maximum £	Minimum £
1 October 1998[3]	250	5–10[2]
1 April 1996–30 September 1998[1]	250	5–10[2]
1 September 1991–31 March 1996[1]	250	10 or under
1 September 1989–31 August 1991	150	10 or under

[1] The Treasury issued a new prospectus in April 1996: Booklet IR98 para 5.4.
[2] The company may choose a minimum savings contribution between £5 and £10.
[3] The Treasury issued a new prospectus applying from 1 October 1998 (see (1998) SWTI 1118).

Approved SAYE contracts: bonus and interest payments on termination

Date of termination	Amount payable – contracts to 30 September 1998	Amount payable – contracts from 1 October
3-year contract		
After at least 1 but less than 3 years	Refund of contributions plus simple interest at 3% p.a.	Refund of contributions plus simple interest at 3% p.a.
After 3 years	Refund of contributions plus bonus of 3 months' contributions	Refund of contributions plus bonus of 2.75 times the monthly contributions
5-year contract		
After at least 1 but less than 5 years	Refund of contributions plus simple interest at 3% p.a.	Refund of contributions plus simple interest at 3% p.a.
After 5 years	Refund of contributions plus bonus of 9 months' contributions	Refund of contributions plus bonus of 7.5 times the monthly contributions
After at least 5 but less than 7 years	Refund of contributions plus bonus of 9 months' contributions and compound interest at 3% p.a. for period after first 5 years	Refund of contributions plus bonus of 7.5 times the monthly contributions and compound interest at 3% p.a. for period after first 5 years
After 7 years	Refund of contributions plus bonus of 18 months' contributions	Refund of contributions plus bonus of 13.5 times the monthly contributions

Reliefs
Where the conditions of the scheme are complied with, no Schedule E charge arises on the employee in respect of –
   (a) the grant of an option to acquire shares;
   (b) the exercise of the option; or
   (c) any increase in the value of the shares.
Capital gains tax is chargeable on disposal of the shares: the CGT base cost is the consideration given by the employee for both the shares and the option.

Main conditions for relief
1. All full time employees must be eligible to participate on similar terms (subject to a minimum service requirement of up to 5 years and material interest exclusions).
2. The scheme must provide for shares to be paid for with an amount of money not exceeding the repayments, bonuses and interest payments made under a linked SAYE scheme.
3. The scheme shares must be fully paid up, not redeemable and not subject to special restrictions.
4. Subject to cessation of employment due to injury, disability, redundancy, retirement or death, share options must not be exercised before the bonus date under the SAYE scheme (3, 5 or 7 years after its commencement, see above).
5. The purchase price of the shares must be stated at the time the option is granted and must not be manifestly less than 80% of their market value.

Approved employee share schemes — continued

Approved profit sharing schemes
(TA 1988 ss 186, 187, Sch 9, 10)

Profit sharing schemes will continue to be approved where applications for approval are received by the Revenue before 6 April 2001. Tax free awards of shares under approved schemes will continue to be allowed up to 31 December 2002: FA 2000 s 49.)

Annual limit on shares appropriated

From 1991–92:	Greater of £3,000 or 10% of salary, up to £8,000
1989–90 and 1990–91:	Greater of £2,000 or 10% of salary, up to £6,000
1988–89:	Greater of £1,250 or 10% of salary, up to £5,000

Schedule E charge on early disposal or receipt of capital from shares

Time of disposal or capital receipt	Percentage charge[1]
Before 3rd anniversary of appropriation[2]	100%[3]

[1] Calculated on the appropriate percentage of the initial market value of the shares when appropriated (or the sales proceeds if less).

[2] If that anniversary falls on or after 29 April 1996. If the 3rd anniversary of the appropriation falls before that date but the 5th anniversary falls after it, the 100% charge arises if the disposal or capital receipt takes place before 29 April 1996. Where the 5th anniversary fell before 29 April 1996, the following charges applied:

Time of disposal or capital receipt	Percentage charge
Before 4th anniversary of appropriation	100%[4]
Between 4th and 5th anniversary of appropriation	75%[4]
After 5th anniversary of appropriation	nil

[3] The charge is reduced to 50% where the employee reaches the retirement age specified in the scheme rules or leaves the employment due to injury, disability or redundancy before the shares are sold or capital is received.

[4] The charge was reduced to 50% where the employee reached the retirement age specified in the scheme rules or left the employment due to injury, disability or redundancy within 5 years of the appropriation.

Reliefs

Where the conditions of the scheme are satisfied, no Schedule E charge arises on the employee in respect of –
  (a) the value of the shares at the time of appropriation;
  (b) any increase in the value of the shares; or
  (c) any gain on the disposal of the shares (although capital gains tax is chargeable on any gain over the market value on appropriation).

Main conditions for relief

1. Shares in a company (or its parent company) must be acquired by trustees of the scheme and allocated to employee participants.
2. All employees must be eligible to participate on similar terms (subject to a minimum service requirement of up to 5 years and material interest exclusions).
3. The annual value of shares appropriated must not exceed the statutory maximum (see above).
4. The shares used in the scheme must be fully paid up, not redeemable and not subject to special restrictions.
5. Participants must permit the scheme trustees to hold the shares for the retention period (two years from the date of appropriation, unless the participant ceases to be employed before that date by reason of injury, disability, redundancy, retirement or death).
6. Shares disposed of within a specified period are subject to a Schedule E charge (see above).

Executive share option schemes
(TA 1988 ss 185, 187, Sch 9)

NOTE: The income tax relief in respect of the grant and exercise of options under executive schemes was withdrawn with effect for options granted after 17 July 1995, subject to transitional provisions (see Revenue Press Release dated 28 November 1995). In general, options granted under an approved scheme after 16 July 1995 qualify for tax relief only if they meet the conditions for approved company share option plans (see above).

Limit on market value of unexercised options

Greater of £100,000 or 4 times emoluments subject to PAYE (excluding benefits).

Reliefs

Where the conditions of the scheme are satisfied, no Schedule E charge arises on the employee in respect of –
  (a) the grant or exercise of the option; or
  (b) any increase in value of the shares.

Capital gains tax is chargeable on disposal of the shares: the CGT base cost is the consideration given by the employee for both the shares and the option.

Main conditions for relief
1. The market value of shares over which a participant holds unexercised options must not exceed the statutory limit (see above).
2. The purchase price of the shares must be stated at the time the option is granted and must not be manifestly less than 85% of their market value.
3. The scheme shares must be fully paid up, not redeemable and not subject to special restrictions.
4. Only full time directors or qualifying employees may participate in the scheme.
5. Options must be exercised between 3 and 10 years after the grant, and not less than 3 years after the last exercise by the participator of an option (under the same or another approved executive scheme).

Profit-related pay schemes

(TA 1988 ss 169–184, Sch 8; FA 1997 s 61; FA 1998 s 62)

Limit on tax-free pay

Profit period beginning	*Exempt amount*
After 31 December 1999	no relief
1 January 1999–31 December 1999	lowest of: profit-related pay, 20% of earnings[1] and £1,000
1 January 1998–31 December 1998	lowest of: profit-related pay, 20% of earnings[1] and £2,000
1 April 1991–31 December 1997	lowest of: profit-related pay, 20% of earnings[1] and £4,000
1 April 1989–31 March 1991	lowest of: half profit-related pay, 10% of earnings[1] and £2,000
Before 1 April 1989	lowest of: half profit-related pay, 10% of earnings[1] and £1,500

[1] Emoluments within PAYE (excluding benefits) plus profit-related pay.

Main conditions for relief
1. The scheme must be registered. Schemes can only be established for private sector employments.
2. A scheme must relate to an employment unit (all or part of a business).
3. A scheme must define eligible employees and include at least 80% of the employees in the employment unit.
4. The scheme must operate by reference to defined profit periods and must define the method of calculation of the distributable pool of profit-related pay.

Payments on termination or variation of employment

Exempt lump sum payments

(a) Payments in connection with the cessation of employment on the death, injury or disability of the employee.
(b) Payments under unapproved retirement benefits schemes where the employee has been taxed on the actual or notional contributions to provide the benefit.
(c) Payments under approved retirement benefits schemes which can properly be regarded as a benefit earned by past service.
(d) Certain payments of terminal grants to members of the armed forces.
(e) Certain benefits under superannuation schemes for civil servants in Commonwealth overseas territories.
(f) Payments in respect of foreign service where the period of foreign service comprises –
  (i) 75% of the whole period of service; or
  (ii) the whole of the last 10 years of service; or
  (iii) where the period of service exceeded 20 years, one-half of that period, including any 10 of the last 20 years.
Otherwise, a proportion of the payment is exempt, as follows –

$$\frac{\text{length of foreign service}}{\text{length of total service}} \times \text{amount otherwise chargeable}$$

(g) The first £30,000 of genuine ex gratia payments (where there is no 'arrangement' by the employer to make the payment): TA 1988 s 148.
(h) Statutory redundancy payments (included in computing £30,000 limit in (f) above).

Personal pension schemes, stakeholder pensions and retirement annuities

1 July 1988: Retirement annuity contracts were replaced by personal pension schemes, although retirement annuity premiums may continue to be paid, and tax relief obtained (TA 1988 ss 618-629). There are provisions for the carrying back (TA 1988 s 619) and the carrying forward (TA 1988 s 625) of relief, and these are not affected by FA 2000.

6 April 2001: The personal pension scheme rules were adapted to accommodate the stakeholder pensions provisions (TA 1988 ss 630-655, FA 2000 s 61, Sch 13). From that date, personal pension and stakeholder pension contributions are subject to the same rules.

Tax relief on contributions

Retirement annuities: Premiums continue to be deducted from or set off against relevant earnings (TA 1988 s 619). The amount of relief available is based on a percentage of net relevant earnings (see maximum amount, below).

Personal pension schemes: Before 6 April 2001, premiums were deducted from or set off against relevant earnings (TA 1988 s 639, as enacted). The amount of relief available was based on a percentage of net relevant earnings (see maximum amount, below).

Personal pension schemes/stakeholder pensions:

Contributions not exceeding the earnings threshold:

(1) Contributions of up to £3,600 gross ('the earnings threshold') may be paid into a stakeholder pension by anyone who is not a member of an occupational pension scheme, regardless of the amount (if any) of their earnings (TA 1988 s 632A).

(2) An individual who is a member of an occupational pension scheme but who is not a controlling director and whose total annual remuneration is no more than £30,000 is allowed to pay into both an occupational scheme and a stakeholder pension and will receive tax relief on an annual contribution of up to £3,600 (gross) into the stakeholder pension (TA 1988 s 632B).

Contributions exceeding the earnings threshold:

(1) Contributions in excess of the earnings threshold may be made. Tax relief is given on contributions up to a maximum based on a percentage of net relevant earnings (see maximum percentage below).

(2) For the purpose of supporting contributions in excess of the earnings threshold, a tax year for which evidence of relevant earnings can be provided may be nominated as the basis year and contributions based on the amount of those earnings may be paid in each of the next 5 years (TA 1988 s 646B). The provisions enable an individual to make pension contributions for up to 5 years after the relevant earnings ceased, by reference to the net relevant earnings of a basis year which may be any one of the 6 tax years preceding the first year for which there are no relevant earnings (TA 1988 s 646D).

Carry-back of relief:

Carry-back of relief is provided for in TA 1988 s 641A. There is no carry forward of relief (FA 2000 Sch 13 para 19).

Basic and higher rate relief:

From 6 April 2001, contributions are payable net of basic rate tax relief. Tax relief at the higher rate is given by extending the basic rate band by the amount of the contribution paid in the year of assessment (TA 1988 s 639, as amended by FA 2000 Sch 13 para 15).

From 2001-02, relief for contributions is given up to a maximum which is the greater of:
(a) the 'earnings threshold'; and
(b) the 'maximum percentage' of net relevant earnings for the year

(TA 1988 s 640, as amended by FA 2000 Sch 13 para 16). For the purposes of calculating the maximum percentage, net relevant earnings are subject to an earnings cap (TA 1988 s 640A).

Earnings threshold: from 6 April 2001 onwards £3,600 (TA 1988 s 630(1), as amended)

Maximum amount

Personal pension schemes/ stakeholder pensions (TA 1988 s 640)		
	Age in years at beginning of year of assessment	Maximum percentage
	35 and below	17½
	36 to 45	20
	46 to 50	25
	51 to 55	30
	56 to 60	35
	61 or more	40
Earnings cap	£	
2001-02	95,400	
2000-01	91,800	
1999-00	90,600	
1998-99	87,600	
1997-98	84,000	
1996-97	82,200	

Retirement annuities (TA 1988 s 626)

Age in years at beginning of year of assessment	Maximum percentage
50 and below	17½
51 to 55	20
56 to 60	22½
61 or more	27½

Life insurance element (TA 1988 s 640(3), as amended)

The maximum amount of contributions in respect of life insurance on which tax relief can be given is limited to a percentage of net relevant earnings (retirement annuities; personal pension contracts taken out before 6 April 2001) or of total amount of relevant pension contributions (personal pensions/stakeholder pension contracts taken out after 5 April 2001).

	Maximum percentage of net relevant earnings
Retirement annuities (contracts for dependents or life insurance)	5%
Personal pension schemes (contract of life insurance made before 6 April 2001)	5%

	Maximum percentage of total relevant pension contributions
Personal pension schemes/stakeholder pensions Contract of life insurance made after 5 April 2001	10%

Approval of contracts

Trades and professions for which an early retirement age has been agreed by the Revenue under TA 1988 s 620(4)(c) for the purpose of the approval of retirement annuity contracts are set out below. Under the personal and stakeholder pensions legislation, individuals may not take benefits from their pension arrangements before the age of 50. The trades and professions listed below for which the Revenue has approved an earlier retirement age of 30, 35, 40 or 45 have been approved under TA 1988 s 634(3)(b) for the purposes of personal pension schemes and stakeholder pensions.

Retirement age	Profession or occupation		
30	skiers (downhill)		
35	athletes	ice hockey players	table tennis players
	badminton players	models	tennis players (including real tennis)
	boxers	national hunt jockeys	
	cyclists	Rugby League players	wrestlers
	dancers	Rugby Union players	
	footballers	squash players	
40	cricketers	golfers	motor racing drivers
	divers (saturation, deep sea and free swimming)	motocross motorcycle riders	speedway riders
		motorcycle road racing riders	trapeze artists
			WPBSA snooker players
45	jockeys (flat racing)	members of the reserve forces	
50	circus animal trainers	newscasters (ITV)	Royal Navy reservists
	croupiers	off-shore riggers (mechanical fitters, pipe fitters, riggers, platers, welders and roustabouts)	Rugby League referees
	interdealer brokers		territorial army members
	martial arts instructors		
	moneybroker dealers		
55	air pilots	inshore fishermen	psychiatrists (who are also maximum part time specialists employed within the NHS solely in the treatment of the mentally disordered)
	brass instrumentalists	midwives (female)	
	distant water trawlermen	moneybroker dealer managers and directors responsible for dealers	
	firemen (part-time)		
	health visitors (female)	nurses (female)	singers
		physiotherapists (female)	

Maintenance payments

From 6 April 2000: The transitional relief for payments under pre 15 March 1988 arrangements is ended. Payments are treated in the same way as payments under maintenance arrangements set up on or after 15 March 1988. Tax relief will only be given after 5 April 2000 if one or both parties to the marriage is aged 65 or over at 5 April 2000 (the test that applies for the receipt of a married person's allowance after that date, see p 56).

For court orders or agreements made on or after 15 March 1988, or applied for before 15 March but made after 30 June 1988, relief is given to the payer only up to an amount equal to the minimum annual married couple's allowance (£2,070 for 2001-02) and provided that the payment is to *the divorced or separated spouse*. The payments are made gross and the recipient is exempt from tax in respect of them.

Before 1994–95 the relief was given as a deduction from total income. From 1994–95 onwards it is given as a reduction in tax liability calculated as the appropriate percentage of the amount of the relief.

For 1994–95, the tax relief given to the payer was limited to the 20% lower rate. From 1995–96 the tax relief was limited to 15% and from 1999-2000 it is limited to 10%.

Medical insurance premiums

From 6 April 1990 to 1 July 1997, individuals were entitled to tax relief on premiums paid under an eligible contract for private medical insurance for UK resident individuals aged 60 or over (FA 1989 s 54). For premiums paid after 5 April 1994 relief was restricted to the basic rate, given by deduction from the premium; there was no higher rate relief. Until that date basic rate relief was given by deduction at source and higher rate relief had to be claimed.

Tax relief on such premiums is abolished for policies taken out, or renewed, after **1 July 1997** (except where arrangements were made before 2 July 1997 and the relevant contract was made, with the premium being at least partly paid, before 1 August 1997 or where a contract that had come to an end before 2 July 1997 is renewed before 1 August 1997 and the premium is at least partly paid by that date). See F(No2)A 1997 s 17.

National Savings Bank interest

First £70 of interest on deposits (other than investment deposits) is exempt (TA 1988 s 325).

Rent-a-room scheme

Subject to a maximum, gross annual receipts from letting furnished accommodation in the only or main home are exempt from tax. If the receipts exceed the maximum, the taxpayer can pay tax on the gross receipts after deduction of expenses or on the amount by which the receipts exceed the maximum, without relief for the actual expenses. An individual's maximum is halved if during the basis period for the year some other person received income from letting accommodation in that property. (F(No 2) A 1992 Sch 10.)

	Maximum amount
6 April 1997 onwards	£4,250
6 April 1992–5 April 1997	£3,250

Schedule E assessments

Persons domiciled in UK	Services performed			
	Wholly in UK	Partly in UK	Partly abroad	Wholly abroad
Non-resident	All	That part	None	None
Resident but not ordinarily resident	All	That part	Remittances	Remittances
Resident and ordinarily resident	All	All[1]	All[1]	All[1]

Persons domiciled outside UK		
	UK employer	As for person domiciled in UK.
	Foreign employer	*Non-resident* All UK earnings. *Resident (not ordinarily resident)*—All UK earnings. (Remittances for duties performed outside UK.) *Resident (and ordinarily resident)* All earnings. (Remittances if all duties performed outside UK.)

[1] Before 17 March 1998, exempt if qualifying period of over 364 days mostly abroad. The relief for seafarers continues after that date (FA 1998 s 63). Special relief for employees forced to return early from Kuwait or Iraq who had intended to work abroad for over 364 days.

Thresholds: PAYE and national insurance

	1994–95	1995–96	1996–97	1997–98	1998–99	1999–00	2000–01	2001–02
PAYE[1]: Weekly	£66·50	£68·00	£72·50	£78·00	£80·50	£83·00	£84·00	£87·00
Monthly	£287·00	£294·00	£314·00	£337·00	£350·00	£361·00	£365·00	£378·00
National Insurance[2]: Weekly	£57·00	£58·00	£61·00	£62·00	£64·00	£66·00	£76·00	£87·00
Monthly	£247·00	£252·00	£265·00	£269·00	£278·00	£286·00	£329·00	£378·00

[1] From 1999-2000 these are also the earnings thresholds for employers for national insurance contributions.
[2] For employees only from 1999-2000.

Uniform allowances[1]

	1992–93 £	1993–94 £	1994–95 £	From 1995–96 £
Royal Navy and Royal Marines				
RN officers of flag rank and equivalent RM officers	1,026·72	1,043·52	1,068·94	1,071·00
RN and RM below flag rank	790·68	802·08	798·84	792·12
WRNS officers (non-seagoing)	540·12	583·56	514·20	680·52
WRNS officers (seagoing)	609·12	661·56	646·56	853·80
Women medical and dental officers RN	455·76	516·36	452·16	567·48
QARNNS officers: female officers: matron and above	588·00	731·88	572·88	544·68
below matron	875·64	963·48	821·28	828·00
male officers: chief nursing officer and above	475·08	488·40	527·28	489·36
below chief nursing officer	444·00	454·92	493·56	456·48
Army				
Officers serving at mounted duty with Household Cavalry and King's Troop RHA	909·92	973·93	1,012·88	1,012·88
Male dismounted officers: colonel and above	665·75	720·95	749·78	749·78
below colonel	623·22	566·63	673·19	673·19
Household Division	—	647·30	—	—
except Household Division	—	566·63	589·29	589·29
Female QARANC: nursing officers, colonels and above	623·24	627·76	671·48	671·48
non-nursing officers, colonels and above	—	—	—	—
nursing officers below colonel	606·18	645·66	652·87	652·87
non-nursing officers below colonel	—	—	—	—
Female officers: colonels and above (except QARANC above)	—	480·62	499·84	499·84
below colonel (except QARANC above)	—	469·52	488·30	488·30
WRAC women officers: colonel and above	466·35	—	—	—
below colonel	438·03	—	—	—
RAMC and RADC women officers: colonel and above	—	—	—	—
below colonel	—	—	—	—
Male officers SSVC, SSLC	167·44	179·38	186·55	186·55
Women officers SSVC, SSLC	186·54	193·47	201·20	201·20
RAF				
RAF and PMRAFNS (male): air officers	375·48	375·48	445·68	422·76
group captains	363·60	363·60	427·56	402·72
wing commanders and below	336·36	336·36	392·52	361·10
PMRAFNS (female): air officers	461·16	461·16	624·00	589·16
group captains	445·20	445·20	621·00	586·00
wing commanders and below	439·68	439·68	615·24	579·70
WRAF and RAF (female): air officers	406·56	406·56	500·16	477·98
group captains	392·64	392·64	452·40	460·74
wing commanders and below	347·52	347·52	443·40	421·69

[1] Allowances have not changed from 1995-96 pending a review of the system for the provision of allowances.

Charities

Gift aid
(FA 1990 s 25)

The gift aid scheme was introduced with effect from 1 October 1990. It gives higher rate relief for an individual donor and corporation tax relief for a corporate donor. The charity claims repayment of basic rate income tax on the grossed up amount of the donation.

Extension of gift aid from 6 April 2000
(FA 2000 ss 39, 40)

From 6 April 2000 for individuals and from 1 April 2000 for companies, gift aid is extended to all donations to charity, including one-off gifts, made by UK-taxpayers. There is no minimum limit for donations. Donors (who may be resident or non-resident) will have to make a declaration that they are UK taxpayers if the charity is to claim the repayment of basic rate income tax on the gift. One declaration can cover a series of donations to the same charity. Donors will be able to join the scheme by phone or the internet. It is no longer necessary for companies to deduct income tax from their donations and for the recipient charity to claim back the tax.

Limits on relief

Individuals and close companies	Minimum	Maximum
From 6 April 2000	—	—
16 March 1993–5 April 2000	£250	—
7 May 1992–15 March 1993	£400	—

Millennium gift aid

Introduced by FA 1998 s 48 and extended by FA 1999 s 56. Tax relief is given on donations by individuals to charities undertaking education and anti-poverty projects in 80 'low income countries'. The charities must be registered with the Revenue. The scheme was set up to run from 31 July 1998 to 31 December 2000 (SI 1998 No 1868). FA 1999 extended Millennium gift aid to gifts of money to relieve refugee poverty. Gifts made by instalment are aggregated and treated as a single payment made in the tax year in which the first instalment was made (FA 1999 s 57). With effect from 6 April 2000, all donations under this scheme fall within the provisions for the gift aid scheme (FA 2000 s 42).

Limits on relief

Single gift or aggregate of smaller gifts made by individual in one tax year	Minimum £100

See now 'Extension of gift aid from 6 April 2000' above.

Covenants
(FA 2000 s 41)

Because of the extension of the gift aid scheme from 6 April 2000, charitable covenants are in effect treated as regular donations by gift aid. For payments under a charitable covenant falling due before 6 April 2000 to be tax-effective, the covenant had to be for a period capable of exceeding three years (there are no monetary limits). With the introduction of the extended gift aid provisions, however, the separate tax relief for payments under covenants is withdrawn and all relief for such payments falling due on or after 6 April 2000 is given under the gift aid scheme.

Payroll giving
(TA 1988 s 202; SI 1986 No 2211; FA 2000 s 38)

Under the payroll giving scheme, employees authorise their employer to deduct charitable donations from their pay and receive tax relief on their donation at their top rate of tax. The government will add a supplement to donations for three years from April 2000.

Limits on relief

	Maximum
From 6 April 2000	—
6 April 1996–5 April 2000	£1,200
6 April 1993–5 April 1996	£900
6 April 1990–5 April 1993	£600

Government supplement

6 April 2000–5 April 2003	10%

Gifts in kind

Relief available for gifts by traders to educational establishments of plant or machinery either manufactured and sold or used for the purposes of the trade. (TA 1988 s 84; CAA 2001 s 63(2)–(4)).

Millennium Gift Aid Scheme, tax relief introduced by FA 1998 s 47 for businesses to donate goods to help education projects and projects undertaken for medical purposes in eighty 'low income countries' from 31 July 1998. From 27 July 1999, this relief was extended by FA 1999 s 55 to donations of goods or plant and machinery to any type of charity. (TA 1988 s 83A; CAA 2001 s 63(2)–(4)).

Gifts of shares and securities

From 6 April 2000, relief is available where a person disposes of listed shares and securities, unit trust units, AIM shares, etc to a charity by way of a gift or sale at an undervalue. The amount deductible from total income is the market value of the shares etc on the date of disposal plus incidental disposal costs less any consideration or value of benefits received by the donor or a connected person. This is in addition to any capital gains tax relief. (TA 1988 s 587B; FA 2000 s 43).

Inheritance tax relief see p 81.
Capital gains tax see p 40.

Reliefs for investments

Enterprise investment scheme
(Shares issued after 31 December 1993: TA 1988 ss 289–312; FA 1997 Sch 8 as revised from 1998–99 by FA 1998 ss 70, 71, 74, Sch 13 and as amended from 1999–2000 by FA 1999 ss 71–73, Schs 7, 8; FA 2000 s 64, Sch 17; FA 2001 s 63, Sch 15.)

Relief on investment

Maximum investment:	From 1998–99	£150,000
	1994–95	£100,000
	1993–94	£40,000[1]
Minimum investment:	From 1993–94	£500
Maximum carryback to preceding year	From 1998–99	½ amount invested between 6 April and 5 October (maximum £25,000)
	1994–95	½ amount invested between 6 April and 5 October (maximum £15,000)
Rate of relief	From 1993–94	20%[2]

[1] Applied to total enterprise investment and business expansion scheme investments for 1993–94.
[2] Given as a reduction in income tax liability.

Other reliefs
(a) A gain on a disposal of shares on which EIS relief has been given and not withdrawn is exempt from capital gains tax.
(b) Reinvestment relief (ie deferral relief under TCGA 1992 Sch 5B) is available for gains on assets where the disposal proceeds are reinvested in eligible shares in a qualifying company. (CGT taper relief is calculated in accordance with the combined periods of ownership of the first and second investments (and any subsequent qualifying periods of reinvestment) where the shares in the first EIS company were issued after 5 April 1998 and disposed of after 5 April 1999: TCGA 1992 Sch 5BA.)
(c) A loss on a disposal of shares on which EIS relief has been given may be relieved against income tax or capital gains tax.

Main conditions for relief
1. The relief is available for subscriptions in cash to new ordinary fully paid-up shares in a qualifying company with no present or future right of redemption and no present or future preferential right to dividends or to the company's assets on a winding-up, throughout a five-year period from the date of issue.
2. The investor must hold the shares for three years from the date of issue (or from the commencement of trade, if later) where shares are issued after 5 April 2000. (The previous limit was five years from date of issue.) The investor must not be connected with the issuing company at any time in the period beginning two years before the issue of the shares and ending immediately before the third anniversary of the issue date (or, if later, the date of commencement of trade) (for shares issued after 5 April 2000). He must not receive value from the company at any time in the period beginning one year before the issue date and ending immediately before the third anniversary of the issue date (or, if later, the date of commencement of trade) (for shares issued after 6 March 2001 and also as regards value received after that date in respect of shares issued on or before that date). From 7 March 2001 such receipts may be ignored where the amount is insignificant or if equivalent replacement value is given.
3. The money subscribed must be used wholly for the purpose of a qualifying business activity within 12 months of the share issue date (or, where the company commences a qualifying trade within 12 months of the share issue date, within 12 months of the commencement). From 7 March 2001 only 80% of the money subscribed has to be used in a qualifying business within that time limit, though the remainder must be used within the subsequent 12 months.
4. The business activity must be carried on wholly or mainly in the UK for three years after the share issue date (or after the commencement of the trade, if later), unless there is a bona fide liquidation or receivership.
5. Throughout the period beginning with the share issue date and ending three years after that date (or, if later, three years after the date on which its qualifying business activity commences), the company must
   (a) exist for a qualifying purpose;
   (b) have fully paid up capital; and
   (c) not be controlled by another company, or control another company (apart from a qualifying subsidiary).
   Under the provisions of FA 1997 Sch 8, a parent company may qualify if non-qualifying activities do not form a substantial part of the group's activities *as a whole*.
   Before 7 March 2001 it was a condition for relief that the company be unquoted throughout the three-year period. From that date it is necessary only that the company be unquoted at the time the shares are issued, provided that there are at that time no arrangements for the company to cease to be unquoted.
6. For shares issued after 1 July 1997, no arrangement must exist before or at the time of issue for the disposal of shares in the company, the disposal of the company's assets, the ending of the company's trade or a guarantee of the shareholders' investment.

Corporate venturing scheme see p 51.

Reliefs for investments — continued
Venture capital trusts
(TA 1988 ss 332A, 842AA, Sch 15B, Sch 28B; TCGA 1992 ss 151A, 151B, Sch 5C; FA 1997 Sch 9; FA 1998 ss 70, 72, 73, Sch 12; FA 1999 ss 69, 70; FA 2000 s 65, Sch 18.)

Relief on investment

Maximum annual investment:	From 1995–96	£100,000
Rate of relief:	From 1995–96	20%[1]
[1] Given as a reduction in income tax liability. The rate of relief is an amount equal to the 'lower rate' of income tax for the year of assessment in respect of which the claim is made (TA 1988 Sch 15B para 1). The lower rate of income tax is 20% as defined by TA 1988 ss 1A, 832(1); FA 1999 s 22.		

Other reliefs

(a) Dividends on shares within investment limit exempt from income tax (unless the investor's main purpose is tax avoidance – from 9 March 1999).
(b) Gains on share disposals exempt from capital gains tax (subject to investment limit).
(c) Reinvestment relief is available for gains on assets where the disposal proceeds are reinvested in a venture capital trust.

Main conditions for relief

1 The investment must be in new eligible shares: that is, ordinary shares which, in the five-year period from the issue date, carry no present or future preferential right to dividends or to a return of assets on the winding-up of the trust and no present or future right to redemption.
2 The investor must be an individual, aged 18 or over. He or she must hold the shares for three years from the date of issue where the shares are issued after 5 April 2000. (The previous minimum holding period was five years.)
3 The trust must satisfy the following conditions for approval by the Revenue –
   (a) it must not be a close company;
   (b) its income must be derived wholly or mainly (at least 70%) from investments in shares or securities;
   (c) at least 70% by value of its investments must comprise 'qualifying holdings' (newly issued shares in unquoted companies carrying on qualifying trades – the provisions relating to parent companies are relaxed by FA 1997). Special provisions apply where a company in which the VCT has invested goes into bona fide liquidation or receivership, or where the company is sold, merges or undergoes a capital reconstruction;
   (d) at least 30% by value of its qualifying holdings must comprise 'eligible shares' (see above);
   (e) it may not hold more than 15% by value of its total investment portfolio in any one company;
   (f) each class of its shares must be quoted on the Stock Exchange;
   (g) it must distribute at least 85% of the income derived from shares and securities and 100% of income derived from other sources in each accounting period;
   (h) at least 10% of the total investment in any one company must be held in ordinary, non-preferential shares (accounting periods ending after 1 July 1997);
   (i) no part of a qualifying holding may consist of securities relating to a guaranteed loan (accounting periods ending after 1 July 1997).

Business expansion scheme
(Shares issued before 1 January 1994: TA 1988 ss 289–312 as originally enacted)

Relief on investment

Maximum investment:	£40,000[1]
Minimum investment:	£500
Maximum carryback to preceding year:	½ amount invested between 6 April and 5 October (maximum £5,000)
Rate of relief:	Up to 40%[2]
[1] Applied to total enterprise investment and business expansion scheme investments for 1993–94. [2] Given as a deduction from total income.	

Other reliefs

Capital gains relief: gains on the first disposal of shares on which BES relief has not been withdrawn are exempt from capital gains tax.
Loss relief (shares issued after 18 March 1986): none.

Main conditions for relief

As for the enterprise investment scheme (see above), except that the investor had to be UK resident and ordinarily resident in the year in which the shares were issued and the company had to be UK resident throughout the three-year period from the share issue date. There was no time limit for using the funds raised.

Reliefs for investments — continued

Individual savings accounts

(TA 1988 s 333; FA 1998 s 75; SI 1998/1870; SI 1998/1871; SI 1998/1869; SI 1998/1872; SI 2000/809; SI 2001/908)

The overall annual subscription limit will remain at £7,000 and the cash limit will remain at £3,000 until 2005-06 inclusive.

(From 6 April 1999)

Overall annual subscription limit	1999–2000 to 2005-06	£7,000
	6 April 2006 onwards	£5,000
Cash limit	1999-2000 to 2005-06	£3,000
	6 April 2006 onwards	£1,000
Life insurance limit	6 April 1999 onwards	£1,000

Reliefs

(a) Investments under the scheme are free from income tax and capital gains tax.
(b) 10% tax credit paid until 5 April 2004 on dividends from UK equities.
(c) Withdrawals may be made without loss of tax relief.

Main conditions for relief

1 The account can include three components:
   (a) cash (including National Savings),
   (b) life insurance,
   (c) stocks and shares.
2 Savers are subject to the subscription limits set out above. If the subscription limit is reached in a year, no further subscriptions can be made in that year, irrespective of any amounts withdrawn.
3 Accounts must be administered by a single manager or by separate managers for each component.

Tax exempt special savings accounts

(Accounts opened **before 6 April 1999**: TA 1988 ss 326A–326C; FA 1998 s 78)

Maximum deposit (from 1 January 1991)

First 12 months	£3,000[1]
Subsequent 12 month periods	£1,800
Overall limit	£9,000
[1] But the full amount of capital invested in a mature TESSA can be immediately reinvested in a new TESSA.	

Reliefs

Interest and bonuses payable on the account over a five-year period from the date on which it was opened are exempt from income tax.

Main conditions for relief

1 An individual aged 18 or over may hold one TESSA.
2 The TESSA must be a bank or building society deposit account or a building society share account. From 2 January 1996 European authorised institutions may operate TESSAs (SI 1995/3239 and concession A92).
3 No capital may be withdrawn from the account during the initial five-year period.
4 After five years the account ceases to be tax exempt, but the capital (ie a maximum of £9,000) may be reinvested in full within six months in another TESSA.
5 TESSAs could be opened until 5 April 1999. Payments into them may be made under the above rules for the full five-year period. The capital in a TESSA that matured between 6 January 1999 and 5 April 1999 could be transferred into an ISA after 5 April 1999 rather than invested into another TESSA before that date. (See below.)

Reliefs for investments — continued

Personal equity plans

(Subscriptions made **before 6 April 1999**: TA 1988 s 333; FA 1998 s 76; SI 1989/469; SI 1998/1869)

Subscription limit

	General plan £	Single company plan £
From 1991–92	6,000	3,000[1]
1990–91	6,000	—
1989–90	4,800	—

[1] Available from 1 January 1992.

Limit on investments in unit and investment trusts

	Qualifying investments £	Permitted non-qualifying investments £
From 1993–94	6,000	1,500
1992–93	6,000[1]	1,500[1]
1991–92	3,000[1]	1,500[1]
1990–91	3,000[1]	900[1]
1989–90	2,400	—

[1] For the years 1990–91 to 1992–93, the limit on investments in permitted non-qualifying holdings operated as an alternative to the limit on investments in qualifying unit and investment trusts. For 1993–94 and subsequent years, investment in one category does not preclude investment in the other category up to the respective limits.

Individuals aged 18 or over who are UK resident and ordinarily resident could subscribe to one general plan and one single company plan in any tax year.

Reliefs

(a) Dividends on shares held in a plan are exempt from income tax.
(b) Interest on plan investments is exempt from income tax if reinvested; interest on cash deposits is paid gross.
(c) Gains on the disposal of assets held in a plan are exempt from capital gains tax.
(d) PEPs held at 5 April 1999 can be held outside the new ISA, but with the same tax advantages as the ISA: (1998) SWTI 388; FA 1998 ss 75, 76.
(e) 10% tax credits paid until 5 April 2004 on dividends from UK equities.

Inheritance tax

Delivery of accounts: due dates

Type of transfer	Due date
Chargeable lifetime transfers	Later of – (a) 12 months after the end of the month in which the transfer took place; and (b) 3 months after the date on which the person delivering the account became liable
PETs which become chargeable	12 months after the end of the month in which the transferor died
Gifts with reservation chargeable on death	12 months after the end of the month in which the death occurred
Transfers on death	Later of – (a) 12 months after the end of the month in which the death occurred; and (b) 3 months after the date on which the personal representatives first act or the person liable first has reason to believe that he is liable to deliver an account
National heritage property	6 months after the end of the month in which the chargeable event occurred

Delivery of accounts: excepted estates

Date of transfer or death	1 April 1991– 5 April 1995	6 April 1995– 5 April 1996	6 April 1996– 5 April 1998	6 April 1998– 5 April 2000	After 5 April 2000
Excepted transfers:	*Value below:*	*Value below:*	*Value below:*	*Value below:*	*Value below:*
Total chargeable transfers since 6 April	£10,000	£10,000	£10,000	£10,000	£10,000
Total chargeable transfers during last 10 years[2]	£40,000	£40,000	£40,000	£40,000	£40,000
Excepted estates:					
Total gross value	£125,000	£145,000	£180,000[1]	£200,000[1]	£210,000[1]
Total gross value of property outside UK	£15,000	£15,000	£30,000	£50,000	£50,000
Total gross value of chargeable transfers of cash, quoted shares or quoted securities within 7 years before death	nil	nil	£50,000	£75,000	£75,000

[1] This limit applies to the aggregate gross value of the estate and of chargeable transfers of cash, quoted shares and quoted securities within 7 years before death.
[2] This limit remains the same for applicable periods prior to 1 April 1991.

Rates of tax

From 6 April 2001: Death rates

Cumulative chargeable transfers (gross)	Rate on gross	Tax on band	Cumulative tax	Cumulative chargeable transfers (net)	Rate on net fraction
£	%	£	£	£	
0 – 242,000	0	0	0	0 – 242,000	nil
242,000 +	40	—	—	242,000 +	2/3

Lower rates

Cumulative chargeable transfers (gross)	Rate on gross	Tax on band	Cumulative tax	Cumulative chargeable transfers (net)	Rate on net fraction
£	%	£	£	£	
0 – 242,000	0	0	0	0 – 242,000	nil
242,000 +	20	—	—	242,000 +	1/4

6 April 2000–5 April 2001: Death rates

Cumulative chargeable transfers (gross)	Rate on gross	Tax on band	Cumulative tax	Cumulative chargeable transfers (net)	Rate on net fraction
£	%	£	£	£	
0 – 234,000	0	0	0	0 – 234,000	nil
234,000 +	40	—	—	234,000 +	²⁄₃

Lower rates

Cumulative chargeable transfers (gross)	Rate on gross	Tax on band	Cumulative tax	Cumulative chargeable transfers (net)	Rate on net fraction
£	%	£	£	£	
0 – 234,000	0	0	0	0 – 234,000	nil
234,000 +	20	—	—	234,000 +	¼

6 April 1999–5 April 2000: Death rates

Cumulative chargeable transfers (gross)	Rate on gross	Tax on band	Cumulative tax	Cumulative chargeable transfers (net)	Rate on net fraction
£	%	£	£	£	
0 – 231,000	0	0	0	0 – 231,000	nil
231,000 +	40	—	—	231,000 +	²⁄₃

Lower rates

Cumulative chargeable transfers (gross)	Rate on gross	Tax on band	Cumulative tax	Cumulative chargeable transfers (net)	Rate on net fraction
£	%	£	£	£	
0 – 231,000	0	0	0	0 – 231,000	nil
231,000 +	20	—	—	231,000 +	¼

6 April 1998–5 April 1999: Death rates

Cumulative chargeable transfers (gross)	Rate on gross	Tax on band	Cumulative tax	Cumulative chargeable transfers (net)	Rate on net fraction
£	%	£	£	£	
0 – 223,000	0	0	0	0 – 223,000	nil
223,000 +	40	—	—	223,000 +	²⁄₃

Lower rates

Cumulative chargeable transfers (gross)	Rate on gross	Tax on band	Cumulative tax	Cumulative chargeable transfers (net)	Rate on net fraction
£	%	£	£	£	
0 – 223,000	0	0	0	0 – 223,000	nil
223,000 +	20	—	—	223,000 +	¼

6 April 1997–5 April 1998 : Death rates

Cumulative chargeable transfers (gross)	Rate on gross	Tax on band	Cumulative tax	Cumulative chargeable transfers (net)	Rate on net fraction
£	%	£	£	£	
0 – 215,000	0	0	0	0 – 215,000	nil
215,000 +	40	—	—	215,000 +	²⁄₃

Lower rates

Cumulative chargeable transfers (gross)	Rate on gross	Tax on band	Cumulative tax	Cumulative chargeable transfers (net)	Rate on net fraction
£	%	£	£	£	
0 – 215,000	0	0	0	0 – 215,000	nil
215,000 +	20	—	—	215,000 +	¼

Reliefs

The following is a summary of the main reliefs and exemptions for 2001–02 under the Inheritance Tax Act 1984. The legislation should be referred to for conditions and exceptions.

Agricultural property
Transfer with vacant possession (or right to obtain it within 12 months); transfer on or after 1 September 1995, of land let (or treated as let) on or after that date. 100% of agricultural value
Any other case 50% of agricultural value
(Under IHTA 1984 s 124C, as inserted by FA 1997 s 94, land managed according to terms of certain Habitat Schemes is treated as farm land, and qualifies for relief after 26 Nov. 1996.)

Charges arising and transfers occurring after 9 March 1992 and before 1 September 1995:
Transfer with vacant possession (or right to obtain within 12 months) 100% of agricultural value
Most other cases 50% of agricultural value

Note: The 100% relief is extended in limited circumstances by Concession F17.

Annual exemption
From 6 April 1981 £3,000

Business property

Unincorporated business Unquoted shares (including shares in AIM or USM companies) (held for 2 years or more)[1] Unquoted securities which alone, or together with other such securities and unquoted shares, give the transferor control of the company (held for 2 years or more)[1] Settled property used in life tenant's business	100%	Controlling holding in fully quoted companies Land, buildings, machinery or plant used in business of company or partnership } 50%

[1] Tax charges arising and transfers occurring after 5 April 1996. 10 March 1992–5 April 1996 minority holding of shares or securities of up to 25% in unquoted or USM company qualified for 50% relief; larger holdings qualified for 100% relief.

Charities, gifts to
From 15 March 1983 Exempt

Marriage gifts
Made by: parent £5,000
remoter ancestor £2,500
party to marriage £2,500
other person £1,000

Political parties, gifts to
From 15 March 1988 Exempt

Quick succession relief
Estate increased by chargeable transfer followed by death within 5 years
Death within first year 100%
Each additional year: decreased by 20%

Small gifts to same person
From 6 April 1981 £250

Spouses with separate domicile (one not being in the UK)
Total exemption £55,000

Tapering relief
The value of the estate on death is taxed as the top slice of cumulative transfers in the 7 years before death. Transfers on or within 7 years of death are taxed on their value at the date of the gift on the death rate scale, but using the scale in force at the date of death, subject to the following taper—

Years between gift and death	Percentage of full charge at death rates
0–3	100
3–4	80
4–5	60
5–6	40
6–7	20

Penalties see page 19.

National insurance: State benefits

Taxable and non-taxable state benefits
State benefits of an income nature are in principle taxable in the same way as other sources of income, but the majority of such benefits are not in fact taxed.

Benefits taxed under Schedule E as earned income
(Income support[1] payments made to people who had to sign on,[2] or to certain claimants[3] involved in a trade dispute)
Incapacity benefit[4]
Industrial death benefit pensions
Invalid care allowance[5]
Jobseeker's allowance
Retirement pension[5]
Statutory maternity pay
Statutory sick pay
(Unemployment benefit[1 and 6])
Widowed parents' allowance[5 and 7]
Bereavement allowance[8]

Notes:
[1] Income support paid to unemployed people and unemployment benefit were replaced by the jobseeker's allowance in October 1996.
[2] Although taxable, income support paid to an unemployed person who is aged 60 or over, or is a lone parent with a child under 16 or is someone who has to stay at home to look after a severely disabled person, is not in fact taxed (leaflet IR41: Income tax and the unemployed, now superseded).
[3] Where the claimant was one of a married or unmarried couple and he (though not his partner) was involved in a trade dispute.
[4] Payments made during the initial 28-week period, and that part of the benefit which represents a child addition, are exempt (see below).
[5] Child dependency additions are not taxable (see (2) below).
[6] Additions for children, housing and exceptional circumstances were excluded.
[7] Replaces widowed mother's allowance from 9 April 2001.
[8] Replaces widow's pension from 9 April 2001.

Benefits which are not taxed
(1) *Short-term benefits*
   Maternity allowance
(2) *Benefits in respect of children*
   Child benefit
   Child dependency additions paid with retirement pension, widows' benefit, incapacity benefit, invalidity benefit, invalid care allowance, severe disablement allowance, higher-rate industrial death benefit, unemployability supplement and sickness (or, formerly, unemployment benefit) if beneficiary over pension age
   Child's special allowance
   Guardian's allowance
   One-parent benefit
(3) *Industrial injury benefits*
   Constant attendance allowance
   Industrial disablement benefit
   Pneumoconiosis, byssinosis and miscellaneous disease benefits
   Workmen's compensation supplement
(4) *War disablement benefits*
   Constant attendance allowance
   Disablement pension
   Severe disablement allowance
(5) *Other benefits*
   Attendance allowance
   Bereavement payment
   Christmas bonus
   Council tax benefit
   Disability living allowance
   Disability working allowance (replaced by disabled person's tax credit from 5 October 1999)
   Earnings top-up
   Family credit (replaced by working families' tax credit from 5 October 1999)
   Housing benefit
   Incapacity benefit (initial 28-week period *only*)
   Income support (other than payments made to people who had to sign on or strikers before 7 October 1996: introduction of jobseeker's allowance. In practice, payments to an unemployed person who was (a) aged 60 or over, (b) a lone parent with a child under 16, or (c) someone staying at home to look after a severely disabled person, were not taxed: IR41.)
   Jobfinder's grant
   Redundancy payment
   Social fund payments
   Television licence payment
   Vaccine damage (lump sum)
   War widow's or dependant's pension
   Widow's payment (replaced by bereavement payment from 9 April 2001)
   Winter fuel payment

Statutory maternity pay
Rates: from 9 April 2001

Higher weekly rate of statutory maternity pay	Lower weekly rate of statutory maternity pay	Daily rate of statutory maternity pay
9/10ths of employee's average weekly earnings	£62·20	—
Paid for a maximum of 18 weeks.	Earnings threshold: £72	

Statutory sick pay
Rates: from 9 April 2001

Average weekly earnings	Weekly rate of statutory sick pay	Daily rate of statutory sick pay
Under £72·00	nil	Weekly rate divided by number of qualifying days in week[1] in which day to be paid occurs
£72·00 or more	£62·20 (standard)	

[1] Commencing on the Sunday

Benefits taxed under Schedule E

	Weekly 10.4.00 onwards £	Total 2000-01 (52 weeks) £	Weekly 9.4.01 onwards £	Total 2001-02 (52 weeks) £
Retirement pensions				
Single person	67.50	3,510.00	72.50	3,770.00
Married couple:				
both contributors—each	67.50	3,510.00	72.50	3,770.00
wife not contributor—addition	40.40	2,100.80	43.40	2,256.80
wife not contributor—joint	107.90	5,610.80	115.90	6,026.80
Age addition (over 80)—each	0.25	13.00	0.25	13.00
Hospital downrating				
20% rate (persons with dependants)	13.50	varies	14.50	varies
40% rate (no dependants)	27.00	varies	29.00	varies
Bereavement (widow's) benefits*				
Bereavement allowance (widow's pension)—standard	67.50	3,510.00	72.50	3,770.00
Widowed parent's (mother's) allowance	67.50	3,510.00	72.50	3,770.00
Non-contributory retirement pension				
Single person (category C or D)	40.40	2,100.80	43.40	2,256.80
Married couple (category C)	64.55	3,356.60	68.35	3,554.20
Married couple (category D—over 80)	80.80	4,201.60	86.80	4,513.60
Age addition	0.25	13.00	0.25	13.00
Incapacity benefit				
Long-term	67.50	3,510.00	69.75	3,627.00
Increased for age: Higher rate	14.20	738.40	14.65	761.80
Lower rate	7.10	369.20	7.35	382.20
Short-term[1] (under pension age) higher rate	60.20	—	62.20	—
(over pension age) higher rate	67.50	—	69.75	—
Invalidity allowance when paid with retirement pension				
Higher rate	14.20	738.40	14.65	761.80
Middle rate	9.00	468.00	9.30	483.60
Lower rate	4.50	234.00	4.65	241.80
Industrial death benefit				
Widow's pension:				
Higher permanent rate	67.50	3,510.00	72.50	3,770.00
Lower permanent rate	20.25	1,053.00	21.75	1,131.00
Invalid care allowance				
Each qualifying individual	40.40	2,100.80	41.75	2,171.00
Earnings limit	50.00	—	72.00	—
Adult dependency increase	24.15	1,255.80	24.95	1,297.40
Jobseeker's allowance				
Single: under 18	31.45	—	31.95	—
18 to 24	41.35	—	42.00	—
25 or over	52.20	—	53.05	—

[1] Lower rate (tax-free) paid up to week 28 (see below). Higher rate (taxable) paid weeks 29 to 52. New claims cannot be made by persons over pensionable age.

Child dependency additions (from 9.4.01): £9·70 a week for child for whom higher rate child benefit payable
£11·35 a week for each other child (tax free).

The Revenue generally apply the basis of 52 weeks at the new rate. In certain cases, however, it may be to the advantage of the recipient to calculate the amount actually received within the year of assessment where this includes one week at the old rate.

Tax-free rates (from 9.4.01):

Attendance allowance:
| | Higher rate | £55·30 a week |
| | Lower rate | £37·00 a week |

Child benefit: £15·50 for eldest eligible child (couple)
£17·55 for eldest eligible child (lone parent, existing claimants only)
£10·35 (each) for other eligible children

Disability living allowance:
Care component: Higher rate £55·30 a week
Middle rate £37·00 a week
Lower rate £14·65 a week
Mobility component: Higher rate £38·65 a week
Lower rate £14·65 a week

Incapacity benefit:
Short term (under pension age) Lower rate £52·60 a week

Maternity allowance:
Lower earnings limit £72·00 a week (average)
Standard rate £62·20 a week
Earnings threshold £30·00 a week (average)
Lower rate 90% average weekly earnings

Bereavement payment:* £2,000 lump sum

* A new system is introduced from 9 April 2001. The new benefit and lump sum payment are claimable by both widows and widowers.

Contributions
From 6 April 2001

Lower earnings limit:	£72 a week £312 a month £3,744 a year	Secondary earnings threshold: (employers)	£87 a week £378 a month £4,535 a year
Primary earnings threshold: (employees)	£87 a week £378 a month £4,535 a year	Upper earnings limit: (employees only)	£575 a week £2,492 a month £29,900 a year

	Employees from 6.4.01	Employers from 6.4.01	
Class 1 Contributions standard rate		(Earnings above £87 a week)	
Earnings: £87–£575	10%	11·9%	
Over £575	no additional liability	11·9%	
Contracted out*		$SR^{1,3}$	$MP^{2,3}$
Earnings: £87–£575	8·4%[4]	8·9%	11·3%
Over £575	no additional liability	11·9%	11·9%
Reduced rate for married women and widows with valid certificate of election	3·85% (earnings £87 to £575)	(As above)	
Men over 65 and women over 60	Nil	(As above)	
Children under 16	Nil	Nil	

Class 1A and Class 1B Contributions: 11·9%

Class 2 Contributions: Self employed
Flat rate: £2·00 a week.
Share fishermen's special rate: £2·65 a week.
Small earnings exception: earnings under £3,955 a year.

Class 3 Voluntary Contributions: £6·75 a week.

Class 4 Contributions: 7% of profits or gains between £4,535 and £29,900 a year.
Exempt if pensionable age reached by beginning of year of assessment.

[1] Rates apply to salary-related schemes.
[2] Rates apply to money-purchase schemes.
[3] The lower rates apply to earnings between the earnings threshold of £87 and the upper earnings limit of £575. A deduction is made for the rebate that would have applied to NICs on earnings between the lower earnings limit of £72 and the earnings threshold of £87. The rebate is 3% for salary-related schemes and 0.6% for money purchase schemes.
[4] A deduction is made from employee contributions for the rebate of 1.6% that would have applied to NICs on earnings between the lower earnings limit of £72 and the primary earnings threshold of £87. Where the rebate reduces the employee's contributions to nil, the balance is offset against the employer's contributions.

6 April 2000–5 April 2001

Lower earnings limit:	£67 a week £291 a month £3,484 a year	Secondary earnings threshold: (employers)	£84 a week £365 a month £4,385 a year
Primary earnings threshold: (employees)	£76 a week £329 a month £3,952 a year	Upper earnings limit: (employees only)	£535 a week £2,319 a month £27,820 a year

	Employees from 6.4.00	Employers from 6.4.00	
Class 1 Contributions standard rate		(Earnings above £84 a week)	
Earnings: £76–£535	10%	12·2%	
Over £535	no additional liability	12·2%	
Contracted out*		$SR^{1,3}$	$MP^{2,3}$
Earnings: £76–£535	8·4%[4]	9·2%	11·6%
Over £535	no additional liability	12·2%	12·2%
Reduced rate for married women and widows with valid certificate of election	3·85% (earnings £76 to £535)	(As above)	
Men over 65 and women over 60	Nil	(As above)	
Children under 16	Nil	Nil	

Class 1A and 1B Contributions: 12·2%

Class 2 Contributions: Self employed
Flat rate: £2 a week.
Share fishermen's special rate: £2·65 a week.
Small earnings exception: earnings under £3,825 a year.

Class 3 Voluntary Contributions: £6·55 a week.

Class 4 Contributions: 7% of profits or gains between £4,385 and £27,820 a year.
Exempt if pensionable age reached by beginning of year of assessment.

[1] Rates apply to salary-related schemes.
[2] Rates apply to money-purchase schemes.
[3] The lower rates apply to earnings between the earnings threshold of £84 and the upper earnings limit of £535. A deduction is made for the rebate that would have applied to NICs on earnings between the lower earnings limit of £67 and the earnings threshold of £84. The rebate is 3% for salary-related schemes and 0.6% for money purchase schemes.
[4] A deduction is made from employee contributions for the rebate of 1.6% that would have applied to NICs on earnings between the lower earnings limit of £67 and the primary earnings threshold of £76. Where the rebate reduces the employee's contributions to nil, the balance is offset against the employer's contributions.

Contributions — continued

6 April 1999–5 April 2000

Lower earnings limit: £66 a week £286 a month £3,432 a year		**Upper earnings limit: (employees only)**	£500 a week £2,167 a month £26,000 a year	
	Employees from 6.4.99		**Employers from 6.4.99**	
Class 1 Contributions standard rate			*(Earnings above £83 a week)*	
Earnings: £66–£500	10%		12·2%	
Over £500	no additional liability		12·2%	
Contracted out*			SR[1,3]	MP[2,3]
Earnings: £66–£500	8·4%		9·2%	11·6%
Over £500	no additional liability		12·2%	12·2%
Reduced rate for married women and widows with valid certificate of election	3·85% (earnings £66 to £500)		(As above)	
Men over 65 and women over 60	Nil		(As above)	
Children under 16	Nil		Nil	

Class 1A and 1B Contributions: 12·2%
Class 2 Contributions: Self employed Flat rate: £6·55 a week. Share fishermen's special rate: £7·20 a week. Small earnings exception: earnings under £3,770 a year.
Class 3 Voluntary Contributions: £6·45 a week.
Class 4 Contributions: 6% of profits or gains between £7,530 and £26,000 a year. Exempt if pensionable age reached by beginning of year of assessment.

Notes: The employer NI contribution holiday of up to a year, which applied from 6 April 1996 (see p 86), is restricted to employments which began before 1 April 1999: (1998) SWTI 1705.
[1] Rates apply to salary-related schemes.
[2] Rates apply to money-purchase schemes.
[3] The lower rates apply to earnings between the earnings threshold of £83 and the upper earnings limit of £500. A deduction is made for the rebate that would have applied to NICs on earnings between the lower earnings limit of £66 and the earnings threshold £83. The rebate is 3% for salary-related schemes and 0·6% for money-purchase schemes.

6 April 1998–5 April 1999

Lower earnings limit: £64 a week £278 a month £3,328 a year			**Upper earnings limit: (employees only)**		£485 a week £2,102 a month £25,220 a year	
	Employees from 6.4.98			**Employers from 6.4.98**		
Class 1 Contributions standard rate	On first £64	Remainder		*(Rate applying to all earnings)*		
Earnings: £ 64·00–£109·99	2%	10%		3%		
£110·00–£154·99	2%	10%		5%		
£155·00–£209·99	2%	10%		7%		
£210·00–£485·00	2%	10%		10%		
Over £485	no additional liability			10%		
Contracted out*	On first £64	Remainder	On first £64	Remainder		
				SR[1]		MP[2]
Earnings: £ 64·00–£109·99	2%	8·4%	3%	Nil		1·5%
£110·00–£154·99	2%	8·4%	5%	2		3·5%
£155·00–£209·99	2%	8·4%	7%	4		5·5%
£210·00–£485·00	2%	8·4%	10%	7		8·5%
Over £485	no additional liability		10% 10%	7% (to £485) 10% (over £485)		8·5% (to £485) 10% (over £485)
Reduced rate for married women and widows with valid certificate of election	3·85% (earnings to £485)			(As above)		
Men over 65 and women over 60	Nil			(As above)		
Children under 16	Nil			Nil		

Class 1A Contributions: 10%
Class 2 Contributions: Self employed Flat rate: £6·35 a week.   Share fishermen's special rate: £7 a week. Small earnings exception: earnings under £3,590 a year.
Class 3 Voluntary Contributions: £6·25 a week.
Class 4 Contributions: 6% of profits or gains between £7,310 and £25,220 a year. Exempt if pensionable age reached by beginning of year of assessment.

[1] Rates apply to salary-related schemes. [2] Rates apply to money-purchase schemes.

Contributions — continued

6 April 1997–5 April 1998

Lower earnings limit: £62 a week £269 a month £3,224 a year		**Upper earnings limit:** **(employees only)**	£465 a week £2,015 a month £24,180 a year	
Class 1 Contributions	**Employees from 6.4.97**		**Employers from 6.4.97**	
standard rate	On first £62	Remainder	(Rate applying to all earnings)	
Earnings: £ 62·00–£109·99	2%	10%	3%	
£110·00–£154·99	2%	10%	5%	
£155·00–£209·99	2%	10%	7%	
£210·00–£465·00	2%	10%	10%	
Over £465	no additional liability		10%	
Contracted out*	On first £62	Remainder	On first £62	Remainder
				SR^1 MP^2
Earnings: £ 62·00–£109·99	2%	8·4%	3%	Nil 1·5%
£110·00–£154·99	2%	8·4%	5%	2 3·5%
£155·00–£209·99	2%	8·4%	7%	4 5·5%
£210·00–£465·00	2%	8·4%	10%	7 8·5%
Over £465	no additional liability		{ 10% { 10%	7% (to £465) 8·5% (to £465) 10% (over £465) 10% (over £465)
Reduced rate for married women and widows with valid certificate of election	3·85% (earnings to £465)		(As above)	
Men over 65 and women over 60	Nil		(As above)	
Children under 16	Nil		Nil	

Class 1A Contributions: 10%

Class 2 Contributions: Self employed Flat rate: £6·15 a week. Share fishermen's special rate: £6·80 a week. Small earnings exception: earnings under £3,480 a year.

Class 3 Voluntary Contributions: £6·05 a week.

Class 4 Contributions: 6% of profits or gains between £7,010 and £24,180 a year. Exempt if pensionable age reached by beginning of year of assessment.

[1] Rates apply to salary-related schemes. [2] Rates apply to money-purchase schemes.

6 April 1996–5 April 1997

Lower earnings limit: £61 a week £265 a month £3,172 a year		**Upper earnings limit:** **(employees only)**	£455 a week £1,972 a month £23,660 a year
Class 1 Contributions	**Employees from 6.4.96**		**Employers from 6.4.96**
standard rate	On first £61	Remainder	(Rate applying to all earnings)
Earnings: £ 61·00–£109·99	2%	10%	3%
£110·00–£154·99	2%	10%	5%
£155·00–£209·99	2%	10%	7%
£210·00–£455·00	2%	10%	10·2%
Over £455	no additional liability		10·2%
Contracted out*	On first £61	Remainder	On first £61 Remainder
Earnings: £ 61·00–£109·99	2%	8·2%	3% Nil
£110·00–£154·99	2%	8·2%	5% 2%
£155·00–£209·99	2%	8·2%	7% 4%
£210·00–£455·00	2%	8·2%	10·2% 7·2%
Over £455	no additional liability		{ 10·2% 7·2% (to £455) { 10·2% (earnings over £455)
Reduced rate for married women and widows with valid certificate of election	3·85% (earnings to £455)		(As above)
Men over 65 and women over 60	Nil		(As above)
Children under 16	Nil		Nil

Class 1A Contributions: 10·2%

Class 2 Contributions: Self employed Flat rate: £6·05 a week. Share fishermen's special rate: £7·20 a week. Small earnings exception: earnings under £3,430 a year.

Class 3 Voluntary Contributions: £5·95 a week.

Class 4 Contributions: 6% of profits or gains between £6,860 and £23,660 a year. Exempt if pensionable age reached by beginning of year of assessment.

* Contracted out rates apply to members of contracted out occupational schemes only.
Note: From 6 April 1996 there is an employer NI contribution holiday of up to a year for individuals taken on who have been out of work for two years or more, trainees, and certain people who work intermittently during the qualifying period, who satisfy the conditions.

Employers' contributions: benefits in kind

From *6 April 2000,* Class 1A national insurance contributions are payable by employers (at 11·9% for 2001-02) on most taxable benefits in kind, excluding benefits:
(1) which are covered by a dispensation; or
(2) included in a PAYE settlement agreement; or
(3) provided for employees not earning more than £8,500 pa (including benefits in kind and expenses payments); or
(4) otherwise not required to be included on a P11D; or
(5) on which Class 1 national insurance contributions were due.

Expenses payments and certain benefits are not liable to Class 1A national insurance contributions. The first returns and payments are due under the new arrangements in July 2001 (see (1999) SWTI pp 400, 409, 1844).

Before 6 April 2000, national insurance contributions were payable by employers only where the benefits in kind were of cars and free fuel provided for the private use of employees (where the latter were liable to the income tax charge on cars). The benefit of cars and free fuel continues to be chargeable (see above). From 6 April 1994 the car benefit figure is calculated by reference to the list price of the car rather than by use of a table (see p 58), although a car fuel benefit table continues to be used.

From *6 April 1999,* Class 1B contributions are payable by employers by reference to the value of any items included in a PAYE settlement agreement (PSA) which would otherwise be earnings for Class 1 or Class 1A, including the amount of tax paid. Income tax and Class 1B contributions on a PSA are payable by 19 October after the end of the tax year to which the PSA relates.

Car benefits: private use
1994–95 onwards Calculated by reference to the list price of the car, see p 58.

Car benefits: free fuel:—Class 1A national insurance contributions	
2001–02	
Cylinder capacity: 1,400cc or less	£229·67
(non-diesel cars) Over 1,400cc up to 2,000cc	£292·74
Over 2,000cc	£430·78
Cylinder capacity: 2,000cc or less	£292·74
(diesel cars) Over 2,000cc	£430·78
No internal combustion engine —	£430·78
2000–01	
Cylinder capacity: 1,400cc or less	£207·40
(non-diesel cars) Over 1,400cc up to 2,000cc	£264·74
Over 2,000cc	£390·40
Cylinder capacity: 2,000cc or less	£264·74
(diesel cars) Over 2,000cc	£390·40
No internal combustion engine —	£390·40
1999–2000	
Cylinder capacity: 1,400cc or less	£147·62
(non-diesel cars) Over 1,400cc up to 2,000cc	£187·88
Over 2,000cc	£276·94
Cylinder capacity: 2,000cc or less	£187·88
(diesel cars) Over 2,000cc	£276·94
No internal combustion engine —	£276·94
1998–99	
Cylinder capacity: 1,400cc or less	£101·00
(non-diesel cars) Over 1,400cc up to 2,000cc	£128·00
Over 2,000cc	£189·00
Cylinder capacity: 2,000cc or less	£128·00
(diesel cars) Over 2,000cc	£189·00
No internal combustion engine —	£189·00
1997–98	
Cylinder capacity: 1,400cc or less	£80·00
(non-diesel cars) Over 1,400cc up to 2,000cc	£101·00
Over 2,000cc	£149·00
Cylinder capacity: 2,000cc or less	£74·00
(diesel cars) Over 2,000cc	£94·00
No internal combustion engine —	£149·00
1996–97	
Cylinder capacity: 1,400cc or less	£72·42
(non-diesel cars) Over 1,400cc up to 2,000cc	£90·78
Over 2,000cc	£134·64
Cylinder capacity: 2,000cc or less	£65·28
(diesel cars) Over 2,000cc	£83·64
No internal combustion engine —	£134·64

National insurance contributions leaflets

Leaflets regarding National Insurance contributions are issued by the Inland Revenue. They are available from the Inland Revenue website: http://www.inlandrevenue.co.uk and can be obtained from local Inland Revenue offices (including those which were Contributions Agency offices before 1 April 1999) except where indicated:
*Coastal Inland Revenue offices
**End of Year Section, HM Inspector of Taxes Cardiff 2, 15 North, Government Buildings, Ty LGlas Road, Llanishen, Cardiff CF4 5FN
†International Services, NICO, Longbenton, Newcastle-Upon-Tyne NE98 1ZZ
‡Contracted-out Employment Group, Inland Revenue National Insurance Contributions Office, Business Support, Room K2104, Newcastle-Upon-Tyne NE98 1ZZ

National Insurance

Leaflet	Date	Title
CA01	2000	National insurance contributions for employees
CA02	2000	National insurance contributions for self-employed people with small earnings
CA04	2000	National insurance contributions, Class 2 and Class 3: direct debit – the easier way to pay
CA07	2000	National insurance: unpaid and late-paid contributions
CA08	2000	NIC voluntary contributions
CA09	2000	NIC for widows
CA10	2000	NIC for divorced women
CA11*	2000	National insurance for share fishermen
CA12	2000	Training for further employment and your National Insurance record
CA13	2000	NIC for married women
CA14‡	1999	Termination of contracted-out employment: manual for salary related pension schemes and salary related parts of mixed benefits schemes
CA14A‡	1999	Termination of contracted-out employment: manual for money purchase pension schemes and money purchase parts of mixed benefits schemes
CA14B‡	1997	Contracted-out guidance for re-elections for salary related pension schemes and salary related overseas schemes
CA14C‡	1999	Contracted-out guidance for SR pension schemes and SR overseas schemes
CA14D‡	1999	Contracted-out guidance for money purchase pension schemes and money purchase overseas schemes
CA14E‡	1999	Contracted-out guidance for mixed benefit pension schemes and mixed benefit overseas schemes
CA14F‡	1999	Technical guidance on contracted-out decision making and appeals
CA15‡	1999	Cessation of contracted-out pension schemes manual
CA16‡	1999	Appropriate personal pension scheme manual – procedural guidance
CA16A‡	1999	Appropriate personal pension scheme manual – guidance for scheme managers
CA17‡	2000	Employees' guide to minimum contributions
CA17F‡	2001	How to calculate your minimum contribution
CA19‡	1999	Using the accrued GMP liability service
CA20‡	1999	Using the contracted-out contributions/earnings information service
CA21‡	1999	Using the National Insurance number/date of birth checking service
CA22‡	2001	Contracted-out data transactions using magnetic media
CA23*	2001	NIC for mariners
CA24*	2001	NIC for masters and employers of mariners
CA25	2000	Agencies and people working through agencies
CA26	2000	NIC for examiners, lecturers, teachers and instructors
CA29	2001	Statutory Maternity Pay manual for employers (with supplement)
CA29 (Supp)	2000	Supplement to the CA29, Statutory Maternity Pay manual for employers
CA30	2001	Statutory Sick Pay manual for employers
CA33	2001	Employer's manual on Class 1A NICs on cars and fuel
CA35	2001	Statutory sick pay tables
CA36	2001	Statutory maternity pay tables
CA37	2001	Simplified deduction scheme for employers
CA38	2001	Not contracted out contributions for employers: important changes to the national insurance system
CA39‡	2001	Tables: contracted out contributions (for employers with contracted-out salary related schemes)
CA40	2001	Employee-only contributions for employers
CA42**	2000	Foreign going mariner's and deep-sea fisherman's contributions for employers
CA43‡	2001	Tables: contracted-out contributions and minimum payments for employers with contracted out money purchase schemes
CA44	2001	National insurance for company directors
CA47	1999	Charter for national insurance contributors
CA50	1999	Making year end returns on tape or disc.
CA51/52	2001	Making year end returns on tape. Technical guide. PAYE income tax and national insurance
CA65†	2001	NIC for people working for embassies, consulates and overseas employers
CA72	2001	National insurance contributions – deferring payments
CA76	1999	National insurance abroad – a guide for employers of employees from abroad
CA78A	2001	International services employers' pack
CA83	2000	NIC office – quality service through people
CA84	2001	Stakeholder pension scheme manual
CA86	2001	Employees' guide to statutory sick pay
CA87	2000	National insurance contributions and the Welsh language
CA88	2000	Payroll cleansing: what is it and what can it do for you?
CA89	2001	Payroll cleansing – a free service offered by the Inland Revenue
CA90	2000	Convention on social security between the UK and the Republic of Korea
CA91	2001	Agreement between the UK and Japan on social security
CA1437	1999	Employer's guide to centralised payments of national insurance contributions
CWG2	2001	Employer's further guide to PAYE and NICs. Some of the fine points
P/SE/1	2001	Starting your own business
CWL2	2001	NI for self-employed people, Class 2 and Class 4
CAT1		A catalogue of information, leaflets and posters
IR37	1999	Appeals against tax, NI contributions, SSP and SMP
IR 56	1999	Employed or self-employed? A guide for tax and national insurance
IR 120	2000	You and the Inland Revenue – National Insurance Contributions Office
IR 148	1999	Are your workers employed or self-employed? – construction workers
NE1	2000	First steps as a new employer
NI38	2000	Social security abroad – national insurance contributions, social security benefits, health care in certain overseas countries
NI132	2000	National insurance for employers of people working abroad
NIC2	1999	NIC holiday scheme

Stamp duties

Ad valorem duty

Rounding. With effect from 1 October 1999, the charging provisions will be standardised to provide for the rounding up to the nearest £5 in all cases (where duty is currently rounded up to multiples of between 50p and £12) other than for SDRT. FA 1999 s 112, Sch 14.

Rates of duty (FA 1963 s 55; FA 1999 s 111, Sch 13; FA 2000 ss 114, 116 (Excluding transfers of intellectual property after 27 March 2000, transfers to registered social landlords after 28 July 2000 and property transactions in disadvantaged parts of the UK designated for this purpose: FA 2000 ss 129, 130; FA 2001 s 92)).

Consideration certified as:	Conveyance or transfer on sale with certificate of value	Lease premium where rent exceeds £600 p.a.	Conveyance etc without certificate of value	Stock transfers
28 March 2000[1] and after				
Not exceeding £60,000	Nil	1%	4%	0·5%
£60,001–£250,000	1%	1%	4%	0·5%
£250,001–£500,000	3%	3%	4%	0·5%
£500,001 or more	4%	4%	4%	0·5%
16 March 1999[2] to 27 March 2000				
Not exceeding £60,000	Nil	1%	3·5%	0·5%
£60,001–£250,000	1%	1%	3·5%	0·5%
£250,001–£500,000	2·5%	2·5%	3·5%	0·5%
£500,001 or more	3·5%	3·5%	3·5%	0·5%
17 March 1998[3] to 15 March 1999				
Not exceeding £60,000	Nil	1%	3%	0·5%
£60,001–£250,000	1%	1%	3%	0·5%
£250,001–£500,000	2%	2%	3%	0·5%
£500,001 or more	3%	3%	3%	0·5%

Unless transfer is pursuant to a contract made before: [1] 22 March 2000 [2] 10 March 1999 [3] 18 March 1998.

Leases
Any agreement for a lease entered into after 19 March 1984 is chargeable to duty as if it were the actual lease irrespective of the length of the term.

Premiums. If the consideration for the lease includes a premium, this is charged to ad valorem duty in accordance with the Table above. The nil rate of duty does not apply if the average rent reserved by the lease exceeds £600 p.a.

Rent. From 28 March 2000: *Leases not exceeding 7 years*, or for an indefinite term, are not chargeable to duty on the rent where this does not exceed £5,000[4] p.a. If the rent exceeds £5,000[4] p.a., the duty is—
For a lease of furnished residential
accommodation for a definite term of
less than 1 year .... £5 from 1 October 1999 (previously £1)[5]
Other cases .... 1% from 1 October 1999 (previously 50p per £50 or part)

[4] The previous limit was £500 (FA 2000 s 115).

Leases exceeding 7 years—

Rent	Over 7 yrs up to 35 yrs	Over 35 yrs up to 100 yrs	Over 100 yrs
From 1 October 1999	2%	12%	24%
Previously	£	£	£
£5 or less	0·10	0·60	1·20
Over £5 up to £10	0·20	1·20	2·40
Over £10 up to £15	0·30	1·80	3·60
Over £15 up to £20	0·40	2·40	4·80
Over £20 up to £25	0·50	3·00	6·00
Over £25 up to £50	1·00	6·00	12·00
Over £50 up to £75	1·50	9·00	18·00
Over £75 up to £100	2·00	12·00	24·00
Over £100 up to £150	3·00	18·00	36·00
Over £150 up to £200	4·00	24·00	48·00
Over £200 up to £250	5·00	30·00	60·00
Over £250 up to £300	6·00	36·00	72·00
Over £300 up to £350	7·00	42·00	84·00
Over £350 up to £400	8·00	48·00	96·00
Over £400 up to £450	9·00	54·00	108·00
Over £450 up to £500	10·00	60·00	120·00
Over £500; for every £50 or fraction of £50	1·00	6·00	12·00

Fixed duties

Stamp Act 1891 Sch 1

	From 1 October 1999[5]	Previously
Leases (other than as described above)	£5	£2
Declaration of trust; duplicate or counterpart exchange or partition; release or renunciation; surrender	£5	50p

CREST: For instruments executed after 30 June 1996 there is no fixed stamp duty charge on deposits of shares into CREST, although there may be a liability to SDRT: see FA 1996 s 186.

[5] The minimum fixed stamp duty is £5 with effect from 1 October 1999 (previously 50p) (FA 1999 s 112, Sch 14).

Interest and penalties

For instruments executed from 1 October 1999, interest is payable on the amount of unpaid duty where the instrument is not stamped within 30 days of execution. A penalty applies where the instrument is not presented for stamping within 30 days after execution (or if executed outside the UK, the day on which it is first received in the UK). If presented within one year after the end of the 30 day period, the penalty is the lower of £300 or the amount of the unpaid duty, and if presented more than one year after the end of the 30 day period, it is the greater of £300 or the amount of the unpaid duty (Stamp Act 1891 ss 15-15B). The Stamp Duty (Collection and Recovery of Penalties) Regulations SI 1999/2537 came into effect on 1 October 1999.

Value added tax

Annual accounting scheme

The taxable person must have been registered for at least one year at the date of application for authorisation (SI 1995/2518 Pt VII as amended). The taxable person must have reasonable grounds for believing that the value of taxable supplies in the year beginning at the date of application will not exceed a prescribed figure.

	Taxable turnover
9.4.91–31.3.01	£300,000
1.4.01 onwards	£600,000

Businesses already operating the scheme may continue to use it until their annual turnover exceeds a higher prescribed figure.

	Higher limit
1.4.96–31.3.01	£375,000
1.4.01 onwards	£750,000

Registration limits
UK taxable supplies

	Past turnover[1]		Future turnover[1]
	1 year	Unless turnover for next year will not exceed:	30 days[2]
29.11.95–26.11.96	£47,000	£45,000	£47,000
27.11.96–30.11.97	£48,000	£46,000	£48,000
1.12.97–31.3.98	£49,000	£47,000	£49,000
1.4.98–31.3.99	£50,000	£48,000	£50,000
1.4.99–31.3.00	£51,000	£49,000	£51,000
1.4.00–31.3.01	£52,000	£50,000	£52,000
1.4.01 onwards	£54,000	£52,000	£54,000

[1] Value of taxable supplies (at zero and positive rates).
[2] Where there are reasonable grounds for believing that limit will be exceeded in this period.

Supplies from other EC countries

	Cumulative total[1] from beginning of calendar year
1.1.93 onwards	£70,000

[1] Value of supplies made by persons in other EC member states to non-taxable persons in the UK.

Acquisitions from other EC countries
VATA 1994 Sch 3

	Past acquisitions[1]	Future acquisitions[1]
	Cumulative total from 1 January	30 days[2]
1.1.96–31.12.96	£47,000	£47,000
1.1.97–31.12.97	£48,000	£48,000
1.1.98–31.3.98	£49,000	£49,000
1.4.98–31.3.99	£50,000	£50,000
1.4.99–31.3.00	£51,000	£51,000
1.4.00–31.3.01	£52,000	£52,000
1.4.01 onwards	£54,000	£54,000

[1] Value of acquisitions of taxable goods from suppliers in other EC member states.
[2] Where there are reasonable grounds for believing that limit will be exceeded in this period.

Deregistration limits

UK taxable supplies

Future turnover	Annual limit
29.11.95–26.11.96	£45,000
27.11.96–30.11.97	£46,000
1.12.97–31.3.98	£47,000
1.4.98–31.3.99	£48,000
1.4.99–31.3.00	£49,000
1.4.00–31.3.01	£50,000
1.4.01 onwards	£52,000
Unless during the year, the person will cease making taxable supplies (or suspend making taxable supplies for 30 days or more).	

Supplies from other EC countries

	Past supplies[1]	Future supplies[1]
	Supplies in preceding calendar year	*Supplies in following calendar year[2]*
1.1.93 onwards	£70,000	£70,000

[1] Value of supplies made by persons in other EC member states to non-taxable persons in the UK.
[2] Where C & E are satisfied that limit will not be exceeded in this period.

Acquisitions from other EC countries
VATA 1994 Sch 3

	Past acquisitions[1]	Future acquisitions[1]
	Acquisitions in preceding calendar year	*Acquisitions in following calendar year[2]*
1.1.95–31.12.95	£46,000	£46,000
1.1.96–31.12.96	£47,000	£47,000
1.1.97–31.12.97	£48,000	£48,000
1.1.98–31.3.98	£49,000	£49,000
1.4.98–31.3.99	£50,000	£50,000
1.4.99–31.3.00	£51,000	£51,000
1.4.00–31.3.01	£52,000	£52,000
1.4.01 onwards	£54,000	£54,000

[1] Value of acquisitions of taxable goods from suppliers in other EC member states.
[2] Where C & E are satisfied that limit will not be exceeded in this period.

Rate of tax

	Standard rate	VAT fraction	Reduced rate	VAT fraction
1.9.97 onwards	17.5%	7/47	5%	1/21
1.4.94–31.8.97	17.5%	7/47	8%	2/27
1.4.91–31.3.94	17.5%	7/47	n/a	n/a
18.6.79–31.3.91	15%	3/23	n/a	n/a

Flat rate scheme for farmers: 4% flat rate addition to sale price.

Penalties and surcharges

Offence	Penalty
Failure to pay tax due under the payment on account scheme on time (VATA 1994 s 59A)	(From 1.6.96) Default surcharge

Failure to submit return or pay tax due within time limit. (Where a return is late but the tax is paid on time or no tax is due, a default is recorded but no surcharge arises) (VATA 1994 s 59)	Default surcharge: the greater of £30 and a specified percentage of outstanding VAT for period, depending on number of defaults in surcharge period–
	  1st default in period: 2%
	  2nd default: 5%
	  3rd default: 10%
	  4th default: 15%
	  Further defaults: 15%
	NB: Surcharge assessments are not issued for sums of less than £200 unless the rate of the surcharge is 10% or more

Evasion of VAT: conduct involving dishonesty (VATA 1994 s 60)	Amount of tax evaded or sought to be evaded (subject to mitigation)
Issuing incorrect certificate as to zero-rating (or, from 27 July 1999, as to eligibility to receive reduced-rate for fuel and power) (VATA 1994 s 62; FA 1999 s 17)	Difference between tax actually charged and tax which should have been charged
Misdeclaration or neglect (VATA 1994 s 63)	15% of VAT which would have been lost if inaccuracy had not been discovered
Repeated misdeclarations (VATA 1994 s 64)	15% of VAT which would have been lost if second and subsequent inaccuracies within penalty period had not been discovered
Material inaccuracy in EC sales statement (VATA 1994 s 65)	£100 for each material inaccuracy in 2 year penalty period (which commences following notice of second material inaccuracy)

Failure to submit an EC sales statement (VATA 1994 s 66)	Greater of £50 and a daily penalty (for no more than 100 days) depending on number of failures in default period–
	  1st failure: £5
	  2nd failure: £10
	  3rd and further failures: £15

Failure to notify liability for registration or change in nature of supplies by person exempted from registration (VATA 1994 s 67)
(From 1.1.96 reintroduced for failure to notify liability for registration when business transferred as going concern)
	Greater of £50 and a specified percentage of the tax for which the person would have been liable, depending on the period of failure–
	  9 months or less: 5%
	  Over 9, up to 18 months: 10%
	  Over 18 months: 15%

Unauthorised issue of invoices (VATA 1994 s 67)	Greater of £50 and 15% of amount shown as or representing VAT
Breach of walking possession agreement (VATA 1994 s 68)	50% of VAT due and amount recoverable
Failure to preserve records for prescribed period (VATA 1994 s 69)	£500

Breaches of regulatory provisions, including failure to notify cessation of liability or entitlement to be registered, failure to keep records and non-compliance with any regulations made under VATA 1994 (VATA 1994 s 69)	Greater of £50 and a daily penalty (for no more than 100 days) of a specified amount depending on number of failures in preceding two years–
	  No previous failures: £5 per day
	  1 previous failure: £10 per day
	  2 or more: £15 per day

Breaches of regulatory provisions involving failure to pay VAT or submit return by due date (VATA 1994 s 69)	Greater of £50 and a daily penalty (for no more than 100 days) of a specified amount depending on number of failures in preceding two years–
	  No previous failures: greater of £5 and $\frac{1}{6}$% of VAT due
	  1 previous failure: greater of £10 and $\frac{1}{3}$% of VAT due
	  2 or more: greater of £15 and $\frac{1}{2}$% of VAT due

Failure to comply with statutory responsibility to pay correct amount of tax on time (FA 1997 ss 51,52)	(From 1 July 1997) Distress (diligence, ie poinding and sale and arrestment, in Scotland)
Failure to comply with VAT tribunal directions or summons (VATA 1994 Sch 12 para 10)	Up to £1,000
Failure by person to whom an attachment notice has been given and who is or becomes indebted to the defaulter to pay the required amount (FA 1997)	£250 plus £20 for each day failure continues after payment has become due
Failure to comply with the accounting, invoicing, record-keeping and notification requirements for supplies involving investment gold (FA 2000 s137).	(From 28 July 2000) 17.5% of the value of transactions concerned.

Default interest

The prescribed rate of interest for the purposes of VATA 1994 s 74 (the provisions of which were operative from 1 April 1990) has varied as follows:

	Rate
From 6 May 2001	7.5%
6 February 2000–5 May 2001	8.5%
6 March 1999–5 February 2000	7.5%
6 January 1999–5 March 1999	8.5%
6 July 1998–5 January 1999	9.5%
6 February 1996–5 July 1998	6.25%
6 March 1995–5 February 1996	7%
6 October 1994–5 March 1995	6.25%
6 January 1994–5 October 1994	5.5%
6 March 1993–5 January 1994	6.25%
6 December 1992–5 March 1993	7%
6 November 1992–5 December 1992	7.75%
6 October 1991–5 November 1992	9.25%

Interest on VAT overpaid in cases of official error
(VATA 1994 s 78)

	Rate		Rate
From 6 May 2001	4%	1 January 1989–31 October 1989	13%
6 February 2000–5 May 2001	5%	1 November 1988–31 December 1988	12.25%
6 March 1999–5 February 2000	4%	1 August 1988–31 October 1988	11%
6 January 1999–5 March 1999	5%	1 May 1988–31 July 1988	9.5%
1 April 1997–5 January 1999	6%	1 December 1987–30 April 1988	11%
6 February–31 March 1997	8%	1 November 1987–30 November 1987	11.25%
16 October 1991–5 February 1993	10.25%	1 April 1987–31 October 1987	11.75%
1 April 1991–15 October 1991	12%	1 January 1987–31 March 1987	12.25%
1 November 1989–31 March 1991	14.25%		

Zero-rated supplies

A zero-rated supply is a taxable supply, but the rate of tax is nil.
(References are to VATA 1994 Sch 8)

Group 1—Food.
Group 2—Sewerage services and water.
Group 3—Books etc.
Group 4—Talking books for the blind and handicapped and wireless sets for the blind.
Group 5—Construction of buildings etc.
Group 6—Protected buildings.
Group 7—International services.
Group 8—Transport.
Group 9—Caravans and houseboats.
Group 10—Gold.
Group 11—Bank notes.
Group 12—Drugs, medicines, aids for the handicapped etc.
Group 13—Imports, exports etc.
Group 15—Charities etc.
Group 16—Clothing and footwear.

Reduced rate supplies
(References are to VATA 1994 Sch 7A)

Group 1—Domestic fuel and power.
Group 2—Installation of energy-saving materials.
Group 3—Grant-funded installation of heating equipment or security goods or connection of a gas supply.
Group 4—Women's sanitary products.
Group 5—Children's car seats.
Group 6—Residential conversions.
Group 7—Renovation and alteration of dwellings.

Exempt supplies

No tax is chargeable on an exempt supply, and input tax cannot be recovered except as allowed under the partial exemption provisions (SI 1995/2518 Pt XIV; VAT Notice 706).
(References are to VATA 1994 Sch 9)

Group 1—Land.
Group 2—Insurance.
Group 3—Postal services.
Group 4—Betting, gaming and lotteries.
Group 5—Finance.
Group 6—Education.
Group 7—Health and welfare.
Group 8—Burial and cremation.
Group 9—Subscriptions to trade unions, professional and other public interest bodies.
Group 10—Sport, sports competitions and physical education.
Group 11—Works of art etc.
Group 12—Fund-raising events by charities and other qualifying bodies.
Group 13—Cultural services etc.
Group 14—Supplies of goods where input tax cannot be recovered.
Group 15—Investment gold.

Partial exemption

De minimis limit for application of partial exemption rules
SI 1995/2518 reg 106

	Exempt input tax not exceeding
Tax years beginning after 30.11.94	(a) £625 per month on average; and (b) 50% of total input tax for prescribed accounting period
Periods beginning between 1.4.92 and 30.11.94	£600 per month on average

Capital goods scheme

Input tax adjustment following change in taxable use of capital goods
VATA 1994 s 34, SI 1995/2518 regs 112–116 (77/388/EEC art 20), SI 1999/599 reg 6.
From 1 April 1990

Item	*Value*	*Adjustment period*
Computer equipment	£50,000 or more	5 years
Land and buildings	£250,000 or more	10 years (5 years where interest had less than 10 years to run on acquisition)

Adjustment formula

$$\frac{\text{Total input tax on item}}{\text{Length of adjustment period}} \times \text{adjustment percentage}$$

The adjustment percentage is the percentage change in the extent to which the item is used (or treated as used) in making taxable supplies between the first interval in the adjustment period and a subsequent interval. (The first interval generally ends on the last day of the tax year in which the input tax was incurred.)

Car fuel

VAT-inclusive scale figures are used to assess VAT due on petrol provided at below cost price for private journeys by registered traders or their employees, where the petrol has been provided from business resources.

	12 months	VAT due per car	3 months	VAT due per car	1 month	VAT due per car
2001–02						
Diesel engine						
Cylinder capacity: 2,000cc or less	£900	£134.04	£225	£33.51	£75	£11.17
more than 2,000cc	£1,145	£170.53	£286	£42.59	£95	£14.14
Any other type of engine						
Cylinder capacity: 1,400cc or less	£970	£144.46	£242	£36.04	£80	£11.91
Over 1,400cc up to 2,000cc	£1,230	£183.19	£307	£45.72	£102	£15.19
Over 2,000cc	£1,815	£270.31	£453	£67.46	£151	£22.48
2000–01						
Diesel engine						
Cylinder capacity: 2,000cc or less	£930	£138.51	£232	£34.55	£77	£11.46
more than 2,000cc	£1,180	£175.74	£295	£43.93	£98	£14.59
Any other type of engine						
Cylinder capacity: 1,400cc or less	£1,025	£152.65	£256	£38.12	£85	£12.65
Over 1,400cc up to 2,000cc	£1,300	£193.61	£325	£48.40	£108	£16.08
Over 2,000cc	£1,915	£285.21	£478	£71.19	£159	£23.68
1999–2000						
Diesel engine						
Cylinder capacity: 2,000cc or less	£785	£116.91	£196	£29.19	£65	£9.68
more than 2,000cc	£995	£148.19	£248	£36.93	£82	£12.21
Any other type of engine						
Cylinder capacity: 1,400cc or less	£850	£126.59	£212	£31.57	£70	£10.42
Over 1,400cc up to 2,000cc	£1,075	£160.10	£268	£39.91	£89	£13.25
Over 2,000cc	£1,585	£236.06	£396	£58.97	£132	£19.65
1998–99						
Diesel engine						
Cylinder capacity: 2,000cc or less	£785	£116.91	£196	£29.19	£65	£9.68
more than 2,000cc	£995	£148.19	£248	£36.93	£82	£12.21
Any other type of engine						
Cylinder capacity: 1,400cc or less	£850	£126.59	£212	£31.57	£70	£10.42
Over 1,400cc up to 2,000cc	£1,075	£160.10	£268	£39.91	£89	£13.25
Over 2,000cc	£1,585	£236.06	£396	£58.97	£132	£19.65

HM Customs and Excise: VAT notices

New notices no longer carry a designation of the year of issue or revision, but this is retained here as a guide to the year of publication of the latest version. Several leaflets and notices contain Update inserts, published from time to time.

(Cancelled leaflets have been deleted from the list.)

Notice		Date	Title
48		1999	**Extra-statutory concessions**
60		1998	**The Intrastat general guide**
400		1999	**HM Customs and Excise Charter Standards**
431		1999	**Visiting forces**
700		2000	**The VAT guide**
	700/1	2001‡	Should I be registered for VAT?
	700/1W	1997	Ddylwnifod wedi fy nghofrestru am TAW?
	700/1A	1997	Should I be registered for VAT? Distance selling
	700/1AW	1997	Ddylwnifod wedify nghofrestru am TAW? – Gweythmo bell
	700/1B	1997	Should I be registered for VAT? Acquisitions
	700/1BW	1997	Ddylwnifod wedify nghofrestru am TAW? – Caffaeliadau
	700/2	1999	Group treatment
	700/3	1998	Registration for VAT: Corporate bodies organised in divisions
	700/4	1997	Registration for VAT: non-established taxable persons
	700/7	1994	Business promotion schemes
	700/9	1996	Transfer of a business as a going concern
	700/9W	1996	Trosglwyddo busnes fel busnes byw
	700/11‡	2001	Cancelling your registration
	700/12	2001	Filling in your VAT return
	700/12W	1995	Llanwi'ch ffurflen TAW
	700/14	1999	Video cassette films: rental and part-exchange
	700/15	2000	The ins and outs of VAT
	700/15W	1995	Manylion TAW
	700/17	1996	Funded pension schemes
	700/18	1997	Relief from VAT on bad debts
	700/18W	1997	Rhyddhad rhag TAW ar ddrwg-ddyledion
	700/21	1995	Keeping records and accounts
	700/21W	1995	Cadw cofnodion a chyfrifon
	700/22	1989	Admissions
	700/24	1994	Postage and delivery charges
	700/25	2000	Taxis and hire cars
	700/28	1994	Estate agents
	700/31	1999	Pawnbrokers: disposals of pledged goods
	700/33	1995	Government funded training programmes and schemes to help the unemployed
	700/34	1994	Staff
	700/35	1997	Business gifts and samples
	700/41	1995	Late registration penalty
	700/41W	1995	Dirwy am gofrestru yn hwyr
	700/42	2000	Misdeclaration penalty and repeated misdeclaration penalty
	700/43	1996	Default interest
	700/44	2000	Barristers and advocates who cease to practise
	700/45	2000	How to correct VAT errors and make adjustments or claims
	700/45W	1999	Sut i gywiro gwallau y dewch o hyd iddynt ar eich ffurflenni TAW
	700/46	1993	Agricultural flat rate scheme
	700/47	1993	Confidentiality in VAT matters (Tax advisers) – Statement of practice
	700/50	1997	Default surcharge
	700/50W	1997	Gordal diffyg talu
	700/51	1995	VAT enquiries guide
	700/51W	1995	Arweiniad ar ymholiadau TAW
	700/52	1996	Notice of requirement to give security to Customs and Excise
	700/52W	1996	Hysbysiad o'r angen i roi gwarant i'r Tollau Tramor o Chartref
	700/55	1993	VAT input tax appeals: luxuries, amusements and entertainment
	700/56	1999	Insolvency
	700/57	1999	VAT – administrative agreements entered into with trade bodies
	700/58	1998	Treatment of VAT repayment returns and VAT repayment supplements
	700/58W	1998	Triniaeth ffurflenni ad-dalu TAW ac ychwanegiad at ad-dallad TAW
	700/60	1996	Payments on account
	700/61	1997	Artificial separation of business activities: statement of practice
	700/64	1996	Motoring expenses
	700/65	1996	Business entertainment
	700/67	1997	The VAT registration scheme for racehorse owners
701	701/1	1995‡	Charities
	701/5	1990	Clubs and associations
	701/6	1997	Charity-funded equipment for medical, veterinary etc. uses
	701/7	1994‡	VAT reliefs for people with disabilities
	701/8	1997	Postage stamps and philatelic supplies
	701/9	1985	Terminal markets: dealings with commodities
	701/10	1999	Liability of printed and similar matter
	701/12	2000	Sales of antiques, works of art etc from historic houses
	701/13	1995	Gaming and amusement machines
	701/14	1997	Food
	701/15	1995	Food for animals
	701/16	1999	Water and sewage services
	701/18	2001	Reduced rate of VAT on women's sanitary protection products
	701/19	1995	Fuel and power
	701/20	1996†	Caravans and houseboats
	701/21	2000	Gold
	701/21A	2000	Investment gold coins
	701/22	1995	Tools for the manufacture of goods for export

HM Customs and Excise: VAT notices — continued

Notice		Date	Title
	701/23	1995	Protective boots and helmets
	701/24	1992	Parking facilities
	701/26	1995	Betting and gaming
	701/27	1997	Bingo
	701/28	1997	Lotteries
	701/29	1992	Finance
	701/30	2000	Education and vocational training
	701/31	1992	Health
	701/32	1997	Burial, cremation and the commemoration of the dead
	701/33	1997	Trade unions, professional bodies and learned societies
	701/34	1989	Competitions in sport and physical recreation
	701/35	1995	Youth clubs
	701/36	1997	Insurance
	701/37	1994	Live animals
	701/37W	1994	Anifeiliaid byw
	701/38	1999	Seeds and plants
	701/39	2000	VAT liability law
	701/40	1999	Abattoirs
	701/41	1995	Sponsorship
	701/43	1993	Financial futures and options
	701/44	1998	Securities
	701/45	1994	Sport and physical education
	701/47	1996	Culture
	701/48	1997	Corporate purchasing cards
	701/58	2001	Charity advertising and goods connected with collecting donations
702		1998	**Imports** (Single Market supplement)
	702/4	1994	Importing computer software
	702/6	1991	Import VAT certificates
	702/7	1993	Import VAT relief for goods supplied onward to another country in the European Community
	702/9	1998	Warehousing and free zones
703		1996	**Exports**
	703/1	1995	Supply of freight containers for export or removal from the UK
	703/2	1999	Sailaway boats supplied for export outside the European Community
	703/3	1999	Sailaway boat scheme
704		1999	**Retail exports**
	704/1	1999	VAT refunds for travellers departing from the European Community
	704/2	1999	Traveller's guide to the retail export scheme
705		1995	**Personal exports of new motor vehicles to destinations outside the European Community from 1 January 1993**
705A		1995	**VAT: Supplies of vehicles under the personal export scheme for removal from the EC**
706		1999	**Partial exemption**
	706/1	1992	Self-supply of stationery
	706/2	2001	Capital goods scheme
708		1997	**Buildings and construction**
	708/5	1997	Registered social landlords (Housing Associations, etc)
709	709/1	1987	Industrial, staff and public sector catering
	709/2	1991	Catering and take-away food
	709/3	1993	Hotels and holiday accommodation
	709/4	1988	Package holidays and other holiday services
	709/5	1998	Tour operators' margin scheme
	709/6	1997	Travel agents
710	710/1	1991	Theatrical agents and Nett Acts
	710/2	1983	Agencies providing nurses and nursing auxiliaries
714		1995	**Young children's clothing and footwear**
714A		1995	**Young children's clothing and footwear: schedule of maximum sizes for zero-rating**
718		1999	**Margin schemes for secondhand goods, works of art, antiques and collectors' items**
719		1996	**VAT refunds for DIY builders and converters**
719W		1996	**Ad-daliadau TAW i adeiladwyr ac addaswyr 'ymdopi' ch hun'**
723		2000	**Refunds of VAT in the European Community for EC and non-EC businesses**
725		1998	**VAT: the Single Market**
727		1997	**Retail schemes†**
727W		1997	**Cynlluniau Manwerthu**
	727/2	1997	Bespoke retail schemes
	727/3	1997	How to work the point of sale scheme
	727/4	1997	How to work the apportionment schemes
	727/5	1997	How to work the direct calculation schemes
	727/6	1997	Choosing your retail scheme
728		2000	**Motor vehicles, boats, aircraft: intra-EC movements by persons not registrable for VAT**
730		1994	**Civil evasion penalty investigations: Statement of practice**
731		1999	**Cash accounting†**
731W		1999	**Cyfrifo arian**
732		1996	**Annual accounting**
732W		1996	**Cyfrifo blynyddol**
741		1998	**Place of supply of services**
742		1995	**Land and property†**
	742/1	1990	Letting of facilities for sport and physical recreation
	742/2	1992	Sporting rights
	742/3	1995	Scottish land law terms
742C		1995	**Land and property: law**
744A		1996	**Passenger transport**

HM Customs and Excise: VAT notices — continued

Notice	Date	Title
744B	1997	**Freight transport and associated services**
744C	1997	**Ships, aircraft and associated services**
744D	1996	**International services – zero rating**
747	2000	**VAT notices having the force of law**
749	2000	**Local authorities and similar bodies**
749W	2000	**Awdurdodau lleol a chyrff tebyg**
750	1998	**Community/Common transit**
759	1998	**An introduction to Customs Freight Simplified Procedures**
760	1998	**Customs freight simplified procedures (CFSP)**
761	1998	**Visits by Customs and Excise Officers to traders using Customs Freight Simplified Procedures**
770	1998	**Imported goods: End-use relief**
915	2001	**Assessments and time limits: statement of practice**
920	1999	**The single currency**
930	1999	**What if I don't pay?**
989	1997	**Visits by Customs and Excise officers**
989W	1997	**Ymweliadau gan Swyddogion y Tollau Tramor a Chartref**
999	2001	**Catalogue of publications**
1000	2001	**Complaints and putting things right**
1000W	1999	**Cwynion a sut i ddatrys problemau: ein côd ymarfer**
CWLI	1999	Starting your own business?
CWL4	2001	Fund-raising events: exemption for charities and other qualifying bodies
M/L19	2000	What is VAT?
–	1995	Welcome to VAT
Explanatory leaflet:	1999	Appeals and applications to the tribunals

Information sheets: available also at http://www.hmce.gov.uk.

4/93	Intra-EC processing of goods: simplification
5/95	VAT – changes to tour operators' margin scheme
6/95	VAT – NHS dispensing doctors
1/96	VAT – filling in your EC sales list (Form VAT 101)
3/96	Tour operators' margin scheme – practical implementation of the airline charter option following the changes which came into effect on 1 January 1996
4/96	Tour operators' margin scheme – practical implementation of the agency option following the changes which came into effect on 1 January 1996
5/96	VAT – supplies by dentists
1/97	Tour operators' margin scheme – practical implementation of the 'trader to trader (wholesale) option' following the changes which came into effect on 1 January 1996
6/97	Drugs, medicine and aids for the handicapped – liability with effect from 1 January 1998
2/98	Export house VAT provisions: withdrawal
3/98	Local authorities and NHS joint stores depots
5/98	Local authorities: supplies to new unitary authorities under local government reorganisation (transitional arrangements)
6/98	Local authority pension funds: VAT treatment and administrative concession
8/98	Charities – supply, repair and maintenance of relevant goods (including adapted motor vehicles)
9/98	VAT relief on the installation of energy saving materials
2/99	Local Authorities: agreement of section 33 recovery methods
3/99	VAT: new deal programme
6/99	Charities: liabilities of routine domestic tasks
7/99	Construction services: new rule for accounting for VAT
8/99	Opticians: Apportionment of charges for supplies of spectacles and dispensing
9/99	Imported works of art, antiques and collectors' pieces: changes to the reduced rate of VAT
10/99	Financial exemptions: changes brought about by the 1999 Finance Order
11/99	VAT - exemption of subscriptions to political, religious, patriotic, philosophical, philanthropic and civic bodies
12/99	VAT on business cars–changes to take effect on 1 December 1999
1/00	VAT: Reduced rate for the installation of energy saving materials
2/00	Exports and removals: Conditions for zero-rating
3/00	Supplies through undisclosed agents: revised VAT treatment
4/00	Civil evasion cases: Trial of a new approach to investigations – statement of practice
5/00	Construction and building materials
1/01	VAT relief for young children's clothing and footwear
3/01	VAT: Digitised publications
4/01	VAT Budget changes: VAT reduced rate – urban regeneration
7/01	VAT: Motor vehicles adapted for disabled people
Video and booklet	1995 Welcome to VAT

† Publications having legal or quasi-legal force.   ‡ Now available in large print.

22% grossing-up table

Am't	Grossed at 22%	Am't	Grossed at 22%	Am't	Grossed at 22%	Am't	Grossed at 22%	Am't	Grossed at 22%	Am't	Grossed at 22%	Am't	Grossed at 22%	Am't	Grossed at 22%	Am't	Grossed at 22%	Am't	Grossed at 22%
£	£	£	£	£	£	£	£	£	£	£	£	£	£	£	£	£	£	£	£
1	1·28	71	91·03	141	180·77	211	270·51	281	360·26	351	450·00	421	539·74	491	629·49				
2	2·56	72	92·31	142	182·05	212	271·79	282	361·54	352	451·28	422	541·03	492	630·77				
3	3·85	73	93·59	143	183·33	213	273·08	283	362·82	353	452·56	423	542·31	493	632·05				
4	5·13	74	94·87	144	184·62	214	274·36	284	364·10	354	453·85	424	543·59	494	633·33				
5	6·41	75	96·15	145	185·90	215	275·64	285	365·38	355	455·13	425	544·87	495	634·62				
6	7·69	76	97·44	146	187·18	216	276·92	286	366·67	356	456·41	426	546·15	496	635·90				
7	8·97	77	98·72	147	188·46	217	278·21	287	367·95	357	457·69	427	547·44	497	637·18				
8	10·26	78	100·00	148	189·74	218	279·49	288	369·23	358	458·97	428	548·72	498	638·46				
9	11·54	79	101·28	149	191·03	219	280·77	289	370·51	359	460·26	429	550·00	499	639·74				
10	12·82	80	102·56	150	192·31	220	282·05	290	371·79	360	461·54	430	551·28	500	641·03				
11	14·10	81	103·85	151	193·59	221	283·33	291	373·08	361	462·82	431	552·56	510	653·85				
12	15·38	82	105·13	152	194·87	222	284·62	292	374·36	362	464·10	432	553·85	520	666·67				
13	16·67	83	106·41	153	196·15	223	285·90	293	375·64	363	465·38	433	555·13	530	679·49				
14	17·95	84	107·69	154	197·44	224	287·18	294	376·92	364	466·67	434	556·41	540	692·31				
15	19·23	85	108·97	155	198·72	225	288·46	295	378·21	365	467·95	435	557·69	550	705·13				
16	20·51	86	110·26	156	200·00	226	289·74	296	379·49	366	469·23	436	558·97	560	717·95				
17	21·79	87	111·54	157	201·28	227	291·03	297	380·77	367	470·51	437	560·26	570	730·77				
18	23·08	88	112·82	158	202·56	228	292·31	298	382·05	368	471·79	438	561·54	580	743·59				
19	24·36	89	114·10	159	203·85	229	293·59	299	383·33	369	473·08	439	562·82	590	756·41				
20	25·64	90	115·38	160	205·13	230	294·87	300	384·62	370	474·36	440	564·10	600	769·23				
21	26·92	91	116·67	161	206·41	231	296·15	301	385·90	371	475·64	441	565·38	610	782·05				
22	28·21	92	117·95	162	207·69	232	297·44	302	387·18	372	476·92	442	566·67	620	794·87				
23	29·49	93	119·23	163	208·97	233	298·72	303	388·46	373	478·21	443	567·95	630	807·69				
24	30·77	94	120·51	164	210·26	234	300·00	304	389·74	374	479·49	444	569·23	640	820·51				
25	32·05	95	121·79	165	211·54	235	301·28	305	391·03	375	480·77	445	570·51	650	833·33				
26	33·33	96	123·08	166	212·82	236	302·56	306	392·31	376	482·05	446	571·79	660	846·15				
27	34·62	97	124·36	167	214·10	237	303·85	307	393·59	377	483·33	447	573·08	670	858·97				
28	35·90	98	125·64	168	215·38	238	305·13	308	394·87	378	484·62	448	574·36	680	871·79				
29	37·18	99	126·92	169	216·67	239	306·41	309	396·15	379	485·90	449	575·64	690	884·62				
30	38·46	100	128·21	170	217·95	240	307·69	310	397·44	380	487·18	450	576·92	700	897·44				
31	39·74	101	129·49	171	219·23	241	308·97	311	398·72	381	488·46	451	578·21	710	910·26				
32	41·03	102	130·77	172	220·51	242	310·26	312	400·00	382	489·74	452	579·49	720	923·08				
33	42·31	103	132·05	173	221·79	243	311·54	313	401·28	383	491·03	453	580·77	730	935·90				
34	43·59	104	133·33	174	223·08	244	312·82	314	402·56	384	492·31	454	582·05	740	948·72				
35	44·87	105	134·62	175	224·36	245	314·10	315	403·85	385	493·59	455	583·33	750	961·54				
36	46·15	106	135·90	176	225·64	246	315·38	316	405·13	386	494·87	456	584·62	760	974·36				
37	47·44	107	137·18	177	226·92	247	316·67	317	406·41	387	496·15	457	585·90	770	987·18				
38	48·72	108	138·46	178	228·21	248	317·95	318	407·69	388	497·44	458	587·18	780	1,000·00				
39	50·00	109	139·74	179	229·49	249	319·23	319	408·97	389	498·72	459	588·46	790	1,012·82				
40	51·28	110	141·03	180	230·77	250	320·51	320	410·26	390	500·00	460	589·74	800	1,025·64				
41	52·56	111	142·31	181	232·05	251	321·79	321	411·54	391	501·28	461	591·03	810	1,038·46				
42	53·85	112	143·59	182	233·33	252	323·08	322	412·82	392	502·56	462	592·31	820	1,051·28				
43	55·13	113	144·87	183	234·62	253	324·36	323	414·10	393	503·85	463	593·59	830	1,064·10				
44	56·41	114	146·15	184	235·90	254	325·64	324	415·38	394	505·13	464	594·87	840	1,076·92				
45	57·69	115	147·44	185	237·18	255	326·92	325	416·67	395	506·41	465	596·15	850	1,089·74				
46	58·97	116	148·72	186	238·46	256	328·21	326	417·95	396	507·69	466	597·44	860	1,102·56				
47	60·26	117	150·00	187	239·74	257	329·49	327	419·23	397	508·97	467	598·72	870	1,115·38				
48	61·54	118	151·28	188	241·03	258	330·77	328	420·51	398	510·26	468	600·00	880	1,128·21				
49	62·82	119	152·56	189	242·31	259	332·05	329	421·79	399	511·54	469	601·28	890	1,141·03				
50	64·10	120	153·85	190	243·59	260	333·33	330	423·08	400	512·82	470	602·56	900	1,153·85				
51	65·38	121	155·13	191	244·87	261	334·62	331	424·36	401	514·10	471	603·85	910	1,166·67				
52	66·67	122	156·41	192	246·15	262	335·90	332	425·64	402	515·38	472	605·13	920	1,179·49				
53	67·95	123	157·69	193	247·44	263	337·18	333	426·92	403	516·67	473	606·41	930	1,192·31				
54	69·23	124	158·97	194	248·72	264	338·46	334	428·21	404	517·95	474	607·69	940	1,205·13				
55	70·51	125	160·26	195	250·00	265	339·74	335	429·49	405	519·23	475	608·97	950	1,217·95				
56	71·79	126	161·54	196	251·28	266	341·03	336	430·77	406	520·51	476	610·26	960	1,230·77				
57	73·08	127	162·82	197	252·56	267	342·31	337	432·05	407	521·79	477	611·54	970	1,243·59				
58	74·36	128	164·10	198	253·85	268	343·59	338	433·33	408	523·08	478	612·82	980	1,256·41				
59	75·64	129	165·38	199	255·13	269	344·87	339	434·62	409	524·36	479	614·10	990	1,269·23				
60	76·92	130	166·67	200	256·41	270	346·15	340	435·90	410	525·64	480	615·38	1,000	1,282·05				
61	78·21	131	167·95	201	257·69	271	347·44	341	437·18	411	526·92	481	616·67	2,000	2,564·10				
62	79·49	132	169·23	202	258·97	272	348·72	342	438·46	412	528·21	482	617·95	3,000	3,846·15				
63	80·77	133	170·51	203	260·26	273	350·00	343	439·74	413	529·49	483	619·23	4,000	5,128·20				
64	82·05	134	171·79	204	261·54	274	351·28	344	441·03	414	530·77	484	620·51	5,000	6,410·26				
65	83·33	135	173·08	205	262·82	275	352·56	345	442·31	415	532·05	485	621·79	6,000	7,692·31				
66	84·62	136	174·36	206	264·10	276	353·85	346	443·59	416	533·33	486	623·08	7,000	8,974·36				
67	85·90	137	175·64	207	265·38	277	355·13	347	444·87	417	534·62	487	624·36	8,000	10,256·41				
68	87·18	138	176·92	208	266·67	278	356·41	348	446·15	418	535·90	488	625·64	9,000	11,538·46				
69	88·46	139	178·21	209	267·95	279	357·69	349	447·44	419	537·18	489	626·92	10,000	12,820·51				
70	89·74	140	179·49	210	269·23	280	358·97	350	448·72	420	538·46	490	688·21	11,000	14,102·56				

34% grossing-up table

(*The rate applicable to trusts remains at 34% for 2001-02.*)

Am't	Grossed at 34%	Am't	Grossed at 34%	Am't	Grossed at 34%	Am't	Grossed at 34%	Am't	Grossed at 34%	Am't	Grossed at 34%	Am't	Grossed at 34%	Am't	Grossed at 34%	Am't	Grossed at 34%	Am't	Grossed at 34%
£	£	£	£	£	£	£	£	£	£	£	£	£	£	£	£	£	£	£	£
1	1·52	71	107·58	141	213·64	211	319·70	281	425·76	351	531·82	421	637·88	491	743·94				
2	3·03	72	109·09	142	215·15	212	321·21	282	427·27	352	533·33	422	639·39	492	745·45				
3	4·55	73	110·61	143	216·67	213	322·73	283	428·79	353	534·85	423	640·91	493	746·97				
4	6·06	74	112·12	144	218·18	214	324·24	284	430·30	354	536·36	424	642·42	494	748·48				
5	7·58	75	113·64	145	219·70	215	325·76	285	431·82	355	537·88	425	643·94	495	750·00				
6	9·09	76	115·15	146	221·21	216	327·27	286	433·33	356	539·39	426	645·45	496	751·52				
7	10·61	77	116·67	147	222·73	217	328·79	287	434·85	357	540·91	427	646·97	497	753·03				
8	12·12	78	118·18	148	224·24	218	330·30	288	436·36	358	542·42	428	648·48	498	754·55				
9	13·64	79	119·70	149	225·76	219	331·82	289	437·88	359	543·94	429	650·00	499	756·06				
10	15·15	80	121·21	150	227·27	220	333·33	290	439·39	360	545·45	430	651·52	500	757·58				
11	16·67	81	122·73	151	228·79	221	334·85	291	440·91	361	546·97	431	653·03	510	772·73				
12	18·18	82	124·24	152	230·30	222	336·36	292	442·42	362	548·48	432	654·55	520	787·88				
13	19·70	83	125·76	153	231·82	223	337·88	293	443·94	363	550·00	433	656·06	530	803·03				
14	21·21	84	127·27	154	233·33	224	339·39	294	445·45	364	551·52	434	657·58	540	818·18				
15	22·73	85	128·79	155	234·85	225	340·91	295	446·97	365	553·03	435	659·09	550	833·33				
16	24·24	86	130·30	156	236·36	226	342·42	296	448·48	366	554·55	436	660·61	560	848·48				
17	25·76	87	131·82	157	237·88	227	343·94	297	450·00	367	556·06	437	662·12	570	863·64				
18	27·27	88	133·33	158	239·39	228	345·45	298	451·52	368	557·58	438	663·64	580	878·79				
19	28·79	89	134·85	159	240·91	229	346·97	299	453·03	369	559·09	439	665·15	590	893·94				
20	30·30	90	136·36	160	242·42	230	348·48	300	454·55	370	560·61	440	666·67	600	909·09				
21	31·82	91	137·88	161	243·94	231	350·00	301	456·06	371	562·12	441	668·18	610	924·24				
22	33·33	92	139·39	162	245·45	232	351·52	302	457·58	372	563·64	442	669·70	620	939·39				
23	34·85	93	140·91	163	246·97	233	353·03	303	459·09	373	565·15	443	671·21	630	954·55				
24	36·36	94	142·42	164	248·48	234	354·55	304	460·61	374	566·67	444	672·73	640	969·70				
25	37·88	95	143·94	165	250·00	235	356·06	305	462·12	375	568·18	445	674·24	650	984·85				
26	39·39	96	145·45	166	251·52	236	357·58	306	463·64	376	569·70	446	675·76	660	1,000·00				
27	40·91	97	146·97	167	253·03	237	359·09	307	465·15	377	571·21	447	677·27	670	1,015·15				
28	42·42	98	148·48	168	254·55	238	360·61	308	466·67	378	572·73	448	678·79	680	1,030·30				
29	43·94	99	150·00	169	256·06	239	362·12	309	468·18	379	574·24	449	680·30	690	1,045·45				
30	45·45	100	151·52	170	257·58	240	363·64	310	469·70	380	575·76	450	681·82	700	1,060·61				
31	46·97	101	153·03	171	259·09	241	365·15	311	471·21	381	577·27	451	683·33	710	1,075·76				
32	48·48	102	154·55	172	260·61	242	366·67	312	472·73	382	578·79	452	684·85	720	1,090·91				
33	50·00	103	156·06	173	262·12	243	368·18	313	474·24	383	580·30	453	686·36	730	1,106·06				
34	51·52	104	157·58	174	263·64	244	369·70	314	475·76	384	581·82	454	687·88	740	1,121·21				
35	53·03	105	159·09	175	265·15	245	371·21	315	477·27	385	583·33	455	689·39	750	1,136·36				
36	54·55	106	160·61	176	266·67	246	372·73	316	478·79	386	584·85	456	690·91	760	1,151·52				
37	56·06	107	162·12	177	268·18	247	374·24	317	480·30	387	586·36	457	692·42	770	1,166·67				
38	57·58	108	163·64	178	269·70	248	375·76	318	481·82	388	587·88	458	693·94	780	1,181·82				
39	59·09	109	165·15	179	271·21	249	377·27	319	483·33	389	589·39	459	695·45	790	1,196·97				
40	60·61	110	166·67	180	272·73	250	378·79	320	484·85	390	590·91	460	696·97	800	1,212·12				
41	62·12	111	168·18	181	274·24	251	380·30	321	486·36	391	592·42	461	698·48	810	1,227·27				
42	63·64	112	169·70	182	275·76	252	381·82	322	487·88	392	593·94	462	700·00	820	1,242·42				
43	65·15	113	171·21	183	277·27	253	383·33	323	489·39	393	595·45	463	701·52	830	1,257·58				
44	66·67	114	172·73	184	278·79	254	384·85	324	490·91	394	596·97	464	703·03	840	1,272·73				
45	68·18	115	174·24	185	280·30	255	386·36	325	492·42	395	598·48	465	704·55	850	1,287·88				
46	69·70	116	175·76	186	281·82	256	387·88	326	493·94	396	600·00	466	706·06	860	1,303·03				
47	71·21	117	177·27	187	283·33	257	389·39	327	495·45	397	601·52	467	707·58	870	1,318·18				
48	72·73	118	178·79	188	284·85	258	390·91	328	496·97	398	603·03	468	709·09	880	1,333·33				
49	74·24	119	180·30	189	286·36	259	392·42	329	498·48	399	604·55	469	710·61	890	1,348·48				
50	75·76	120	181·82	190	287·88	260	393·94	330	500·00	400	606·06	470	712·12	900	1,363·64				
51	77·27	121	183·33	191	289·39	261	395·45	331	501·52	401	607·58	471	713·64	910	1,378·79				
52	78·79	122	184·85	192	290·91	262	396·97	332	503·03	402	609·09	472	715·15	920	1,393·94				
53	80·30	123	186·36	193	292·42	263	398·48	333	504·55	403	610·61	473	716·67	930	1,409·09				
54	81·82	124	187·88	194	293·94	264	400·00	334	506·06	404	612·12	474	718·18	940	1,424·24				
55	83·33	125	189·39	195	295·45	265	401·52	335	507·58	405	613·64	475	719·70	950	1,439·39				
56	84·85	126	190·91	196	296·97	266	403·03	336	509·09	406	615·15	476	721·21	960	1,454·55				
57	86·36	127	192·42	197	298·48	267	404·55	337	510·61	407	616·67	477	722·73	970	1,469·70				
58	87·88	128	193·94	198	300·00	268	406·06	338	512·12	408	618·18	478	724·24	980	1,484·85				
59	89·39	129	195·45	199	301·52	269	407·58	339	513·64	409	619·70	479	725·76	990	1,500·00				
60	90·91	130	196·97	200	303·03	270	409·09	340	515·15	410	621·21	480	727·27	1,000	1,515·15				
61	92·42	131	198·48	201	304·54	271	410·61	341	516·67	411	622·73	481	728·79	2,000	3,030·30				
62	93·94	132	200·00	202	306·06	272	412·12	342	518·18	412	624·24	482	730·30	3,000	4,545·45				
63	95·45	133	201·52	203	307·58	273	413·64	343	519·70	413	625·76	483	731·82	4,000	6,060·61				
64	96·97	134	203·03	204	309·09	274	415·15	344	521·21	414	627·27	484	733·33	5,000	7,575·76				
65	98·48	135	204·55	205	310·61	275	416·67	345	522·73	415	628·79	485	734·85	6,000	9,090·91				
66	100·00	136	206·06	206	312·12	276	418·18	346	524·24	416	630·30	486	736·36	7,000	10,606·06				
67	101·52	137	207·58	207	313·64	277	419·70	347	525·76	417	631·82	487	737·88	8,000	12,121·21				
68	103·03	138	209·09	208	315·15	278	421·21	348	527·27	418	633·33	488	739·39	9,000	13,636·36				
69	104·55	139	210·61	209	316·67	279	422·73	349	528·79	419	634·85	489	740·91	10,000	15,151·52				
70	106·06	140	212·12	210	318·18	280	424·24	350	530·30	420	636·36	490	742·42	11,000	16,666·67				

17.5% VAT (tax included in amount) – VAT fraction 7/47

Am't	VAT incl. in Am't	Am't	VAT incl. in Am't	Am't	VAT incl. in Am't	Am't	VAT incl. in Am't	Am't	VAT incl. in Am't	Am't	VAT incl. in Am't
£ or p	£ or p	£ or p	£ or p	£ or p	£ or p	£ or p	£ or p	£ or p	£ or p	£ or p	£ or p
1	0.15	71	10.57	141	21.00	211	31.43	281	41.85	810	120.64
2	0.30	72	10.72	142	21.15	212	31.57	282	42.00	820	122.13
3	0.45	73	10.87	143	21.30	213	31.72	283	42.15	830	123.62
4	0.60	74	11.02	144	21.45	214	31.87	284	42.30	840	125.11
5	0.74	75	11.17	145	21.60	215	32.02	285	42.45	850	126.60
6	0.89	76	11.32	146	21.74	216	32.17	286	42.60	860	128.09
7	1.04	77	11.47	147	21.89	217	32.32	287	42.74	870	129.57
8	1.19	78	11.62	148	22.04	218	32.47	288	42.89	880	131.06
9	1.34	79	11.77	149	22.19	219	32.62	289	43.04	890	132.55
10	1.49	80	11.91	150	22.34	220	32.77	290	43.19	900	134.04
11	1.64	81	12.06	151	22.49	221	32.91	291	43.35	910	135.53
12	1.79	82	12.21	152	22.64	222	33.06	292	43.49	920	137.02
13	1.94	83	12.36	153	22.79	223	33.21	293	43.64	930	138.51
14	2.09	84	12.51	154	22.94	224	33.36	294	43.79	940	140.00
15	2.23	85	12.66	155	23.09	225	33.51	295	43.94	950	141.49
16	2.38	86	12.81	156	23.23	226	33.66	296	44.09	960	142.98
17	2.53	87	12.96	157	23.38	227	33.81	297	44.23	970	144.47
18	2.68	88	13.11	158	23.53	228	33.96	298	44.38	980	145.96
19	2.83	89	13.26	159	23.68	229	34.11	299	44.53	990	147.45
20	2.98	90	13.40	160	23.83	230	34.26	300	44.68	1,000	148.94
21	3.13	91	13.55	161	23.98	231	34.40	310	46.17	1,100	163.83
22	3.28	92	13.70	162	24.13	232	34.55	320	47.66	1,200	178.72
23	3.43	93	13.85	163	24.28	233	34.70	330	49.15	1,300	193.62
24	3.57	94	14.00	164	24.43	234	34.85	340	50.64	1,400	208.51
25	3.72	95	14.15	165	24.57	235	35.00	350	52.13	1,500	223.40
26	3.87	96	14.30	166	24.72	236	35.15	360	53.62	1,600	238.30
27	4.02	97	14.45	167	24.87	237	35.30	370	55.11	1,700	253.19
28	4.17	98	14.60	168	25.02	238	35.45	380	56.60	1,800	268.08
29	4.32	99	14.74	169	25.17	239	35.60	390	58.09	1,900	282.98
30	4.47	100	14.89	170	25.32	240	35.74	400	59.57	2,000	297.87
31	4.62	101	15.04	171	25.47	241	35.89	410	61.06	2,100	312.77
32	4.77	102	15.19	172	25.62	242	36.04	420	62.55	2,200	327.66
33	4.91	103	15.34	173	25.77	243	36.19	430	64.04	2,300	342.55
34	5.06	104	15.49	174	25.91	244	36.34	440	65.53	2,400	357.45
35	5.21	105	15.64	175	26.06	245	36.49	450	67.02	2,500	372.34
36	5.36	106	15.79	176	26.21	246	36.64	460	68.51	2,600	387.23
37	5.51	107	15.94	177	26.36	247	36.79	470	70.00	2,700	402.13
38	5.66	108	16.09	178	26.51	248	36.94	480	71.49	2,800	417.02
39	5.81	109	16.23	179	26.66	249	37.09	490	72.98	2,900	431.91
40	5.96	110	16.38	180	26.81	250	37.23	500	74.47	3,000	446.81
41	6.11	111	16.53	181	26.96	251	37.38	510	75.96	3,100	461.70
42	6.26	112	16.68	182	27.11	252	37.53	520	77.45	3,200	476.60
43	6.40	113	16.83	183	27.26	253	37.68	530	78.94	3,300	491.49
44	6.55	114	16.98	184	27.40	254	37.83	540	80.43	3,400	506.38
45	6.70	115	17.13	185	27.55	255	37.98	550	81.91	3,500	521.28
46	6.85	116	17.28	186	27.70	256	38.13	560	83.40	3,600	536.17
47	7.00	117	17.43	187	27.85	257	38.28	570	84.89	3,700	551.06
48	7.15	118	17.57	188	28.00	258	38.43	580	86.38	3,800	565.96
49	7.30	119	17.72	189	28.15	259	38.57	590	87.87	3,900	580.85
50	7.45	120	17.87	190	28.30	260	38.72	600	89.36	4,000	595.74
51	7.60	121	18.02	191	28.45	261	38.87	610	90.85	4,100	610.64
52	7.74	122	18.17	192	28.60	262	39.02	620	92.34	4,200	625.53
53	7.89	123	18.32	193	28.74	263	39.17	630	93.83	4,300	640.43
54	8.04	124	18.47	194	28.89	264	39.32	640	95.32	4,400	655.32
55	8.19	125	18.62	195	29.04	265	39.47	650	96.81	4,500	670.21
56	8.34	126	18.77	196	29.19	266	39.62	660	98.30	4,600	685.11
57	8.49	127	18.91	197	29.34	267	39.77	670	99.79	4,700	700.00
58	8.64	128	19.06	198	29.49	268	39.91	680	101.28	4,800	714.89
59	8.79	129	19.21	199	29.64	269	40.06	690	102.77	4,900	729.79
60	8.94	130	19.36	200	29.79	270	40.21	700	104.26	5,000	744.68
61	9.09	131	19.51	201	29.94	271	40.36	710	105.74	6,000	893.62
62	9.23	132	19.66	202	30.09	272	40.51	720	107.23	7,000	1,042.55
63	9.38	133	19.81	203	30.23	273	40.66	730	108.72	8,000	1,191.49
64	9.53	134	19.96	204	30.38	274	40.81	740	110.21	9,000	1,340.42
65	9.68	135	20.11	205	30.53	275	40.96	750	111.70	10,000	1,489.36
66	9.83	136	20.26	206	30.68	276	41.11	760	113.19	11,000	1,638.30
67	9.98	137	20.40	207	30.83	277	41.26	770	114.68	12,000	1,787.23
68	10.13	138	20.55	208	30.98	278	41.40	780	116.17	13,000	1,936.17
69	10.28	139	20.70	209	31.13	279	41.55	790	117.66	14,000	2,085.11
70	10.43	140	20.85	210	31.28	280	41.70	800	119.15	15,000	2,234.04

INDEX

A

Accounts, inheritance tax	
due dates	79
excepted estates	79
Ad valorem duty, rates	89
Additional personal allowance	56
Additional rate	55
Addresses, approval and clearance applications	31
Advance corporation tax	
due date	10
interest on overdue tax	
rates	13
rates	51
Age allowance	56
Agricultural buildings allowances	52
Agricultural property relief	81
Annual accounting scheme, VAT	90
Annual exemption	
capital gains tax	36
inheritance tax	81
Approval applications, addresses	31
Attendance allowance	83
Average exchange rates	3

B

Basic rate	55
Beneficial loans to employees	64
Benefits, social security	82
Blind person's allowance	56
Bus services	60
Business economic notes	35
Business expansion scheme	76
Business property relief	81

C

Capital allowances	
agricultural buildings	52
claims, time limits	25
dredging	52
elections, time limits	25
industrial buildings	52
know-how	52
machinery and plant	53
mines and oil wells	54
patent rights	54
rates	52
research and development	54
scientific research	54
Capital gains tax	
annual exemption	36
chattel exemption	36
claims, time limits	27
due date	10
elections, time limits	27
exemptions	40
gilt-edged securities	38
hold-over relief for gifts	40
indexation allowance	42
interest on overdue tax	
rates	13
reckonable dates	11
leases	37
offences, penalties	17
principal private residence exemption	40
qualifying corporate bonds	40
rates	36
retirement relief	36
roll-over relief	
business assets	41
reinvestment, on	40
returns, penalties	17
taper relief	37
Capital goods scheme, VAT	94
Cars	
capital allowances	61
capital gains exemption	40
fixed profit car scheme	60
fuel for private use	
national insurance contributions	87
Schedule E charge	59
VAT	94
hired, Schedule D deduction	61
private use	58
national insurance contributions	87
Schedule E charge	58
Certificates of tax deposit	9
Charities	
capital gains exemption	40
covenanted donations to	74
gift aid	74
gifts in kind	74
gifts to, inheritance tax relief	81
millennium gift aid	74
payroll giving scheme	74
Chattels, capital gains exemption	36
Child benefit	83
Claims, time limits	
capital allowances	25
capital gains tax	27
corporation tax only	24
income tax only	22
Income tax and corporation tax	25
Inheritance tax	28
Clearance applications, addresses	31
Close companies	
investment-holding companies	51
Compensation, capital gains exemption	40
Computer equipment	65
Corporation tax	
chargeable gains, on	51
claims, time limits	24
corporate venturing scheme	51
due date	10
elections, time limits	24
interest on overdue tax	
rates	13
reckonable dates	11
marginal relief	51
offences, penalties	17
rates	51
research and development expenditure	51
returns, penalties	17
Covenanted payments to charity	74
Customs & Excise publications	95
Cycles and cycle safety equipment	60

D

Deed of covenant, payments under	74
Default interest	
direct taxes	
rates	13
reckonable dates	11
VAT	93
Default surcharge	92
Department of Social Security publications	88
Deregistration limits, VAT	91
Disability living allowance	83
Disabled person's tax credit	61
Dividends	55
Double taxation agreements	
air transport profits	8
capital taxes	8
income and capital gains	6
shipping profits	8
Dredging allowances	52
Due dates of tax	10

E

Elections, time limits	
capital allowances	25
capital gains tax	27
corporation tax only	24
income tax only	22
Income tax and corporation tax	25
Inheritance tax	28
Employees	
beneficial loans to	64
bus services for	60
business travel, tax-free allowances	60
car benefits	58
cycles and cycle safety equipment	60
expenses, flat rate allowances	62
fuel benefits	59
loan of computer equipment	65
loan benefits	64
mobile phone benefit	60
parking facilities for	60
relocation benefits	65
share schemes	66
uniform allowances, armed forces	73
Enterprise investment scheme	
capital gains exemption	40
income tax relief	75
Enterprise management incentives	66
Enterprise zones	
designated areas	54
industrial buildings allowances	52
Excepted estates, inheritance tax	79
Excepted transfers	79
Exchange rates	
average	3
year end	5

Executive share option schemes	68
Exempt supplies, VAT	93
Expensive cars: restricted allowances	61
Explanatory pamphlets	
Customs & Excise	95
Inland Revenue	32
National Insurance	88
F	
Fixed profit car scheme	60
Flat rate expenses	62
Foreign exchange rates	
average	3
year end	5
Foreign income	
Schedule D Cases IV and V	8
Schedule E	72
Foreign service	
Schedule E relief	72
termination payment for	69
FOTRA securities	8
Fuel for private use	
national insurance contributions	87
Schedule E charge	59
VAT	94
Futures exchanges, recognised	30
G	
Gilt-edged securities	38
Gift aid	74
Gifts in kind	74
Grossing up tables	
17.5%	100
22%	98
34%	99
H	
Higher rate tax	55
interest on overdue tax	
rates	13
reckonable dates	11
table of rates	55
Hired cars, Schedule D deduction	61
Hold-over relief for gifts	40
Hotels, capital allowances	52
I	
Incapacity benefit	83
Income tax	
calendar, 2001-02	inside front cover
claims, time limits	22
due dates	10
elections, time limits	22
interest on overdue tax	
rates	13
reckonable dates	11
offences, penalties	17
personal allowances	56
rates	55
returns, penalties	17
table of reliefs	56
Indexation allowance	42
Individual savings accounts	77
Industrial buildings allowances	
enterprise zones	54
rates	52
Industrial death benefit	83
Inheritance tax	
agricultural property relief	81
annual exemption	81
business property relief	81
charitable gifts, exemption	81
claims, time limits	28
due dates for accounts	79
due dates for tax	11
elections, time limits	28
excepted estates	79
interest on overdue tax	
rates	14
reckonable dates	11
marriage gifts, exemption	81
penalties	19
political parties, gifts exemption	81
quick succession relief	81
rates	79
small gifts exemption	81
tapering relief	81
Inland Revenue publications	32
Insurance premiums	
life	56
medical	72
Interest rates	
certificates of tax deposit	9
default	
direct taxes	13
VAT	93
official, beneficial loans	64
overpaid tax	
direct taxes	15
VAT	93
repayment supplement	15
unpaid tax	
direct taxes	13
VAT	93
Invalid care allowance	83
Invalidity allowance	83
Investment reliefs	
business expansion scheme	76
enterprise investment scheme	75
individual savings accounts	77
personal equity plans	78
tax exempt special savings accounts	78
venture capital trusts	76
K	
Know-how, capital allowances	52
L	
Leaflets	
Customs & Excise	95
Inland Revenue	32
National Insurance	88
Leases	
depreciation table	37
premiums	
capital gains tax	37
Schedule A	37
stamp duties	89
Life assurance premium relief	56
Loan to employee, beneficial interest	64
Lower rate of tax	55
M	
Machinery and plant allowances	53
cars	61
rates	53
Maintenance payments	72
Marginal relief, corporation tax	51
Marriage gifts, inheritance tax relief	81
Married couple's allowance	56
Maternity allowance	83
Maternity pay, statutory	82
Medical insurance premiums	72
Millennium gift aid	74
Mines and oil wells, capital allowances	54
Misdeclarations, VAT	92
Mobile telephone, employee benefit	60
Mortgage interest relief	56
Motorcycles	60
N	
National insurance benefits	82
National insurance contributions	
interest on overdue contributions	
rates	13
reckonable dates	11
leaflets	88
rates	
Class 1,2,3,4	84
Class 1 A	87
Class 4	56, 84
weekly and monthly thresholds	73
National Savings Bank interest	72
Nazi persecution, pensions to victims	8
Non-domiciled individuals	
Schedule D Cases IV and V income	8
Schedule E income	72
spouses, inheritance tax	81
Non-residents	
Schedule D Cases IV and V income	8
Schedule E income	72
O	
Offences	
income and capital gains tax	17
corporation tax	17
Official rate of interest, employee loans	64
One parent benefit	82
Overseas income, basis of assessment	
Schedule D Cases IV and V	8
Schedule E	72
Overseas service	
Schedule E relief	72
termination payment	69
P	
Parking facilities	60
Partial exemption, VAT	94
Patent rights, capital allowances	54

PAYE
- interest on overdue tax
  - rates ... 13
  - reckonable dates ... 11
- penalties ... 18
- weekly and monthly thresholds ... 73

Pay and file
- due date of tax ... 10
- interest on overpaid tax ... 16
- interest on unpaid tax
  - rates ... 13
  - reckonable dates ... 11
- penalties connected with returns ... 17

Payroll giving scheme ... 74

Penalties
- corporation tax returns ... 17
- inheritance tax ... 19
- offences under the Tax Acts ... 18
- PAYE returns ... 18
- personal tax returns ... 17
- special information returns ... 19
- stamp duties ... 89
- standard scale ... 21
- statutory maximum ... 21
- VAT ... 92

Personal allowances ... 92

Personal equity plans
- capital gains reliefs ... 78
- income tax reliefs ... 78
- investment limits ... 78
- qualifying investments ... 78

Personal pension schemes ... 71
- contributions limit ... 71
- earnings cap ... 71
- permitted retirement age ... 70

Personal representatives
- capital gains annual exempt amount ... 41
- expenses allowable for CGT ... 41

Plant and machinery allowances
- cars ... 61
- rates ... 53

Political parties, gifts to ... 81

Premiums on leases
- capital gains tax ... 37
- Schedule A ... 37
- stamp duties ... 89

Profit-related pay schemes
- conditions for exemption ... 69
- exempt pay ... 69

Profit sharing schemes, approved
- limit on shares appropriated ... 68
- reliefs ... 68
- Schedule E charge on early disposal ... 68

Q
Qualifying corporate bonds ... 40
Quick succession relief ... 81

R
Rates of tax
- advance corporation tax ... 51
- capital gains tax ... 36
- corporation tax ... 51
- income tax ... 55
- inheritance tax ... 79
- VAT ... 91

Recognised futures exchanges ... 30
Recognised stock exchanges ... 29
Reduced rate supplies, VAT ... 93
Registration limits, VAT ... 90
Reliefs (capital gains) ... 40
Relocation benefits and expenses ... 65
Remission of tax ... 14
Rent-a-room scheme ... 72
Rent, stamp duties ... 89
Repayment supplement ... 15
Research and development ... 51, 54
Retail prices index ... 50
Retirement annuities contracts ... 70
- permitted retirement age ... 71
- premiums limit ... 70
Retirement pensions ... 83
Retirement relief ... 36
Roll-over relief
- business assets ... 41
- reinvestment, on ... 41

S
Savings-related share option schemes
- contributions to SAYE scheme ... 67
- reliefs ... 67
- SAYE contracts, bonus payments ... 67

Schedule A
- due date of tax ... 10,12

- lease premiums ... 37

Schedule C, due date of tax ... 10,12

Schedule D
- Cases IV and V, basis of assessment ... 8
- due date of tax ... 10,12

Schedule E
- basis of assessment ... 72
- due date of tax ... 10,12

Scientific research allowances ... 54

Securities
- gilt-edged ... 38
- tax-free for non-residents ... 8

Share schemes ... 66
Sick pay, statutory ... 82
Small companies relief ... 51
Small gifts relief ... 81

Social security benefits
- non-taxable ... 82,83
- taxable ... 82,83

Stamp duties
- ad valorem ... 89
- conveyances or transfers ... 89
- fixed ... 89
- interest ... 89
- leases ... 89
- penalties ... 89
- premiums ... 89
- rent ... 89
- stock transfers ... 89

Stakeholder pensions ... 71
Standard scale of penalties ... 21
Statutory maternity pay ... 82
Statutory maximum penalty ... 21
Statutory sick pay ... 82
Stock exchanges, recognised ... 29

T
Taper relief
- capital gains tax ... 37

Tapering relief
- inheritance tax ... 81

Tax exempt special savings accounts
- income tax exemptions ... 77
- maximum deposits ... 77

Tax year 2001-02, calendar ... inside front cover
Telephone, mobile ... 60
Termination payments, exemptions ... 69
Toll roads, capital allowances ... 52

Trustees
- capital gains annual exempt amount ... 36
- expenses allowable for CGT ... 41

U
Unemployment benefit ... 82
Uniform allowances ... 73

V
Van, employee benefit ... 60
Variation of employment, payments on ... 69

VAT
- annual accounting scheme ... 90
- capital goods scheme ... 94
- car fuel for private use ... 94
- default interest ... 93
- default surcharge ... 92
- deregistration limits ... 91
- evasion ... 92
- exempt supplies ... 93
- failure to notify liability ... 92
- interest on overpaid tax ... 93
- misdeclarations ... 92
- notices and leaflets ... 95
- partial exemption ... 94
- penalties ... 92
- rates ... 91
- reduced rate supplies ... 93
- registration limits ... 90
- zero-rated supplies ... 93

Venture capital trusts
- capital gains exemptions ... 40
- conditions for approval ... 76
- income tax reliefs ... 76

W
Widow's benefits ... 83
Widow's payment ... 83
Working families' tax credit ... 61
Workshops, capital allowances ... 52

Z
Zero-rated supplies ... 93

"Anyone contemplating a serious study of their tax position should read Tolley's... quoting from Tolley's tends to impress the Inland Revenue."
The Sunday Times

Tolley's Tax Annuals 2001-02: The only real choice for tax professionals

Tolley's Tax Annuals 2001-02 are the 'must have' reference works for all taxation professionals who want to make the tax advice they provide on behalf of clients more effective. They have served accounting professionals and taxation practitioners for decades and are the most reliable, authoritative, comprehensive and user-friendly tax guides ever published. The latest developments to **Tolley's Tax Annuals 2001-02** include:

- **Full expert coverage of both Finance Acts expected during this election year**
- **Updated case studies**

- **Internet site cross-references for further research**

You can be sure that **Tolley's Tax Annuals 2001-02** will make your working life easier by following the same practical format valued by so many professionals for so many years, including clear alphabetical format, thorough indexing and fully revised and up-to-date worked examples.

Now available with or without Budget supplements for as little as £53.95.

Title	Pub. Date	Price	Code	ISBN
Tolley's Income Tax 2001-02				
With post Budget supplement	Apr / Sept	£69.95	IT01B	0 7545 1195 2
Without supplement	Sept	£54.95	IT01AO	0 7545 1388 2
Tolley's Corporation Tax 2001-02				
With post Budget supplement	Apr / Sept	£69.95	CT01B	0 7545 1189 8
Without supplement	Sept	£54.95	CT01AO	0 7545 1389 0
Tolley's Capital Gains Tax 2001-02				
With post Budget supplement	Apr / Sept	£69.95	CGT01B	0 7545 1190 1
Without supplement	Sept	£54.95	CG01AO	0 7545 1390 4
Tolley's NI Contributions 2001-02				
With post 'Green' Budget supplement	June / Dec	£69.95	NIC01B	0 7545 1187 1
Without supplement	Oct	£54.95	NI01AO	0 7545 1392 0
Tolley's Value Added Tax 2001-02	May / Sept	£95.00*	VAT01	0 7545 1158 8
* Price includes two complete volumes. The first edition will be despatched with an invoice and the second edition will be sent out without charge in September 2001.				
Tolley's Inheritance Tax 2001-02	Sept	£53.95	IHT01	0 7545 1188 X

How To Order

To order, please contact Butterworths Tolley
Customer Service Dept: **Butterworths Tolley,**
FREEPOST SEA 4177, Croydon, Surrey CR9 5WZ
Telephone: 020 8662 2000 Fax: 020 8662 2012

Tolley Tolley is the tax imprint of Butterworths Tolley

Butterworths Tolley, 35 Chancery Lane, London WC2A 1EL

A member of the Reed Elsevier plc group

25 Victoria Street, London SW1H 0EX
VAT number: 730 8595 20
Registered Office Number: 2746621

We like to keep our customers informed of other relevant books, journals and information services produced by Butterworths or by companies approved by Butterworths. If you do not wish to receive such information, please tick the box ☐

Tax Direct Service is the ultimate on-line service that provides you with instant access to the most authoritative information ... all via the internet.
For more information on all of our products, please visit our website at www.butterworths.com